For Matthew and Mary

For Jo, Jamie, Catriona and Hannah

Contents

List of tables, figures and boxes

Tables

Figures

Boxes

Acknowledgements

This book is a substantially revised and updated second edition of *Social Work and Direct Payments*, published in 2002 by The Policy Press.

The authors are grateful to everyone at The Policy Press for their support with this second edition.

In particular, they are grateful to Simon Duffy, in Control, Frances Hasler, Jane Campbell, Roy Taylor, Jenny Owen, Debra Cox and the HSMC library.

Thanks to Kevin Chettle for permission to use his painting on the front cover.

Note on the text

Many thanks to in Control for permission to reproduce text in Boxes 5.2, 5.3, 5.6–5.8, 5.10 and 6.1, Figures 5.1–5.3 and Tables 5.2–5.8. Discussion of conditional resource enhancements also draws directly on the work of Waters and Duffy (2007).

Chapters Three and Four explore the take-up of direct payments. Although this is flagged up later in the book, it is surprisingly difficult to obtain meaningful data on the experiences of different user groups and on progress in the four countries of the UK. Although a lot of data exists, it is often collected and summarised in slightly different ways, making easy comparisons difficult. In response, we have sought to draw on this data as best we can to provide an overview of the key trends; however, experts will recognise that we have had to make some difficult decisions about how best to do this. Wherever possible we have tried to be both accurate *and* accessible – although some trade-offs are inevitably required in striking this balance.

Glossary

As explained below, this is a complex area where the key terms can be a source of confusion. As a result, this glossary seeks to provide some basic definitions to simplify subsequent debates as much as possible.

Direct payments: introduced formally under 1996 legislation, the individual receives the cash equivalent of a directly provided service. This is available for social care only, and can be used to contract with a private/voluntary sector agency or to become an employer by hiring one's own staff – it cannot be used to purchase public sector services.

in Control: a national social enterprise, independent from government, which developed the concept of personal budgets and is supporting local authority members to implement this way of working.

Independent living: a key aim of the disabled people's movement has been to achieve independent living (a situation in which disabled people have as much choice and control over their lives as everyone else). This does not mean doing everything oneself – in practice, no one is truly independent, and we are all interdependent on others to meet our needs as human beings.

Indirect payments: prior to the 1996 Community Care (Direct Payments) Act, many local authorities overcame uncertainties in the legal context by making indirect or third-party payments.

Individual/personal budget: a new way of working pioneered by in Control. At its most simple, it involves being clear with the person from the outset how much money is available to meet their needs, then allowing them maximum choice over how the money is spent/how much control they want over the money. Initially, the individual budgets developed by in Control were for social care funds only. Subsequently, Department of Health pilots began to explore scope for integrating a series of additional funding sources (and their use of the term 'individual budget' therefore tends to refer to a single pot with the potential to bring together all the various funding available to the individual). This book follows current policy rhetoric by referring to 'personal budgets' for adult social care funds only, and to 'individual budgets' for more integrated sources of funding.

Self-directed support: as explained in Chapter Five, personal budgets are only one part of a new system for social care, which in Control has called 'self-directed support'.

Abbreviations

ADSS	Association of Directors of Social Services (now ADASS – Association of Directors of Adult Social Services)
BCODP	British Council of Disabled People
CIL	Centre for Independent Living
CIPFA	Chartered Institute of Public Finance and Accountancy
COS	Charity Organisation Society
CRB	Criminal Record Bureau
CRE	Conditional Resource Enhancement
CSCI	Commission for Social Care Inspection
CSIP	Care Services Improvement Partnership
DfES	Department for Education and Skills
DH	Department of Health
DHSS	Department of Health and Social Security
DHSSPS	Department of Health, Social Services and Public Safety (Northern Ireland)
DPDF	Direct Payments Development Fund
ENIL	European Network on Independent Living
ILF	Independent Living Fund
JRF	Joseph Rowntree Foundation
LSE	London School of Economics and Political Science
MASC	Modernising Adult Social Care research initiative
NCIL	National Centre for Independent Living
NIMHE	National Institute for Mental Health in England
PA	Personal assistant
PSI	Policy Studies Institute
PSSRU	Personal Social Services Research Unit
RAS	Resource Allocation System
SI	Statutory Instrument
SR	Statutory Rule
TAG	Technical Advisory Group
VPST	Valuing People Support Team

ONE

Introduction

This introduction provides:
- an overview of the book and how to use it;
- an explanation of why the time is right for a second edition;
- a brief note on terminology.

The 1996 Community Care (Direct Payments) Act, which came into force on 1 April 1997, has been described as holding out 'the potential for the most fundamental reorganisation of welfare for half a century' (Oliver and Sapey, 1999, p 175). After longstanding pressure from a range of user groups, the Act empowered social services departments to make cash payments to service users aged between 18 and 65 in lieu of direct service provision. Although progress was initially slow, the number of direct payments has continued to increase and the original Act has been extended to include older people, younger people aged 16 and 17, carers and the parents of disabled children. As lessons began to emerge from both research and practice, the first edition of this book (*Social work and direct payments*, 2002) sought to provide an introductory textbook to summarise the history and nature of direct payments, promote good practice and explore the implications of direct payments, both for service users and for social work staff.

Since 2002, adult social care has changed almost beyond recognition. Initially discretionary, direct payments quickly became a national performance indicator and began to be compulsory for all local authorities to offer to those who met the criteria (see Chapter Three). They also quickly became associated with the so-called 'modernisation' of adult social care, viewed by policy makers and other key commentators as a core mechanism for changing and improving social care services. From 2003, the concept of a direct payment was supplemented by the notion of a personal budget. Although technically entirely separate from the advent of direct payments, personal budgets nevertheless have much in common with this agenda and seem to offer an even more powerful tool for reforming the system as a whole (see Chapter Five). Under this approach, the local authority gives the person an immediate indication of how much money is available to spend on meeting their needs, and then allows them to choose how this money is spent and how much direct control they have over the money itself. At the time of writing, an official evaluation has just been published and the concept is being rolled out nationally as part of a cross-government commitment to greater 'personalisation' (HM Government, 2007; DH, 2008a). Signed by all leading health and social care bodies as well as six different government departments, this vision for the future of adult social care (*Putting People First*) pledges to achieve a 'system-wide transformation' in which people using services have 'maximum choice, control and power over the support services they receive' (HM Government, 2007, pp 2–3).

As a result of these changes, there are now around 67,000 people receiving direct payments in England and over 9,000 people receiving a personal budget (see Chapters Four and Five). However, more important than overall numbers is the impetus this has received from policy makers. Essentially, the Department of Health has stated that in future all adult social care will be provided via a personal budget unless there is a very good reason why this should not be done (which transforms the current system where pretty much the opposite is true – all people receive a directly provided service unless there is a good reason to the contrary). As we argue in this book, if this commitment is to be achieved even in part then almost everything about adult social care will need to change – the roles of care staff and social workers, the way we train current and future practitioners, the way we conceive of and organise services, and the way we view the roles of people using services and their families. Against this background, the book seeks to make an early contribution to the range of new approaches to research, teaching and practice that may be required if direct payments and personal budgets continue to transform services and people's lives in the way they have to date.

Current literature

When the first edition of this book was published in 2002, it was thought to be the first mainstream textbook on direct payments. As such, it sought to bring together official policy and practice guidance, the latest research and practical advice from disabled people's organisations. Since then, there has been additional research, further policy developments and, as we argue later, a more critical and questioning approach to the concept of direct payments. In particular, Leece and Bornat's (2006) edited collection on *Developments in direct payments* (also published by The Policy Press) is an excellent summary of many of the key issues and should be read alongside the analysis here.

Several years on from our first edition, we feel that the rapidly changing policy context calls for a new book, condensing some of our earlier material and including lessons from more recent research, policy and practice (concerning both direct payments and personal budgets). Given that the latter is so new, much of the material on personal budgets draws heavily on interviews with those involved in developing and rolling out this concept, and on the policy and practice networks of the authors (who were early and committed advocates of this way of working and hence involved in a number of the early debates). As with the first edition, we believe that this new edition may be the first mainstream book on the topic of direct payments and personal budgets, and we hope that this will be the first of many.

Terminology and approach

As non-disabled writers addressing a topic of considerable interest to disabled people, we follow disabled academics such as Morris (1993a) and Oliver (1990, 1996) in adopting a social model of disability. Whereas previous medical approaches have tended to focus on the physical limitations of individuals, the social model of disability emphasises the physical and attitudinal barriers that exclude disabled people from participating fully in society (Oliver, 1990). Thus, the focus of intervention should be the current social organisation rather than the individual. Central to the social model is the distinction between two key concepts (Oliver, 1990, p 11):

- *impairment:* lacking part or all of a limb; or having a defective limb, organism or mechanism of the body;
- *disability:* the disadvantage or restriction of activity caused by a contemporary social organisation which takes little or no account of people who have physical impairments and thus excludes them from the mainstream of social activities.

As a result, disabled writers have tended to advocate the use of terms such as 'disabled people' to refer to the oppression that people with impairments experience as a result of prejudice and discrimination:

> People are disabled by society's reaction to impairment; this is why the term disabled people is used, rather than people with disabilities. The latter term really means people with impairments whereas the disability movement prefers to use the politically more powerful term, disabled people, in order to place the emphasis on how society oppresses people with a whole range of impairments. (Morris, 1993a, p x)

In keeping with this approach, we use the term **disabled people** to refer to all people with an impairment, retaining **people with physical impairments** as a technical term to distinguish such service users from other user groups (such as people with learning difficulties or people with mental health problems). Thus, the term 'disabled people' is used inclusively to refer to all people with an impairment, whatever their age, whatever the nature of their impairment and whatever category formal services would place the person in.

In addition, it is important for us to be clear from the start about the approach we have taken to many of the issues raised in this book. Having analysed the evidence, talked to disabled people receiving direct payments and personal budgets, worked alongside social care practitioners and engaged with policy makers, we believe that these two ways of working are among the most powerful tools available for increasing the choice and control available to disabled people and for changing the relationship between the state and the individual. While there remain barriers to further progress, we believe that many, if not all, of these are to do with the way in which direct payments and personal budgets have been operationalised either nationally or locally, and are not inherent in the concepts themselves.

While we have tried to write a textbook that will be relevant to readers in England, Wales, Scotland and Northern Ireland (and beyond, we hope), some of the specifics of policy and practice guidance cited in Chapter Three tend to refer primarily to England (albeit with references to equivalent documents in the other countries of the UK).

TWO

History – why direct payments and personal budgets are different from what went before

> **This chapter explores:**
> * the evolution of social care and its relationship with financial issues;
> * ongoing pressure for reform;
> * the relationship between the state and the individual.

To understand the importance of direct payments and personal budgets, it is necessary to have a basic awareness of the history of social work, its relationship with financial/poverty issues and the traditional relationship between the state and the individual recipient of services. As a result, this chapter provides a brief overview of the origins of modern social work in 19th-century philanthropy and the now notorious Poor Law, the build-up to the 1996 Community Care (Direct Payments) Act and some reflections on the post-war evolution of social care.

Social work and finance/poverty

The Charity Organisation Society

Social work, as a profession, has its origins in 19th-century philanthropy and in the pioneering approach of the Charity Organisation Society (COS) (Bosanquet, 1914; Rooff, 1972; Lewis, 1995). Founded in 1869, COS was essentially a reaction against a proliferation of philanthropic activity following the depression of the late 1860s. By offering charity to the poor, it was argued, the rich were encouraging them to become dependent on alms and exacerbating rather than resolving the problem. For leading COS figures such as Charles Loch or Helen Bosanquet, poverty was caused by individual and moral failings – by fecklessness and thriftlessness. As a result, the solution lay in individual casework, with a COS worker assessing whether an individual was worthy or unworthy of assistance. For those deemed deserving, access to charitable resources might be permitted, although the emphasis was still very much on the need for moral reformation and for the individual to change and improve their ways. For the undeserving, charity should be denied and the applicant left to rely on the harsh mechanism of the Poor Law and the workhouse. Although relatively little is known about the reaction of the poor to this form of charity, it seems likely that many felt aggrieved by this patronising and highly judgemental approach to poverty. Certainly when an East End clergyman and his wife sought to abolish almsgiving and establish a local COS, they were besieged by an angry mob on more than one occasion. In the end, such demonstrations became so widespread that the clergyman had to cut a door from the vicarage to his church so that he could slip out and fetch the police whenever the mob gathered outside (Barnett, 1918, p 84).

The Poor Law

For those deemed undeserving of COS assistance, the only other option was the Poor Law. Associated with legislation from the reign of Elizabeth I, the Poor Law levied poor rates and provided support to those in need via the workhouse and via outdoor relief. As Englander (1998, pp 2-3) explains:

> Outdoor relief ... embraced payments for all sorts and conditions – weekly pensions to the aged and infirm, payments for the foster care of village orphans and the upkeep of illegitimate children; casual doles for those in need due to unemployment or sickness; payments for doctor's bills and grants of food, fuel and clothing, particularly during periods of dearth.

Although outdoor relief was technically abolished in 1834, it continued to be paid in practice well into the 20th century (Fraser, 1984; Novak, 1988; Rose, 1988), and was later extended during the 1920s and 1930s to include a complex range of measures to support the poor during the Great Depression (Thane, 1996). Despite this, the Poor Law is most associated with the brutal and dehumanising regime of the workhouse.

To ensure that state support did not encourage the able-bodied to become idle, the 1834 Poor Law Amendment Act promoted the concept of 'less eligibility' (that is, that the workhouse should be made as harsh as possible so that residents were less well off than even the poorest workers outside the workhouse): 'To this end, indoor relief was made as disagreeable as possible by vexatious regulations, want of social amenities, hard labour, poor dietaries and the impact of strict discipline' (Englander, 1998, pp 11-12). Rising at 6am in the summer and 8am in the winter, inmates worked until 6pm, families were separated and distinctive uniforms were enforced to emphasise 'pauper' status and advertise residents' shame (Englander, 1998). Hardly surprisingly, such institutions were bitterly resented by the working classes, many of whom would rather have starved than enter the workhouse (Chinn, 1995). As a result, the 1834 Poor Law Amendment Act was greeted with widespread rioting (Edsall, 1971) and the brutality of the Poor Law has been immortalised by writers such as Charles Dickens (1867).

As unemployment soared in the 1920s and 1930s, new sources of financial assistance were introduced to provide support for the poor (Fraser, 1984). In the 1920s, attempts were made to reduce the cost of such support through the introduction of a stringent 'means test' and a 'genuinely seeking work' test (Thane, 1996). Henceforth, all applicants for state support would have their finances and situations fully assessed, only receiving payments if they were extremely impoverished and if no other source of support was available. Once again, such intrusion into the lives of the poor was heavily resented (Thane, 1996), and the oppressive nature of the system has been widely condemned in literature such as Greenwood's *Love on the dole* (1969).

The abolition of the Poor Law

As pressure mounted to reform the Poor Law, there was a growing awareness that social work should seek to distance itself from its 19th-century origins in order to rid itself of the taint of the Poor Law. Thus, when the Poor Law was finally abolished in 1948, it was replaced by a national scheme for the payment of social security benefits and by new legislation to provide welfare services for older and disabled people. For the first time in its history, social work was separated from the administration of income support and, unlike in most other European countries and the US, social care workers were to play no active part in assessing eligibility for social security payments:

> [The 1948 National Assistance Act] repealed the old Poor Law and replaced it with assistance provided by the National Assistance Board and local authorities. Whereas the Poor Law had dealt with the financial and non-financial welfare of those in need, this Act now divided these up: financial welfare was to be dealt with by the National Assistance Board, whereas it was now the responsibility of local authorities to deal with the non-financial welfare of disabled people, older people and others. Thus, the system developed a sharp separation between cash and in-kind assistance. Social security was to be about the provision of cash, subject to national rules. The social services were to operate locally and apply a much greater degree of discretion in their day-to-day work. This split is not typically found in continental Europe, where local social workers are often involved in the payment of cash benefits. (McKay and Rowlingson, 1999, p 59)

At the time, the separation of social work and social security was seen as a major advance, since social workers would be able to support those in need without the stigma of the old Poor Law (Jordan, 1974). With hindsight, however, the attempt to distance social work from cash payments to those in need has arguably been responsible for practitioners' subsequent failure to address poverty issues. Although the vast majority of people who use social work services are in receipt of social security benefits, many social workers have tended to distance themselves from the material difficulties of their clients and have little 'poverty awareness' (Becker, 1997, p 93), viewing money problems as being the responsibility of other agencies (see Box 2.1). This has contributed to a rapid expansion in specialist money advice services from the early 1970s onwards, often run through voluntary organisations

> **Box 2.1: The lack of poverty awareness**
>
> Social work trainers in Birmingham ask mental health students why most people they
> work with face problems associated with poverty such as debt, homelessness, inadequate
> diets, insufficient clothing and lack of social contacts. Common responses include:
> • Poverty is "a fact of life for people like this".
> • "It's not our job to tackle poverty."
> • "The mentally ill bring it on themselves."
> • "People like this should be grateful for what they get" and "count their blessings".
> • "If these people were given more they would only waste it."
>
> (Davis and Wainwright, 1996, p 49)

and specialist local authority units rather than through social services departments. Despite a growing awareness of the importance of poverty issues (see, for example, Becker and MacPherson, 1988; Burgess, 1994; Davis and Wainwright, 1996), social work has yet to develop a significant anti-poverty perspective (Becker, 1997).

Thus, the desire of the social work profession to distance itself from its 19th-century roots has resulted in a somewhat ambiguous relationship between the profession and cash payments to those in need. Against this background, the introduction of direct payments in 1996 must be seen as a radical departure from previous practice, re-establishing the profession's links to its pre-1948 history. Although direct payments are provided in lieu of services and are therefore very different from outdoor relief or COS charity, the involvement of social workers in making cash payments to disabled people represented a fundamental shift in the nature of the profession, turning the clock back nearly 50 years. This is not only of interest to the social historian, but may also help to explain why some social services departments have been slow to take up the opportunities offered by direct payments (see Chapters Three, Four and Seven).

Certainly, concerns about a potential shift in social work practice were prominent in the early 1990s following a number of attempts to introduce a Private Member's Bill to legalise direct payments (see Chapter Three). In response, the health secretary, Virginia Bottomley, wrote to the MP responsible, suggesting that 'social services legislation is concerned with the arrangements of services and not with direct payments, which is the province of the social security system' (quoted in Hatchett, 1991, pp 14–15). Several years later, the issue was to re-emerge following the passage of the 1996 Community Care (Direct Payments) Act, with fears that social services departments might be turned into 'income maintenance organisations' and that the Benefits Agency might be considering transferring the administration of certain disability benefits to social services (Hirst, 1997). On other occasions, concerns have been reversed – with suggestions that personal budgets could lead to social care funding being transferred to the social security system (see, for example, Gainsbury, 2008). Although these fears have so far proved groundless, they demonstrate the fundamental shift that has taken place as a result of direct payments, and provide an early indication that the social work profession might not necessarily welcome the new reforms with open arms (see Chapters Four and Seven for further details). In many ways, the development of personal budgets makes these issues even more fundamental, and the cultural challenges of self-directed support are explored in more detail in Chapter Five.

Pressure for direct payments

Following the 1948 National Assistance Act, service provision slowly began to evolve away from its initial emphasis on residential care to include a wider range of community services (Means and Smith, 1998a-b; Means et al, 2008). Despite this, pressure for change and for more responsive and flexible services has increased, culminating in 1996 with the passage of the Community Care (Direct Payments) Act. The growing body of research in this area has suggested that the introduction of direct payments can be traced to three separate but interrelated developments (Glendinning et al, 2000a, pp 7-9):

- the shortcomings of directly provided services;
- pressure from the Independent Living Movement;
- the experience of the Independent Living Fund.

As a result, the remainder of this section reviews each of these developments in turn.

Directly provided services

Following the 1990 community care reforms, there is ongoing evidence that services provided directly by the local authority are too inflexible and unresponsive to meet the needs of many service users. In 1994, the British Council of Disabled People (BCODP) published the results of research based on interviews with 70 disabled people from four case study local authorities (Zarb and Nadash, 1994). Although the findings of this study are discussed throughout this book, the research highlighted a number of common criticisms, including lack of control, flexibility and reliability (see Box 2.2).

Under the 1990 NHS and Community Care Act, social services departments were given a specific brief to target scarce resources on those with the greatest needs (DH, 1990). With regard to domiciliary care, this accelerated the trend towards rebranding traditional 'home help' services as 'home care', focusing on personal care rather than housework and often excluding people with 'low-level' needs (Clark et al, 1998). Such changes were frequently accompanied by an increased tendency to define home care interventions in terms of specific tasks, rather than on an hourly basis, leading to complaints of institutionalisation and of reducing opportunities for more generalised social interaction between care staff and service users (Glendinning et al, 2000a). At the same time, reductions in

Box 2.2: Disadvantages of directly provided services

1   Lack of control over times support is supplied:
- disrupts day-to-day routines;
- reduces personal freedom;
- is unreliable.

2   Lack of control over who provides assistance:
- increases feelings of intrusion on privacy;
- reduces choice over characteristics of support workers (for example, age and gender);
- no sanctions to ensure quality of assistance provided (other than complaints procedures adopted by service providers).

3   Inability to control type of assistance and how it is provided:
- leads to inefficiency (for example, workers breaking things, putting household items away in the wrong place, not preparing food to personal tastes);
- increases stress;
- reduces personal dignity and feeling of being in control of one's life.

4   Unreliability:
- increases stress and practical inconvenience;
- reduces ability to control times when assistance is provided;
- can disrupt family life, social life and other activities;
- sanctions available limited if services do not respond to requests for support;
- reduces confidence in support arrangements;
- increases practical demands on other family members.

5   Lack of flexibility:
- can create gaps in assistance provided;
- reduces likelihood of securing back-up and emergency cover for usual sources of support;
- reduces ability to increase support when needs vary;
- can increase vulnerability to breakdown of support arrangements;
- increases reliance on respite services;
- increases reliance on informal support.

6   Interpersonal relationships with staff:
- lack of choice over staff can lead to intrusion on privacy;
- difficulties with changing staff if interpersonal problems arise;
- limited sanctions available if unhappy with attitudes or behaviour of staff;
- larger number of staff to deal with can be inconvenient and/or stressful.

7   Other disadvantages:
- increased vulnerability if service provision reduced or withdrawn;
- uncertainty about future levels of local community care provision;
- concerns about charging and/or means testing.

(Zarb and Nadash, 1994, pp 88–90)

the length of hospital stays and the emphasis on maximising the throughput of patients resulted in patients being discharged to the community with far greater health needs than would once have been the case (Glasby and Littlechild, 2004). This meant that district nurses increasingly dealt with more complex needs and focused much more on technical nursing care, leaving users with fewer health needs to social services home carers (Barret and Hudson, 1997). Throughout all these changes, there is a growing consensus that care remained service- rather than needs-led, and that both health and social care providers were geared more to crisis intervention than to promoting independence and social inclusion (Morris, 1993a; Glasby and Littlechild, 2004). Perhaps the most striking example of the inflexibility of traditional services comes from Morris's (1993a) description of the experiences of 50 disabled people. This research painted a distressing picture of restrictive services that seek to fit the individual to the service and serve only to enhance, rather than reduce, dependency (see Box 2.3). Against this background, direct payments must be seen as a means of enhancing both choice and control, overcoming the traditional limitations of directly provided services.

Box 2.3: Fitting the individual to the service

Marcia's home carers will not assist her with housework or shopping.

Home carers would not assist Mary's husband to have a bath, and the family had to approach their GP to argue that Mary's husband needed a bath for medical reasons.

To get help washing his clothes, William had to argue that this need was created by incontinence.

Catherine's social services department offered to send someone round between 5 and 7 o'clock as this was when they had staff available – even though Catherine did not need assistance at this time.

Elizabeth is Afro-Caribbean and feels that white home carers do not know how to look after her hair properly.

One carer argued with Susan about the way her underwear was placed. Susan tried to deal with this politely, but eventually lost her temper: "Who's fucking wearing it, me or you?"

Vicky feels that the care assistants who visit her are homophobic and do not understand her life.

(Morris, 1993a, ch 7)

Independent living

Although the shortcomings of directly provided services are widely recognised, the most vehement criticisms have often come from the Independent Living Movement. The concept of independent living originated in 1973 in the US, where three disabled students were able to attend university at Berkeley, California, with the support of personal assistants (PAs) provided by the university (Evans, 1993). After graduation, these three students felt that the PA system had been so successful that they established the world's first Centre for Independent Living (CIL), an organisation run and controlled by disabled people, which sought to support other disabled people in taking greater control of their lives and services. Nicknamed the 'quad squad' (since most of the original students were paralysed from the shoulders down), one of the students used an iron lung and went on to become the equivalent of the director of social services in California (Evans, 1993, p 59). Initially, the Berkeley CIL had five key aims, focusing on housing, personal assistance, accessible transport, an accessible environment and peer support. Within ten years, there were 200 CILs in America (Evans, 1993, p 60), and the concept began to spread overseas. In the UK, CILs were founded in Hampshire and in Derbyshire during the early 1980s. Also at this time, the formation of the British Council of Disabled People (established in 1981) and the European Network on Independent Living (ENIL, founded in 1989) provided a national and international focus for the promotion of independent living. More recently, the creation of a National Centre for Independent Living (NCIL) has provided further impetus. From the beginning, the concept of PAs working under the control of disabled people has been a central feature of independent living, pioneering many of the concepts that were later to form part of the direct payments agenda.

The philosophy of the Independent Living Movement is based on four key assumptions (Morris, 1993a, p 21):

- All human life is of value.
- Anyone, whatever their impairment, is capable of exercising choices.
- People who are disabled by society's reaction to physical, intellectual and sensory impairment and to emotional distress have the right to assert control over their lives.
- Disabled people have the right to participate fully in society.

Although definitions of independent living vary, they all emphasise the importance of choice and control (see Box 2.4) – central features of the 1996 Community Care (Direct Payments) Act. Indeed, disabled activists such as Frances Hasler are adamant that direct payments are only a means to achieving the overall goal of independent living: 'Direct payments are a means to an end and that end is independent living. We need to hang on to that. Direct payments are not a good thing or a bad thing in themselves. Direct payments are just a way of getting to independent living' (Hasler, 2000, p 6).

Box 2.4: Independent living

Independent living is the concept of the empowerment of disabled people and their ability to control their own lives.

Independent living is when disabled people live within the community and control the decisions affecting their own lives.

Independent living is a way of choosing and taking control of your own lifestyle. It is all about choosing and controlling what to do, when to do it, and who should do it.

Independent living is a dynamic process. It is about creating choices and identifying solutions. It is a way of life that grows as you grow and develops as you develop.

Independent living is a philosophy and a movement of disabled people who work for equal rights and equal opportunities, self-respect and self-determination. Independent living does not mean that disabled people do not need anybody, that they want to do everything by themselves in isolation. Independent living means that disabled people want the same life opportunities and the same choices in everyday life that their non-disabled brothers and sisters, neighbours and friends take for granted. That includes growing up in their families, going to the neighbourhood school, using the same bus, getting employment that is in line with their education and abilities, having equal access to the same services and establishments of social life, culture and leisure. Most importantly, just like everyone else, disabled people need to be in charge of their own lives, need to think and speak for themselves without interference from others … In order to reach the same control and the same choices in everyday life that non-disabled persons take for granted a number of prerequisites are necessary. For persons with extensive disabilities there are two key requirements: personal assistance and accessibility in the built environment including accessible housing. Without these two necessities persons with extensive disabilities, in many countries, can only choose between being a burden on their families or living in an institution. These extremely limited and limiting options are incompatible with the concept of independent living.

(NCIL, nda; Ratzka, nd)

The Independent Living Fund

Prior to the introduction of direct payments, the Independent Living Fund (ILF) gave disabled people the opportunity to receive cash payments in order to purchase personal assistance. In 1986, the Social Security Act announced measures to replace Supplementary Benefit with Income Support. Whereas recipients of Supplementary Benefit could receive additional payments on the basis of ill-health or disability, the new Income Support would replace such additions with flat-rate disability and severe disability premiums, with much stricter eligibility criteria (Hudson, 1988, 1994). Contemporary estimates suggested that some disabled people would be as much as £50 per week worse off as a result of these changes, and there were fears that some of these people would be forced into residential care (Hudson, 1988; Kestenbaum, 1993a).

In response, disability groups began a sustained lobbying process, eventually succeeding in persuading the then Conservative government to make alternative arrangements for those affected by the 1986 Act. After consulting with representatives of disability groups, Nicholas Scott, minister for social security and the disabled, announced details of a new independent trust fund (the ILF) in early 1988 (Kestenbaum, 1993a). Established for a maximum of five years with an initial budget of £5 million, the ILF would make payments to a small number of disabled people who had to pay for personal assistance. The number of applicants was expected to be 'in the hundreds rather than the thousands' (quoted in Hudson, 1988, p 708), and the Fund was only available to those disabled people on low incomes who had to pay for personal care.

From the beginning, it quickly became apparent that the government had significantly underestimated the demand for the ILF. Although it was initially anticipated that there would be around 300 new awards each year, applications reached the rate of 900 per month in 1989–90 and, by November 1992, 2,000 per month (Kestenbaum, 1993a, pp 29–33). By 1993, some 22,000 people were receiving payments (Zarb and Nadash, 1994, p 6) and the Fund had an annual budget of £82 million (Kestenbaum, 1993a, p 32). Research carried out by the ILF suggested that the popularity of this new form of support was largely due to the enhanced choice and control that it enabled (see Box 2.5). Drawing on semi-structured interviews with ILF recipients and a large-scale postal questionnaire, the ILF research officer found that the most valued aspects of receiving cash to purchase care included (Kestenbaum, 1993b, pp 32-41):

- choice of care assistant;
- continuity of care;
- the flexibility of care arrangements;
- the greater availability of respite options;
- enhanced self-respect;
- control.

As Kestenbaum has demonstrated:

> For many applicants, the ILF was not just about making up for unavailable statutory services. It was the preferred option. From a disabled person's point of view, the provision of cash makes the important difference between having one's personal life controlled by others and exercising choices and control for oneself. Money has enabled ILF clients ... not only to avoid going into residential care,

but also to determine for themselves the help they require and how and when they want it to be provided. (1993a, p 35)

The findings from this research challenge the assumption that disabled people are incapable of exercising effective choice and control over their own care arrangements ... The experience of ILF clients ... shows how, with enough money to have care assistance under their own control, or that of a chosen advocate, many disabled people can greatly improve the quality of their lives as well as stay out of residential care. (1993b, p 78)

Box 2.5: Users' experiences of the Independent Living Fund

"If you're paying for it you can get what you want."

"You can do what you want when you want to do it."

"Having the cash to pay for the things you need means that you have standing. You're more in control of your life. That's what you're trying to achieve all the time."

"Having the cash means you aren't always on the receiving end. You feel better having two-way traffic – give and take."

"I think this is the best way. You're in charge of your own destiny. We're the boss, aren't we?"

(Kestenbaum, 1993b, pp 35-8; see also Lakey, 1994)

Perhaps inevitably, the success of the ILF posed both financial and political problems for the government (Morris, 1993a, p 14). While the Fund had uncovered the need for cash payments to enable disabled people to purchase their own care, the cost was escalating rapidly and local authorities (the lead agencies under the community reforms introduced in 1993) were prohibited from making such payments (see Chapter Three for further details). After tightening eligibility criteria in 1990 and 1992 and introducing an age limit on the Fund (excluding those aged 75 and over), the ultimate response of the government was to terminate the original ILF, and to replace it with two successor bodies (Hudson, 1993; ILF, 2000):

- The Independent Living (Extension) Fund would continue to administer payments to recipients of the original ILF, although awards were not linked to inflation.
- The Independent Living (1993) Fund would accept new applications but on a different basis. Henceforth, disabled people receiving at least £200 worth of services per week from their local authority could receive a maximum of £375 from the Fund. Crucially, the new Fund was to be restricted to people aged under 66 at the time of their application (see Kestenbaum, 1999, appendix A, and ILF, 2000 for eligibility criteria).

Thus, from April 1993, local authority social services departments were responsible for purchasing services to meet the assessed needs of disabled people, using the new ILF to 'top up' existing care packages. This was widely interpreted as a retrograde step that emphasised professional control rather than user-led services and independent living (see, for example, Hudson, 1993; Morris, 1993b). Despite this, the experience of the ILF did reveal a number of significant issues that were later to influence the initial introduction and subsequent expansion of direct payments:

- A number of prominent cases raised the need for adequate support systems to ensure that disabled people purchasing their own care were able to meet their legal and financial obligations. In some cases, ILF recipients were left in thousands of pounds of debt having failed to make National Insurance and other contributions, serving as a powerful reminder of the need to focus on the technicalities of being an employer (Bond, 1996).
- Some disabled people can find it very difficult to recruit PAs, and may value support in this area (Kestenbaum, 1993b, pp 12-13).
- At the same time, concerns were expressed that any payments to disabled people should take additional costs such as recruitment, employers' contributions and other overheads fully into account (Bond, 1996).
- Some ILF recipients were nervous about what would happen when the community care reforms were introduced, and feared that they could lose their payments (Kestenbaum, 1993b, p 41). During the late 1990s, similar issues were to be raised following the tendency of many local authorities to introduce direct payments on a pilot basis, leaving some service users unsure whether or not pilot projects would become part of mainstream service provision (see Chapters Three and Four).
- The ILF revealed the potential conflicts that can arise between the aims of the Independent Living Movement and the desire of central government to limit public expenditure (see Chapter Seven for further details).

Above all, however, the ILF enabled disabled people to purchase their own care and represented a fundamental shift in power between professionals and users. As Hudson has commented:

> The ILF offered precisely what many people wanted – a major weekly cash payment … direct to claimants to buy the support they felt they required. For the first time in Britain, users were calling the shots in the purchase and provision of care … In a major and unintended way, the 1986 Social Security Act produced a visionary glimpse of the reality and feasibility of user-led care packages. (1993, p 28)

This was not the original aim of the government, and Morris (1993a, p 13) uses the phrase 'progress by default' to describe how a small-scale government policy measure could have such significant implications for the Independent Living Movement. While the ILF has continued to evolve, its underlying approach has remained similar since 1993 and, in 2006, the Department for Work and Pensions commissioned an independent review (Henwood and Hudson, 2007a). This described the ILF as 'an organisation created in haste to solve a particular political problem at a particular point in time' (para 12.4), but gave it credit for having 'played a significant part in the short history of independent living' (para 12.37). The review recommended that the ILF should continue to be administered in its current form for the short term, but that it should ultimately be fully incorporated into the personal budgets programme (see Chapter Five). Whatever the future may hold, however, it seems clear (at least with hindsight) that the ILF must be seen as a form of 'Pandora's box' (Hudson, 1993, p 28) that, once opened, would be very difficult to close again.

Post-war evolution of social care

This brief overview is illustrative of a more general change in the relationship between the individual and the state that has evolved in British post-war welfare services. In 1948 the National Assistance Act imposed upon local authorities the duty to provide residential care for those people who, by virtue of 'their age, infirmity or any other circumstances are in need of care and attention which is not otherwise available to them'. The care needs of people living in their own homes were then largely met by voluntary organisations and individuals' families and friends, although the role of local authorities in providing community-based services began to extend during the 1950s and 1960s (Means et al, 2008). Nevertheless, the relationship between the state and the individual was largely based on paternalism, with welfare professionals offering assistance from a limited range of prescribed services and characterising people in need of help as passive recipients of care (Audit Commission, 1992). During the 1970s and 1980s the increasing concern about the cost and quality of residential care resulted in a shift of resources from residential to community-based services. At the same time the Conservative government, with Margaret Thatcher as prime minister, made it clear that it saw a reduced role for the state in the provision of social care and an increased need for individual responsibility. Thus, as the 1981 White Paper,

Growing Older, suggested: 'care in the community must necessarily mean by the community' (DHSS, 1981, p 3).

Although the community care reforms of the 1990s often adopted the rhetoric of citizenship, many of the detailed changes fell far short of a rights-based approach to social welfare (Rummery, 2006; Lister, 2008). Instead, the emphasis was more on introducing notions of consumerism into welfare policies, with people who used social care services recast as 'customers' with the ability to exercise influence and choice over decisions about their care (DH, 1989). Ultimately, if people using services did not like what they were receiving, the reforms implied that they had the right to take their 'custom' elsewhere. However, as Chapter Seven suggests, many commentators are critical of consumerism, claiming that its application to the majority of people who receive social care services is inappropriate and misplaced (see, for example, Barnes and Walker, 1996; M. Barnes, 1997; Rummery, 2006; Means et al, 2008).

With the coming to power of New Labour in 1997, the 'modernisation' of public services sought 'to deliver efficient, high quality and responsive public services' (Butcher, 2002, p 184), based increasingly around the 'principle of "person-centredness"' (Scourfield, 2007, p 110). Despite this change in language, commentators continue to debate the extent to which the modernisation agenda differs significantly from what went before. Certainly in social care there is some evidence to support the view that not a great deal has changed in people's experiences from those outlined in Boxes 2.2 and 2.3 from the early 1990s. While the focus is now less on institutional forms of care and more on intensive support at home, current services often seem just as inflexible and unresponsive as the previous system (see, for example, Raynes et al, 2001; Patmore and McNulty, 2005; CSCI, 2006a). Thus, a national inspection of home care services carried out by the Commission for Social Care Inspection (CSCI, 2006a) found that, despite widespread appreciation of the help they received from individual workers, older people were still concerned about the timing and the lack of reliability of visits, shortness of visits, inadequate time to carry out tasks and frustration about the restriction on what home carers could do (see Box 2.6). Despite service providers' intentions to provide personalised care at home, therefore, the capacity of the older people to exercise choice and control over the services they received remained severely restricted.

How, then, has the introduction of direct payments and personal budgets addressed some of these issues? Chapter Six documents in detail the largely positive messages that have come from the recipients of direct payments and personal budgets. The majority of people report an increase in the control they feel they have over their lives, with greater ability to choose what they receive, how and from whom (see Leece and Bornat, 2006 for various accounts of the experiences of direct payment recipients). Nevertheless, difficulties and barriers to implementation still exist, not least of which are some of the tensions experienced by social workers whose role it is to assess people's eligibility for direct payments.

As Ellis (2007, p 409) explains:

> Social workers also face conflict between their legal obligations to ration access to direct payments and their ethical obligation to value self-determination and empowerment – a tension heightened by the rooting of eligibility criteria in functional and financial definitions of independence rather than on autonomy and full participation.

Box 2.6: Older people's experiences of home care services

"They do the hoovering, sink, toilet. They will open cans, which is a big help. They will not dust."

"Home carers won't clean – it's not allowed."

"They couldn't do this, they couldn't do that – nothing above this level, nothing below that. In the end I told them 'is it worth your while coming? Because it's not a lot of good to me.'"

"They [volunteers] do all the things that paid carers can't or won't do. The big difference is that the carers come and do what someone else has decided I need, and the volunteers come and ask what I want."

"It's silly. They said, 'Can you wash and dress?' And I said 'Yes.' They said, 'Oh, you don't qualify for help.' But I don't want someone to help me wash and dress – I want someone to help me with housework, I don't want to depend on my family."

"I'm terrified of social services – they want to know too much – I struggle on – it's just the fear of not being well."

"I had five different carers in ten days. I have to explain things in detail. One brought me cold water to wash all over. I had to say: there are two taps …"

"There should be a central point for carers training. We have to learn to lift and to care for our relatives because we don't have any other choice. I had to teach the carers how to use a hoist and how to lift a person. This problem needs urgent attention."

(CSCI, 2006a, pp 36-45)

In a study of social workers' approaches to direct payments, Ellis (2007) found that Lipsky's (1980) theory of 'street-level bureaucracy' is still pertinent to the way in which social workers ration their time and resources and act as gatekeepers to direct payments. These issues are explored in more detail in Chapter Seven, but here lies the nub of what Duffy (2005c) sees as one of the key limitations of direct payments: that they are still administered within what he calls 'the professional gift relationship' (see also Figure 5.1, Chapter Five). As Waters and Duffy (2007, p 8) maintain:

> Both these approaches [direct payments and the Independent Living Fund] were still expected to fit within an overall system of Social Care that was not designed to support Independent Living. Although there has been significant progress in moving away from its institutional legacy the assumptions of the past still influence the current system. Today the current system of Social Care is still not designed to treat recipients as citizens who are entitled to support and who can be expected to take control over their own support. Instead support is treated as a 'gift' which is given to people on the basis of an assessment of their needs.

In short, despite the significant changes that have taken place in the design and delivery of services, the underlying ethos of social care and the relationship between the state and the individual have remained remarkably stable over time. In contrast to the professional gift model, Duffy (2005c) advocates a system of self-directed support, based upon citizen entitlement rather than on discretion. These concepts are explored in detail in Chapter Five, but the emerging evidence suggests that self-directed support and personal budgets may address some of the unanswered questions about direct payments – introducing a more even-handed and transparent relationship between the individual and the state, which will address concerns about equity and social justice (Riddell et al, 2005; Rummery, 2006; Ellis, 2007; Scourfield, 2007). However, these issues are contentious – and success is by no means guaranteed. As Waters and Duffy (2007, p 13) caution:

> The approach is a form of co-production – with the [personal budget] forming one part of the new 'contract' between the citizen and the state. However, this shift is not merely technological. It is primarily cultural and it would be wrong to conceive of the cultural change being merely about changes in how professionals think and behave. Self-directed support is a challenge not just to professionals but to the whole of society.

SUMMARY

In order to overcome the stigma of the Poor Law, post-war social work in Britain has been characterised by the separation of social security and social services, with the former focusing on financial needs and the latter on providing welfare services for frail and disabled people. Once widely hailed as a step forward, this separation has since been criticised for enforcing an artificial distinction that does not adequately reflect people's needs, and for depriving social work of an awareness of poverty issues. Against this background, the decision to enable local authorities to make cash payments in lieu of directly provided services represents a major cultural shift that significantly alters the role of social services departments. As a result, those seeking to promote direct payments need to be aware of the magnitude of the task ahead of them in seeking to overcome social workers' opposition to this new way of working (see Chapter Seven for further discussion).

Prior to the introduction of direct payments in 1996, pressure for reform had been mounting for some time. Crucially, key figures in the campaign for change were disabled people themselves, critiquing local authority services, organising themselves into an Independent Living Movement and persuading the government to introduce the ILF. As criticisms of directly provided services increased, the experience of receiving ILF payments began to alter the relationship between service users and service providers, demonstrating the liberating and empowering potential of disabled people purchasing personal assistance directly. Although the government acted in order to limit the scope of the ILF, services could not return to the pre-1988 situation and reform of some description was almost inevitable.

In post-war Britain there have been a number of minor changes and developments in the relationship between the state and people who use welfare services. A largely paternalistic philosophy has gradually been replaced by one that, at least in principle, acknowledges that people want choice and flexibility in the services they receive. However, people using services – even when they can access a direct payment – still remain recipients of a 'professional gift' without necessarily feeling that they are entitled to support as citizens. Against this background, the advent of personal budgets, discussed in further detail in Chapter Five, has the potential to change fundamentally the relationship between the individual and the state – and it is for this reason that the issues discussed in this book are so contentious but also so important.

IMPLICATIONS FOR POLICY AND PRACTICE

- Historically, social workers held an important role in administering cash payments to people in need of financial help. However, the advent of the post-war welfare state meant this was removed when a national system for the payment of social security benefits was established.
- As direct payments are now mandatory in all local authorities and as personal budgets are introduced, social work practice must once again be prepared to engage with financial issues.
- Central to direct payments and personal budgets are the principles of independent living. Some social care professionals may find these challenging to their current practice and so be reluctant to advocate for direct payments and personal budgets.
- The introduction of direct payments and personal budgets represents a fundamental change in the relationship between the state and the individual (which will have implications for service users, families, practitioners, managers and policy makers alike).

Recommended reading and useful websites

For those interested in the historical overview provided above, Payne (2005) offers an interesting account of the origins of social work, with a comprehensive list of references and relevant websites.

Accessible accounts of the development of post–war social care services can also be found in Glasby (2007), Glasby and Littlechild (2004), Means and Smith (1998b) and Means et al (2008).

Morris (1993a) gives an overview of the philosophy of the Independent Living Movement and summarises accounts from disabled people about the inflexibility of directly provided services.

Butcher (2002) and Lister (2008) both explore the concept of citizenship, while Rummery (2006) looks specifically at the role of direct payments in supporting disabled people to become full citizens.

A number of commentators take a more critical look at the role of direct payments and personal budgets in addressing issues of social exclusion; these include Ellis (2007), Riddell et al (2005), Rummery (2006), Ferguson (2007) and Scourfield (2007). Many of the issues raised in these accounts are explored in further detail in Chapters Six and Seven of this book.

Information about independent living and the campaign for direct payments can be found via:

- the UK Disabled People's Council (www.bcodp.org.uk) – formerly the British Council of Disabled People;
- the National Centre for Independent Living (www.ncil.org.uk);

- the Disability Archive (www.leeds.ac.uk/disability-studies/archiveuk) – an excellent source of published and 'grey' literature on disability studies, including a number of hard to access but crucial accounts of the history of the independent living movement.

For personal budgets, access the in Control website (www.in-control.org.uk).

Information about the ILF is available via www.ilf.org.uk. Henwood and Hudson's (2007a) review of the Independent Living Fund can be accessed via the Department for Work and Pensions website (www.dwp.gov.uk/publications/dwp/2007/independentliving/).

Reflective exercises

1. How does an understanding of the history of social work help explain the relationship between social work and financial issues? How has this changed over time and what difference do direct payments and personal budgets make to social work practice?
2. In a group, take it in turns to describe what the term 'independent living' means to you. To what extent do you agree with each other? Compare your answers with the definitions used by NCIL in Box 2.4.
3. How well do you think the description of services in Box 2.2 fits the principles of independent living? How could some of those limitations be addressed by direct payments and personal budgets?
4. What is your understanding of how the relationship between the individual and the state has changed over the last 100 years? In particular, how do you think it has changed since the introduction of direct payments? What other differences do you think the introduction of personal budgets might make to this relationship?

THREE

Direct payments – where they came from and how they developed

This chapter explores:
- indirect payments and the campaign for direct payments;
- the 1996 Community Care (Direct Payments) Act;
- the extension of direct payments and recent policy developments;
- a more recent reaction possibly emerging against direct payments.

Despite the growth of the Independent Living Movement and the popularity of the ILF, direct payments to individual service users were illegal under the 1948 National Assistance Act until the passage of the 1996 Community Care (Direct Payments) Act (see Box 3.1). Although the 1968 Social Work (Scotland) Act did permit direct payments in certain circumstances, these were heavily prescribed and the power to make such payments was rarely used (Zarb and Nadash, 1994; Witcher et al, 2000). Nevertheless, pressure had begun to build for some sort of cash payment to enable disabled people to make their own care arrangements (see Chapter Two). Against this background, this chapter covers the key milestones in the campaign for direct payments, from the growth of indirect payments in the 1980s–1990s to the potential for a reaction against this way of working.

Box 3.1: Direct payments prior to 1996

Nothing in the foregoing provisions of this section shall authorise or require: (a) the payment of money to persons to whom this section applies ... [that is to say, persons who are blind, deaf or dumb, and other persons who are substantially and permanently handicapped by illness, injury, or congenital deformity].

Source: 1948 National Assistance Act, section 29

Indirect payments and the campaign for direct payments

As awareness about the potential advantages of enabling disabled people to purchase their own care increased, both service users and local authorities began to explore methods of circumventing the prohibitions of the National Assistance

Act. For John Evans, then chair of the BCODP Independent Living Committee, it was crucial to get rid of 'that damn silly law from 1948, and accept that direct payments for some people are just common sense' (quoted in George, 1994, p 15). Others agreed, and a range of schemes were developed in different parts of the country to make payments to disabled people, some of doubtful legality (Mandelstam, 1999). Although arrangements varied, the two main approaches were to make payments via a third party (such as a voluntary agency) or via an independent trust (see Box 3.2 for examples).

Probably the first example of indirect payments was in Hampshire in the early 1980s, where a group of disabled people were able to move out of residential care after persuading their local authority to take the pioneering step of making payments to each individual via the original residential home (Project 81, nd; Shearer, 1984; Zarb and Nadash, 1994, pp 5-6; Brindle, 2008a). Although the Hampshire scheme faced closure because of legal concerns raised by the county's solicitor and treasurer, a report from the Audit Commission (1986, p 69) cited Hampshire's payment scheme as an example of innovative good practice (Evans

Box 3.2: Indirect payments

To overcome legal restrictions, Lauren used to receive payments from her local authority via a housing association. This meant that the housing association was the employer, not Lauren. So she took further action to enhance her control of her care package. On the suggestion of a friend, Lauren set up a trust to receive the payments on her behalf. The trust deed was drawn up by a solicitor, and Lauren served as a trustee together with three friends. Lauren now employs four PAs and is able to work and care for her mother. To ensure accountability to the local authority, a social worker sits on the trust.
(Morris, 1993a, p 122)

There are examples of severely disabled people living in the community. One of the best is provided by the Centre for Independent Living based at Lee Court Cheshire Home in Hampshire. The Social Services Department and Health Authority have contributed funds to a trust for purchasing care which is administered by the Leonard Cheshire Foundation. The disabled person buys in the help they need with this money, topped up by his or her own social security benefits. Thus the disabled people construct their own packages of care and employ their own staff in a highly autonomous fashion.
(Audit Commission, 1986, p 69)

One example is that of Lothian Social Work Department who, having assessed someone's personal assistance needs, makes a quarterly cash payment in advance for the cost of paying for that assistance to the Edinburgh Voluntary Organisation Council. The payment is passed on to the individual who then uses it to either employ their own personal assistants, or to employ agency staff.
(Morris, 1995)

and Hasler, 1996). This proved enough to save the project, and Hampshire remained a key player during the implementation of direct payments.

Over time, payment schemes began to expand and, in 1990, research commissioned by RADAR found that 59% of 69 participating local authorities made payments to disabled people, either directly or indirectly through intermediaries (Browne, 1990, quoted in Hatchett, 1991, p 14). The latter included charities, housing associations and national organisations such as the Spinal Injuries Association (Hatchett, 1991, p 14; Craig, 1992, p 47; Morris, 1993a, p 26). Although payment recipients were often individuals who had taken the initiative in putting their case to the local authority (Morris, 1993a), most participating authorities in the study suggested that they would welcome legislation enabling them to make such payments (Craig, 1992, p 47).

In 1994, researchers from the Policy Studies Institute (PSI) carried out a national postal survey of local authorities in England, Wales and Scotland, with a 64% response rate (Zarb and Nadash, 1994). The study found that just under 60% of participating authorities were already operating payments schemes (most of which involved indirect payments through a third party or through trusts). This figure was almost identical to the RADAR study of 1990, the key difference being that there was far less evidence in the 1994 survey of authorities making payments directly to service users than in 1990 (5% and 23% respectively). However, this was felt to be a product of contemporary legal concerns, following government statements on the illegality of direct payments (to be discussed later). As a result, several authorities had taken legal advice, changed from direct to indirect payments or ceased making payments altogether. Despite this, just over 90% of respondents indicated that they would make direct payments if legislation permitted, with only three authorities stating that they were definitely opposed to such changes.

Thwarted reforms

As evidence of the benefits of paying cash sums to individual service users increased, so pressure began to mount for legislation to promote direct payments. Throughout this process, organisations of disabled people and advocates of independent living were at the forefront of the campaign for change, lobbying Members of Parliament, organising meetings and commissioning research (Evans and Hasler, 1996). A good example of the way in which disabled people were able to take the lead in the campaign for direct payments comes from Kingston-upon-Thames, where an early and prominent payments scheme was established on the initiative of two local disabled people. As part of this process, the disabled people approached the social services department with their proposal for a payments scheme, produced formal documentation for the social services committee and participated in a pilot scheme (Macfarlane, 1990; DH, 1998a).

As part of the lobbying process, BCODP quickly found an influential supporter in Andrew Rowe, Conservative MP for Faversham and mid-Kent (Evans and Hasler, 1996). Having encountered the concept of direct payments through a disabled member of his constituency, Rowe became a committed supporter of the Independent Living Movement and was a key player in campaigning for the legislative changes, which were finally introduced under the 1996 Community Care (Direct Payments) Act. During parliamentary debates on the NHS and Community Care Bill in 1990, the issue of direct payments was raised in both the House of Commons and the House of Lords, with a number of proposed amendments to promote direct payments. Unfortunately, this campaign was to backfire, with serious and unintended consequences. Having examined the issue of making cash payments to disabled people, the government found that this practice was illegal under the 1948 National Assistance Act and in the policy guidance accompanying the community care reforms reminded local authorities that current legislation 'prohibit[ed] the making of cash payments in place of arranging services' (DH, 1990, p 26). Thus, a measure designed to promote the concept of direct payments and support existing payment schemes had actually resulted in such schemes being declared illegal (personal communication, Andrew Rowe). This was to cause considerable difficulties for a number of local authorities, who were broadly supportive of direct payments yet were understandably concerned that they should be seen to be operating within the law.

Once direct payments had been declared illegal, the only course of action was to campaign for new legislation to overturn this prohibition. In 1992, Andrew Rowe tried to introduce a Private Member's Bill (the Disabled Persons (Services) Bill), which would have enabled disabled people who were able and willing to do so to employ their own staff with the bills paid by the local authority. While Andrew Rowe's preferred choice was for disabled people to control their own payments, his Bill was designed to overcome considerable Treasury concerns about the danger of public money being misappropriated (personal communication). The Bill failed to become legislation, with key concerns about the perceived difficulty of establishing adequate procedures to ensure that public money was spent appropriately and the possible risk that PAs might exploit or abuse disabled people (Zarb and Nadash, 1994; Campbell, 1996).

Throughout the events described above, considerable lobbying and campaigning was taking place, without much apparent success. While groups of disabled people met key politicians who appeared to support independent living schemes, campaigners perceived that a significant barrier to support for a change in legislation was the government's concern that direct payments schemes would cost too much (Evans and Hasler, 1996). In response, the BCODP Independent Living Committee decided to change its tactics somewhat, commissioning independent research in order to investigate the cost implications and effectiveness of direct payment schemes. With funding from the Joseph Rowntree Foundation (JRF), BCODP was able to commission the PSI to undertake the desired research. The resulting study, *Cashing in on independence* (Zarb and Nadash, 1994), was a key document and is still referred to time and time again throughout this book and other literature on direct payments. While it is difficult to gauge how successful it was in persuading the government to implement direct payments, it must undoubtedly have been a factor in the government's eventual change of heart on the direct payments issue (to be discussed below).

Despite government opposition to direct payments and the defeat of Andrew Rowe's proposed legislation, the BCODP campaign did receive significant support from other bodies, most notably from the Association of Directors of Social Services (ADSS) (Evans and Hasler, 1996). In 1992, ADSS adopted a resolution in support of direct payments and became an increasingly active member of the campaign for a change in the law (Taylor, 1996a). In addition to writing the foreword to *Cashing in on independence* (Zarb and Nadash, 1994), Roy Taylor (then chair of the ADSS Disabilities Committee) was a key player in the struggle for direct payments (see, for example, Taylor, 1994, 1995, 1996a-b, 1997). In addition to the ADSS, other key supporters of direct payments included the Audit Commission, the Prince of Wales Advisory Group on Disability, the British Association of Social Workers and the Association of Metropolitan Authorities (*Hansard*, House of Lords Debates 21 April 1993, col 1642; Evans, 2000). Also at this time, the concept of direct payments received qualified support from the House of Commons Health Committee (1993), which felt that more research was required before direct payments could be implemented, but that such payments were consistent with the emphasis of the community care reforms on user involvement and choice.

Despite widespread support for direct payments, disabled people were not without their concerns about the uncertainty of what the future might hold with regard to independent living. With the legality of payment schemes thrown into doubt and a series of abortive attempts to introduce new legislation, many disabled people were unsure about the future availability of payments (Zarb and Nadash, 1994). This uncertainty was later to continue after the implementation of the 1996 Community Care (Direct Payments) Act, for the initial discretionary nature of the reforms meant that disabled people had no guarantees that the various direct payment schemes that had been piloted would continue and be adopted into mainstream service provision. In many ways, this was similar to events in the early 1990s, when the introduction of the community care reforms led to fears about the longer-term availability of ILF payments. There are also parallels with the more recent situation, where some have viewed the introduction of personal budgets as a potential threat to direct payments (see Chapter Five).

Nevertheless, the government was faced with a considerable dilemma as pressure from influential quarters mounted for change. Members of the government had expressed their support for the concept of independent living, and the rationale for direct payments was in line with the principles of choice and control that underpinned their community care reforms. However, there were also concerns about rapidly rising public expenditure and fears about what might happen if direct payments were introduced. In many ways, this combination of commitment to the underlying principles and concerns about the practical and financial implications has also greeted the advent of personal budgets (see Chapter Five for further discussion).

The 1996 Community Care (Direct Payments) Act

The legislation

In November 1994, the government announced its intention to legislate in order to enable local authorities to make direct payments to service users rather than providing community care services directly:

> I [Virginia Bottomley, health secretary] intend to take … a new power to enable social services authorities and social work departments to make direct cash payments to disabled people in lieu of community care services. Direct payments … will give disabled people greater independence and choice and involve them and their carers more fully in their own care. (DH, 1994, p 1)

While it may never be entirely clear what led to this change of heart, there appear to have been a number of key considerations. The imminent launch of the BCODP/PSI research into direct payments (which showed that direct payments were both cheaper than directly provided services and resulted in higher-quality services) may have been a key factor in persuading the government to reconsider its previous opposition (Zarb and Nadash, 1994; Evans and Hasler, 1996). For Andrew Rowe, direct payments were the result of a dedicated and sustained campaign for reform and the momentum for change was simply too strong for the government to resist. Ultimately, 'direct payments were an idea whose time had long since come' (Andrew Rowe, personal communication).

Once the decision had been taken to introduce direct payments, a number of practical matters needed to be resolved before new legislation could be drawn up. As a result, a Technical Advisory Group (TAG), including representatives from central government, local authorities and organisations of disabled people, met to consider some of the technical issues which implementation would raise, drew up guidance for government ministers and civil servants, and contributed to a 1996 consultation paper on direct payments. Although the group included three disability organisations, only one member of TAG was a personal assistance user running her own direct payment scheme (Evans and Hasler, 1996).

Building on the work of TAG, the Department of Health introduced a consultation paper in January 1996 on its proposals for direct payments (DH/ Scottish Office/Welsh Office/Northern Ireland Office, 1996). In addition to setting out how direct payments would operate, the consultation paper sought views on a number of key issues to be contained within the regulations and guidance. Central to the government's view of how direct payments should function was the belief that recipients must be 'willing' to receive payments instead of services and 'able' to manage them (DH/Scottish Office/Welsh Office/Northern Ireland Office, 1996, p 3). While service users could receive extensive support from others, they would ultimately remain responsible for the management of their payments.

Crucially, the Direct Payments Bill would give the secretary of state the power to specify which groups could receive direct payments, a move justified in terms of the need to restrict the number of direct payment recipients while the scheme was in its infancy (DH/Scottish Office/Welsh Office/Northern Ireland Office, 1996, pp 3-4). As a result, the consultation paper set out six possible groups of people that might be able to benefit from direct payments, emphasising that its own preference was to limit direct payments to people with physical impairments under the age of 65 (DH/Scottish Office/Welsh Office/Northern Ireland Office, 1996, pp 4-5). While this preference was never enacted, it does give an early insight into official thinking and undoubtedly affected the take-up of direct payments by some user groups (see Chapter Four). Another key issue in the consultation paper was a restriction on using direct payments to employ partners or close relatives (to be discussed later; see also Chapter Seven). This was justified by a desire to prevent existing informal care arrangements from becoming too formalised, to prevent the risk of exploitation and to prevent family members from feeling under pressure to give up their jobs and become full-time carers (DH/Scottish Office/Welsh Office/Northern Ireland Office, 1996, p 8). However, a more cynical interpretation might be that it would prove too expensive to pay family carers for work that they had previously been expected to carry out free of charge as part of their family obligations.

As a result of the government's determination to reserve the power to restrict eligibility for direct payments, the 1996 Community Care (Direct Payments) Act was relatively concise, with the bulk of detail provided through accompanying regulations and subsequent policy and practice guidance. As the government had already indicated in its 1996 consultation paper, the user groups eligible for direct payments could be expanded at a later stage if the experiment proved successful, without the need for further legislation. Consequently, the Act itself simply authorised local authorities to make payments directly to disabled people (see Boxes 3.3 and 3.4), with the bulk of the reforms to be set out in much greater detail by the secretary of state.

Box 3.3: The 1996 Community Care (Direct Payments) Act

Be it enacted... as follows:

> Where an authority have decided ... that the needs of a person call for the provision of any community care services ... the authority may, if the person consents, make to him, in respect of his securing the provision of any of the services for which they have decided his needs call, a payment of such amount as ... they think fit.

Box 3.4: Key changes under the 1996 Community Care (Direct Payments) Act

- Local authorities had the *power*, not the *duty* to provide direct payments.
- Direct payments could be paid to all adult user groups under the age of 65.
- Payments were not to be used for more than four weeks' residential care in any period of 12 months.
- Payments could not be used to employ certain types of relatives and household members.

Thanks to ongoing lobbying by disabled people's organisations, the government's original intention to exclude people with learning difficulties and/or with mental health problems from direct payments was defeated and direct payments were to be available to all adult user groups under 65.

Policy and practice guidance

After the passage of the 1996 Community Care (Direct Payments) Act, official policy and practice guidance was issued in May 1997 (DH, 1997; see also DHSSPS, 1997; National Assembly for Wales, 1997; Scottish Office, 1997). In the event, implementation in Northern Ireland was delayed for one year until 1998. However, since 1997/98, the original guidance has been revised and updated as direct payments legislation has been extended and as emerging practice has revealed ongoing barriers to further progress (see, for example, DH, 2000a, 2001a–c, 2003a). Whereas the 1997 policy guidance set out *what* local authorities should do if they chose to exercise their new power to make direct payments, the practice guidance advised on *how* authorities might implement the Act. From the very beginning, the policy guidance emphasised that the government's aim was to enhance the independence of service users by giving them control over the way that community care services are delivered. To maximise this independence, local authorities should work in partnership with disabled people and leave as much choice as possible in the hands of the service user, while at the same time ensuring that the individual's needs are being met and that public money is being used appropriately and cost effectively. Although authorities now had the *power* to make direct payments, this was not a *duty*, and local authorities retained discretion over whether or not to implement direct payments and the detail of how to do so. However, whatever an authority decided to do, the guidance was clear that it should not treat direct payment recipients any more, or less, favourably than people receiving services, and should continue to develop other ways of making services more responsive.

Since payments were only to be made by local authority social services departments in lieu of community care services, the Act did not allow any other body (such as a health or housing authority) to make direct payments, nor for direct payments to be used for health- or housing-related services. Although direct payments could be used for all community care services, this excluded permanent residential care (including a total of more than four weeks' respite care in any 12-month period) and services provided directly by the local authority. Since direct payments are an alternative to community care services, the guidance made it clear that authorities offering payments needed to do so within their existing budgets and should only make a direct payment if this would be at least as cost-effective as the services that would otherwise be arranged.

The original legislation prevented payments to people under 18 or to adults wishing to purchase services for people aged under 18. Although users could ask carers, or other third parties, to help them manage direct payments, the user had to remain in control of the payment and was accountable for the way the money was used. The local authority had to be satisfied that the user consented to receiving payments and understood the financial and legal implications of receiving direct payments (in shorthand, being 'willing and able'). Throughout ongoing debates, it was often re-stated that payments are designed to enhance independence, not to transfer dependence from a local authority to dependence on a third party.

Initially, direct payments were to be made available only to disabled people under 65 (including people with physical impairments, learning difficulties, mental health problems and HIV/AIDS), although people receiving such payments before the age of 65 could carry on receiving them after that age. However, this was to be reviewed after the Act had been in force for one year. In addition, direct payments could not be offered to certain people in the mental health or criminal justice system. The original guidance confirmed that direct payments could not be used to purchase services from a partner or a close relative living in the same household. In addition, services could not be purchased from a close relative living elsewhere or from someone else living in the same household, although authorities could make an exception to this rule if this was the only appropriate way of securing the relevant services. For the purposes of the Act, a close relative was defined as a parent, parent-in-law, aunt, uncle, grandparent, son, daughter, son-in-law, daughter-in-law, step-son or step-daughter, brother, sister or the spouse or partner of any of the above. This restriction has since been revised (see later in this chapter and Chapter Seven for further discussion) and was not meant to prevent disabled people from employing live-in PAs, but to prevent recipients employing people with whom they had a personal, rather than a contractual, relationship.

Drawing on the experience of existing independent living schemes, the practice guidance emphasised that service users are well placed to judge how best to use direct payments and have a vested interest in using their payments properly on necessary services. The guidance acknowledged that direct payments can be complex, but stated that 'the aim should be to set up simple but effective systems, which contain safeguards but are not unnecessarily bureaucratic or time-consuming' (DH, 1997, p 26). Since direct payments are intended to enhance control, this process should begin at the very start through consultations with people with different types of impairment, people from different ethnic backgrounds and people of different ages. In particular, the practice guidance emphasised the importance of adequate support mechanisms, both before an assessment and at the point of making a decision about direct payments. This might include access to someone with employment expertise, a payroll service, lists of local agencies, assistance with drafting advertisements, job descriptions and contracts, rooms for interviewing, training, advocacy or written materials (see Chapter Seven for further discussion of the importance of support services). In particular:

> The experience of users on existing independent living schemes is that they find it easier to seek advice from someone who is independent of the local authority ... People who have experience of managing direct payments themselves are well placed to advise and help others as they begin to receive direct payments. In many areas, people who are managing their own care meet regularly to support one another and to discuss any difficulties which have arisen. This can be an effective way of sharing experience. (DH, 1997, pp 39-40)

The extension of direct payments

When direct payments were implemented in April 1997, policy and practice guidance emphasised that the reforms would be reviewed after one year, with a view to reconsidering the user groups eligible for direct payments (DH, 1997). Since the original 1996 Act, a number of developments have taken place:

- the extension of direct payments to older people, carers, people with parental responsibility for disabled children and disabled young people;
- revised policy and practice guidance;
- changes in legislation to make direct payments mandatory;
- the introduction of a performance indicator on direct payments;
- new forms of support to help people access direct payments;
- a change in legislation about the giving of consent for direct payments.

On 1 February 2000, new regulations removed the age limit that had initially applied to direct payments, enabling people aged 65 and over to benefit from such payments in authorities that decided to take advantage of the new powers available to them (Age Concern, 2000; Statutory Instrument (SI) 2000/11; see also Scottish Statutory Instrument (SSI) 2000/183; SI 2000/1868 (W127); Statutory Rule (SR) 2000/114). Since the original legislation, some policy and practice developments have taken place in Wales and Northern Ireland at a later date than in England but the basic principles have remained largely the same. In Scotland, however, there have been significant similarities, but also some key differences (which are addressed briefly later in this chapter).

In 2000, the Department of Health issued revised guidance to take account of the relatively slow progress to date in implementing direct payments and the recent extension of the scheme to older people (DH, 2000a; see also National Assembly for Wales, 2000; DHSSPS, 2000a-b; Scottish Executive, 2000). Although the guidance was often very similar to its predecessor, there were a number of changes in emphasis that seemed to indicate the government's intention to increase the availability of direct payments and to ensure that particular groups of service users were not excluded. As a result, the guidance stressed from the beginning that direct payments have a very broad potential, improving quality of life, promoting independence, aiding social inclusion and encompassing areas such as rehabilitation, education, leisure and employment. The government was clear that it wanted 'to see more extensive use made of direct payments' (DH, 2000a, p 3) and that authorities would need to consider how to include people with different types of impairment, people from different ethnic backgrounds and people of different ages. When deciding whether or not to offer direct payments to an individual, authorities should not 'fetter their discretion' (that is, they should consider each case on its merits, even where the authority was not currently offering direct payments, and treat all adult client groups equitably) (DH, 2000a, p 4). Although direct payments could still only be offered if they were at least as cost-effective as direct services, there was a recognition that any consideration of cost-effectiveness should consider long-term best value.

At the same time as it issued revised guidance, the government also indicated its intention to introduce legislation to extend direct payments to a range of groups originally excluded from the 1996 Act. The 2000 Carers and Disabled Children Act, accompanied by a raft of policy and practice guidance (DH, 2001a-e), empowered local authorities to make direct payments to:

- carers aged 16 and over (for services that meet their own assessed needs to support them in their caring role);
- people with parental responsibility for disabled children (for services to meet the assessed needs of the disabled child or to provide short-term breaks that meet the needs of both parent and child);
- young disabled people (aged 16 and 17).

While the extension of direct payments to carers was broadly welcomed by many commentators, a number of concerns were raised. Disability organisations, such as NCIL (2000), suggested that there was scope for conflict between users and carers, arguing that extending direct payments to other groups should not undermine the basic goal of increasing users' independence.

Nevertheless, the government remained committed to extending the take-up of direct payments and in 2001 made this way of working mandatory rather than discretionary. Under section 57 of the 2001 Health and Social Care Act, local authorities must offer direct payments to anyone who is eligible for community care services, consents to receiving payments and is able to do so. Shortly after this extension of direct payments came into effect in 2003, moreover, direct payments became one of the Social Services Performance Assessment Framework Indicators (DH, 2003b) and they remain a key benchmark by which performance is assessed (CSCI, 2006b). Although the 2008 Health and Social Care Act has created a new integrated regulator, the Care Quality Commission, it seems likely that increasing the number of direct payments will remain an important task for adult social care. Despite these positive attempts to promote direct payments, however, an unfortunate backwards step came when the Department for Work and Pensions caused widespread confusion with a national campaign to promote their own version of 'direct payments' (social security benefits paid direct into recipients' bank accounts; see CSCI, 2004; DH, 2005a).

To accompany legislative changes under the 2001 Health and Social Care Act, the government produced new guidance in 2003–04 (DH, 2003a; see also Scottish Executive, 2003; DHSSPS, 2004; Welsh Assembly Government, 2004). Now that direct payments were mandatory, the government recognised that 'for some staff/professionals, direct payments may require a significant change from current ways of working with people needing services' and that this may involve a 'cultural leap' (DH, 2003a, p 5). While the principles of direct payments remain largely the same as in previous guidance, there were three areas in the 2003 guidance that received additional attention:

- *The employment of close relatives*: a key change was a relaxation of rules about employing close relatives. While direct payments may not ordinarily be used to pay for services from a close relative living in the *same* household, the restrictions were lifted on employing relatives who lived *elsewhere*. The wording of the guidance does not, however, appear positively to *encourage* the employment of relatives who live in other households, rather it is the omission of the phrase '*living elsewhere*' that signifies the change (see Box 3.5).
- *Issues of cost-efficiency*: in deciding whether or not direct payments represent a cost–effective option, local authorities can consider long-term issues such as whether or not direct payments are likely to prevent a future hospital or residential care admission. As in 2000, this is a much wider definition of cost-efficiency than in the original guidance and includes not only social services expenditure, but also possible savings to the system as a whole (see Box 3.6). Of course, if direct payments can be used to make long-term savings in both health and social care, there may be a case for extending their scope beyond social services provision (see Chapter Five).
- *Additional support*: in an attempt to encourage new groups of people to receive direct payments and increase the overall numbers of recipients, the Department of Health launched a £9 million Direct Payments Development Fund (DPDF) in 2003, available over three years. The Fund was used to pay for voluntary organisations, in partnership with local authorities, to set up additional information and support services. The money was allocated in two rounds: in July 2003 £4.5 million was paid to 43 voluntary organisations; the

following year 42 grants were made (Hasler, 2006, p 150). The DPDF also made a single grant to NCIL, as the key national organisation for disabled people, of £280,000 per year over three years, which included an evaluation of all the projects receiving DPDF funding. In addition, the DPDF was subject to an external evaluation by the Personal Social Services Research Unit (PSSRU) at the London School of Economics (LSE), which assessed whether or not the Fund had reached its primary objective of increasing take-up and whether the process of involving the voluntary sector in the grant allocated had worked (Hasler, 2006, pp 150-1). More limited resources for support organisations to perform similar roles were also made available for Scotland, Wales and Northern Ireland (Pearson, 2006).

Box 3.5: Relaxation of rules on employment of close relatives

Regulations ... prevent people using direct payments to secure services from their partner (i.e. the other member of a married or unmarried couple) or a close relative living in the same household. A close relative in this context is a parent, parent-in-law, aunt, uncle, grandparent, son, daughter, son-in-law, daughter-in-law, step son or daughter, brother, sister or the spouse or partner of any of these. In addition, local authorities should not allow people who use direct payments to secure services from a close relative, living elsewhere or from someone else living in the same household as the direct payment recipient.
(DH, 2000a, paras 23-4)

Unless a council is satisfied that it is necessary to meet satisfactorily a person's needs, a council may not allow people to use direct payments to secure services from a spouse (husband or wife), from a partner (the other member of an unmarried couple with whom they live) or from a close relative (or their spouse or partner) who live in the same household as the direct payment recipient.
(DH, 2003a, para 94)

Box 3.6: Calculating the amount of a direct payment

A preventive strategy may necessitate a higher investment to achieve long-term benefits and savings. Provision of direct payments that allow a person to remain in their own home may represent long-term savings if that person does not then require hospital or residential care. Similarly, the provision of direct payments to a person in need of rehabilitative care may result in a more sensitive and individualised service which may in turn ease a person's recovery.
(DH, 2003a, para 87)

Building on the issue of appropriate support, findings from the NCIL evaluation (2006) showed that the DPDF helped to increase the number of people receiving direct payments and to get direct payments onto local agendas. During the course of the project an additional 8,483 people received direct payments, twice as many as had originally been estimated (NCIL, 2006, p 12). Box 3.7 gives a summary of some of the key factors that the study found can enhance the take-up of direct payments. Despite this, a national survey of support organisations (Davey et al, 2007a) showed a steady increase in the level of support for direct payments recipients across the UK, but a wide variation in the kind of support available. The survey found that over 50% of people receiving direct payments did not receive help from a support scheme, but it was not clear whether this was because they felt they did not need assistance, found help elsewhere or could not access a support scheme (Davey et al, 2007a, p 92). In England, approximately one-third of support schemes did not provide support to all user groups (which raises concerns that a number of user groups may be missing out on accessing appropriate support). A further concern was about the sustainability of support services, given that the DPDF was time limited. In addition, the survey found that most schemes focused on promoting the take-up and setting-up of direct payments, with approximately one-third leaving the maintenance and ongoing management of direct payments to the recipient (which may account for some of the variability in take-up rates between different user groups in Chapter Four).

Box 3.7: Factors likely to enhance the take-up of direct payments

The evaluation of the Development Fund projects has confirmed that the take up of direct payments is enhanced if:

- Sufficient levels of consistent support are provided to individual service users.
- There is good knowledge of direct payments amongst local statutory organisations and voluntary and community groups.
- Local authorities take a strategic lead on direct payments.
- Users are involved in all areas of direct payments.
- There is understanding of the principles of independent living.

(NCIL, 2006, p 84)

Although direct payments were introduced by a Conservative government, they have received whole-hearted support from New Labour. In 2003, Stephen Ladyman, then the community care minister, argued that:

> The assumption should be not only will care be delivered by a direct payment; the assumption should be that the person can manage a direct payment and the only times when care should be delivered,

in my view, other than by a direct payment, is when the individual themselves has made a personal and positive choice to receive the care directly and not via a direct payment. (NCIL, 2003)

More recently, the parliamentary under-secretary of state for care services described direct payments as: 'Crucial to delivering the government's aim to increase independence, choice and control of social services for service users and their carers through allowing them the opportunity to arrange their own personalised care' (DH, 2008b, p 2; see also Box 3.8 for further examples).

Box 3.8: Key policy documents supporting direct payments (see also Chapter Five)

Improving the Life Chances of Disabled People (Prime Minister's Strategy Unit, 2005): in this wide-ranging strategy document, the government identified direct payments as a key mechanism for promoting independent living for disabled people.

Independence, Well-being and Choice (DH, 2005a): one of the key proposals in this Green Paper was 'wider use of direct payments and individual budgets to stimulate the development of modern services delivered in the way people want' (DH, 2005a, para 13.2).

Our Health, Our Care, Our Say (DH, 2006): this White Paper confirmed the government's commitment to expanding direct payments and extending them to groups of people who had previously not been eligible to receive them.

Putting People First (HM Government, 2007): this concordat, produced by central and local government, professional bodies, social care providers and regulators, pledged to increase the number of people receiving direct payments and to roll out personal budgets throughout all adult social care.

The Health and Social Care Act 2008 extended the availability of direct payments to people who lack capacity by enabling a direct payment to be made to a 'suitable person' acting on their behalf.

Although legislation for direct payments was passed for all countries of the UK at the same time, the exact nature and pace of implementation has varied, in Scotland in particular (Pearson, 2004; see also Chapter Four). Direct payments are now seen as one means of 'self-directed support' to enable people to achieve independent living (Scottish Executive, 2007). The Scottish Executive has actively encouraged direct payments and in 2002 allocated a development grant of £530,000 over two years to Direct Payments Scotland. The aims of the project were to set up user-led support organisations, provide training, build confidence, promote awareness of direct payments at local and national levels and facilitate information sharing (Scottish Executive, 2001). Other key developments in Scottish legislation and regulations are highlighted in Box 3.9.

The availability of direct payments has most recently been extended in England by the 2008 Health and Social Care Act. Until lately, a key anomaly was experienced by parents receiving a direct payment for a disabled child. If the child was assessed as lacking capacity to manage a direct payment when they became an adult, the family/individual should technically lose their direct payment. In the 2006 White Paper, *Our Health, Our Care, Our Say*, the government therefore agreed to extend the availability of direct payments to people who lack capacity as defined under the 2005 Mental Capacity Act and so are unable to give consent to receiving a direct payment (DH, 2006). In 2008, the Health and Social Care Act extended the availability of direct payments to such people by enabling a direct payment to

---

Box 3.9: Key developments in Scottish legislation and policy

- The 1968 Social Work (Scotland) Act permitted cash payments in exceptional circumstances.
- The 1996 Community Care (Direct Payments) Act enabled payments to adults aged 18–64.
- 2000 – direct payments extended to older people.
- The 2002 Community Care and Health (Scotland) Act placed a mandatory duty on local authorities to offer direct payments from June 2003.
- Accompanying regulations (SSI 2003/243) specified that direct payments were to be offered to parents with parental responsibility for disabled children but, unlike in England, Wales and Northern Ireland, not to carers.
- In contrast to other parts of the UK, the Act extended direct payments to *all* people assessed as having care needs, including people who are 'frail, receiving rehabilitation after an accident or operation, fleeing domestic violence, refugees, homeless or recovering from drug or alcohol dependence' (Pearson, 2006, p 36). The date for this change was subsequently revised from 2004 to 2005 (SSI 2005/114).
- Unlike the rest of the UK, the 2003 regulations also extended direct payments to attorneys and guardians for people unable to manage their own payments.
- Under the 2003 regulations, close relatives who lived with a person receiving a direct payment could not be paid but relatives living elsewhere were eligible for payment. However, the 2007 Adult Support and Protection (Scotland) Act, section 63, empowered local authorities 'to offer increased flexibility in tailoring individualised self-directed support packages'. The 2007 regulations (SSI 2007/458) changed the rules on employing close relatives and gave local authorities the discretion to allow a close relative to be employed 'if the local authority is satisfied that securing a service from that person is necessary to meet the beneficiary's need for a service, or that securing a service from such a person is necessary to safeguard or promote the welfare of a child in need' (Scottish Executive, 2007, Section 5, p 111).

be made to a 'suitable person' acting on behalf of the person lacking capacity. In addition to benefiting young disabled adults when they become 18, this change may also benefit some adults with head injuries and people with dementia. At the time of writing, the government is also considering extending direct payments to people currently excluded by mental health legislation, although this is expected to have only a limited impact in terms of overall numbers (see DH, 2008b-c).

Finally, the government has also launched a consultation on the future of long-term care. Between May and November 2008 they sought the views of key stakeholders and members of the public about the nature and funding of social care in the 21st century. In setting out their case for reform the government states: 'Person-centred planning and self-directed support will become mainstream, with greater emphasis on self-assessment, and everyone will receive their support through flexible personal budgets' (DH, 2008d, p 40). The results of the consultation will contribute to a forthcoming Green Paper on adult social care and there is every indication that direct payments will be a central feature of this (see Glasby, 2008a for a view on how direct payments and personal budgets could help to shape the future funding of long-term care).

A reaction against direct payments?

Despite widespread enthusiasm about the potential of direct payments, more recent years seem to have witnessed something of a reaction against this way of working. For some commentators, there is a strong sense that the numbers of direct payments have not grown as rapidly as some had hoped and that their impact on the social care system as a whole has been less profound than might have been the case. While it is rare to find this stated openly, such views certainly seem implicit in some of the more recent policy discussion (and can also be aired more explicitly when talking to frontline practitioners). According to CSCI (2004, p 5), for example, 'the number of people receiving direct payments remains disappointingly low'. At the same time, many early studies of direct payments were often very positive (and this is entirely understandable, given the level of policy suspicion and hostility that needed to be overcome). However, more recent research has perhaps started to be more healthily sceptical – still identifying the many positives of direct payments but also spending longer on some of the potential barriers (see, for example, more critical accounts by Scourfield, 2005a, 2007; Spandler, 2004; see also Chapter Seven for discussion of the barriers to direct payments).

While we recognise the importance of adopting a more cautious and critical stance, we also feel that many of the perceived barriers to direct payments are to do with the way in which this policy has been implemented – not necessarily to do with the concept itself. Although there are some important political and philosophical tensions underpinning this way of working (see Chapter Seven for further discussion), the majority of barriers were probably to have been expected, and some of the criticism that direct payments have received sometimes seems a little unfair. To take but three examples:

- While take-up of direct payments varies by user group and by region (see Chapter Four), it depends on your point of view and your initial expectations as to whether recent progress has been disappointing or not. Although the proportion of people receiving direct payments is low in relation to people receiving *all* community-based services – for example in 2006/07 in England, 48,000 adults received direct payments out of a total of 1.52 million adults receiving all community-based services (3.2%) (Health and Social Care Information Centre, 2008, p 14) – nevertheless, the rate of increase in take-up year on year is impressive. Table 3.1 shows the estimated number of adults in England receiving direct payments over time from 2000/01 to 2006/07. The percentage increase in these years varied from 26% to 77%, a considerable achievement for a policy that involves such a significant cultural shift. Indeed, imagine what would happen if the crime rate or if the number of hospital-acquired infections fell by the same numbers – any professional body and any government would be shouting their achievements from the roof-tops!

- Some commentators suggest that direct payments appeal mainly to more confident and articulate disabled people. Debates about equity are dealt with in more detail in Chapter Seven, but to us this may well be an issue of how well direct payments are set up, how accessible they are and how much information and support is available. If a local authority engages only reluctantly with direct payments, fails to support its staff, designs very bureaucratic and unresponsive systems, and fails to provide appropriate advice and support, then we should hardly be surprised if only the most determined and confident people fight their way through the system to get access. Looking forward to discussions about personal budgets (see Chapter Five), an acid test of a new system of self-directed support will be the extent to which adult social care can stay sufficiently faithful to its underlying principles so that it remains inclusive of groups who are often excluded when support and services are difficult to access.

- Some people have been disappointed that direct payments have not transformed the culture of social care to a greater extent. However, because of their design and history, direct payments were seen by some councils as a 'bolt-on' to mainstream activity, and radical change was always unlikely to emerge overnight. In contrast, the more recent advent of personal budgets seems to offer the possibility of building on the legacy of direct payments to bring about more fundamental reform across the system as a whole (see Chapter Five).

Table 3.1: Estimated number of adults in receipt of direct payments in England, 2000/01 to 2006/07

Year	Number	Increase on previous year (%)
2000/01	5,000	n/a
2001/02	6,300	26
2002/03	9,600	52
2003/04	17,000	77
2004/05	24,000	41
2005/06	37,000	54
2006/07	48,000	30

Source: 2000/01–2003/04 figures from DH, 2005b, Table P2f.1; 2004/05–2006/07 figures from the Health and Social Care Information Centre, 2008, p 14.

SUMMARY

After a long and sustained campaign, disabled people were ultimately successful in bringing about the introduction of direct payments. Almost more than any other area of policy and practice, this is a way of working developed by disabled people, lobbied for and promoted by disabled people, and made to work by disabled people. If for no other reason than this, direct payments are worthy of our attention. Since their formal introduction in 1996/97, moreover, their progress has been rapid. Although still small in terms of overall numbers, direct payments have spread to a range of new user groups and have been promoted with enthusiasm by New Labour. Despite this, direct payments remain controversial, and subsequent chapters explore the spread of this new approach (Chapter Four), the positives and negatives of this way of working (Chapters Six and Seven) and the more recent implications of personal budgets and self-directed support (Chapter Five).

IMPLICATIONS FOR POLICY AND PRACTICE

- Direct payments are an example of a policy that has been developed *by* disabled people *for* disabled people.
- As direct payments have developed since 1997, some of the initial restrictions in their implementation have been removed and developments are ongoing. From the very beginning, they have been promoted enthusiastically by New Labour and remain a key feature of adult social care.
- A practical consequence of their rapid growth is that everyone working in social care will need to keep up to date with developments, ensuring that we do not set disabled people up to fail by not informing them of the options available to them.
- The expectations surrounding direct payments were so significant that a degree of disappointment was probably always likely as the practical barriers to change became apparent. However, our contention is that the majority of such barriers are to do with the way in which direct payments were operationalised – not to do with the concept itself (see Chapters Six and Seven for further discussion).

Recommended reading and useful websites

For background reading on direct payments, see:

- Leece (2003): written by a qualified social worker and practice teacher, this provides an accessible overview of the information, knowledge and skills that practitioners need to feel confident about offering direct payments. Other articles and publications by the same author also provide short but accessible summaries of some of the key practice/implementation issues at a local level and some of the key national debates (see, for example, Leece and Leece, 2006; Leece, 2004, 2006a).
- Leece and Bornat (2006), an edited collection, with a series of leading commentators providing contributions on the experience of different user groups, voices of experience, the implementation of direct payments, workforce implications and future developments.
- For those who want to place the development of direct payments in a broader context, Perri 6's (2003) article on the history of consumerism and choice in British public services provides a critical overview of developments in education, housing and health and social care.
- For further detail on how previous boundaries between 'cash' and 'care' are changing, Glendinning and Kemp's (2006) edited collection provides an overview of key national and international developments, including a number of chapters on the implications of direct payments.

More details on the legislation, policy and practice guidance on direct payments in the four countries of the UK can be found in key publications at the following websites:

- www.dh.gov.uk/en/SocialCare/Socialcarereform/Personalisation/ Directpayments/DH_076522 (England);
- www.dhsspsni.gov.uk/index/hss/ec-community-care/directpayments-about. htm (Northern Ireland);
- www.scotland.gov.uk/Topics/Health/care/VAUnit/DirectPayments (Scotland);
- www.wales.gov.uk/topics/health/socialcare/directpayments/?lang=en (Wales).

The Department of Health publishes accessible information for people thinking of accessing direct payments (see, for example, DH, 2008e).

In order to help local authorities to increase the uptake of direct payments, the Department of Health/Care Services Improvement Partnership (CSIP) has published a self-assessment and action-planning guide for local authorities and their partners (Murray et al, 2006). Moreover, CSIP has also devised a web-based national 'solution set', enabling local authorities to share knowledge of 'what works' and to build on the experience of others to promote and provide direct payments (see http://kc.csip.org.uk/solutionset.php?grp=601).

For more detail on the Direct Payments Development Fund, see: NCIL (2006, www.ncil.org.uk/uploads/pdf/DHreport2.pdf) and Davey et al (2007a, www.pssru.ac.uk/pdf/dprso.pdf).

Reflective exercises

1. Identify the key factors that you think led to the introduction of the 1996 Community Care (Direct Payments) Act.
2. In your view, was the introduction of direct payments largely the result of effective campaigning by disabled people or the result of the government wanting to reduce the role of directly provided services?
3. Identify the restrictions that were initially imposed on local authorities in the implementation of direct payments. How have these changed in the decade since they were first introduced?
4. What other measures can you think of that would encourage more people to take up direct payments?
5. Are there any further restrictions that you think could be removed to improve access to direct payments?

6. Think about a locality where you have worked (or where you have been on placement as a student) – what support and information was available to help disabled people find out about direct payments? What training and support was there for staff? What systems were in place within the local authority, and how supportive of direct payments was the council in practice?

FOUR

The lessons of direct payments – how they spread and what they achieved

This chapter explores:
- the spread of direct payments;
- take-up of direct payments by different user groups;
- international perspectives on direct payments.

Although the passage of the 1996 Community Care (Direct Payments) Act was a major victory for disabled campaigners, the legislation was initially permissive rather than mandatory (see Chapter Three). It was therefore perhaps inevitable that while some authorities would choose to implement direct payments almost immediately, others would be more cautious and possibly even hostile. This has resulted in a situation where the rate of implementation has been uneven both across the UK and between different user groups. Even though legislation has now made direct payments mandatory, major barriers still remain. Against this background, this chapter reviews the pace of implementation and the experiences of different user groups, highlighting key obstacles to progress. For comparative purposes, brief reference is also made to the international literature in order to summarise emerging lessons from other systems.

The spread of direct payments

Early days

As noted in Chapter Three, research carried out by the PSI two years prior to the Community Care (Direct Payments) Act suggested that many authorities were already making payments to service users and that many more would do so if legislation permitted. Despite this, there were considerable regional variations, with availability generally much lower in the north and the west of Britain. While 80% of respondents in London were making payments, this was true of only 17% in the north-west, 25% in Wales, 33% in the south-west and 40% in the West Midlands (Zarb and Nadash, 1994, p 27). The researchers were also at pains to stress that many local authorities were only making payments to a small number of people (Zarb and Nadash, 1994, p 27). Overall, the only exception to the concentration of payment schemes in the south was Scotland, where 64% of local authorities were making payments (albeit with low numbers overall) and where such payments had been legal in exceptional circumstances for some time (see Chapter Three).

Immediately after the 1996 Act, progress was not as rapid as Zarb and Nadash's (1994) initial research might have suggested. In 1997, the PSI and NCIL published preliminary findings from a research study into the implementation and management of direct payments (Zarb et al, 1997). Based on a survey of all UK local authorities and on more detailed consultations with ten selected authorities, the research suggested that only 48% of local authorities were operating some form of payments scheme, with about one-third unsure whether to introduce such payments in the future. Although London, the south-west and Scotland had been relatively proactive, provision was very low in the north of England and in Wales and non-existent in Northern Ireland (where implementation was delayed until 1998; Zarb et al, 1997, p 3). This was consistent with the findings of other early studies (see for example, Auld, 1999; Fruin, 2000). In 2000, ADSS surveyed all 171 social services departments in England and Wales with a response rate of 100% (Jones, 2000). This study found that 80% of authorities had introduced direct payment schemes and that all bar one of the remaining 20% planned to follow suit. Despite this, strong regional variations remained, with direct payments most prominent in London and the south. Around 3,500 people were then receiving direct payments, although a number of authorities had excluded people with mental health problems and/or learning difficulties from their schemes. The report concluded in upbeat fashion:

> The survey results ... indicated some regional variations in the availability of direct payments, but if the authorities currently not providing direct payments follow up on their plans *there should soon be almost total availability across England and Wales of direct payments* ... The task now is for social services to work with disabled people to increase the take-up of direct payments, and to make direct payments a mainstream opportunity, as one means of promoting independent living. (Jones, 2000, p 5; emphasis in the original)

It was clear from this research that there were a number of individual authorities that heavily influenced the national overview. For example, Hampshire alone had 400 people receiving direct payments (approximately 11% of all recipients in England and Wales at that time).

In Scotland, the Scottish Executive commissioned a key study on the early implementation of direct payments. By combining a telephone survey of 31 Scottish authorities with in-depth interviews with service users, social workers and managers in four case study authorities, the study identified considerable confusion among local authorities about what direct payments were and how they operated (Witcher et al, 2000). Only 13 (less than half the authorities in Scotland) were making direct payments to a total of 143 people, 125 (87%) with a physical or sensory impairment, 17 (12%) with a learning difficulty and one person with Asperger's syndrome. There were no recipients with mental health problems and no users from a minority ethnic group. Although support schemes were often available, these varied considerably in form and scope and there were concerns about possible gaps, particularly for people with learning difficulties. Funding was also very varied and was often hindered by a lack of flexibility between budgets. Payments to individuals ranged widely as did hourly rates to PAs. Recruiting workers was difficult in most authorities, particularly in rural areas. While most authorities were positive about the principles of direct payments, Box 4.1 highlights the main barriers to implementation identified.

Box 4.1: Barriers to implementation in Scotland

Barriers included:

- confusion in some local authorities about what constitutes direct payments;
- perceived need on the part of local authorities to limit demand;
- demands on care managers' time;
- absence of operational infrastructure for direct payments within local authorities;
- lack of information and publicity;
- lack of active recruitment policies, or restrictive recruitment policies;
- the national 'ban' on direct payments to older people;
- the national 'ban' on employing relatives as PAs;
- the application of additional and restrictive local criteria;
- funding restraints;
- the fact that direct payments were discretionary rather than rights based and mandatory.

(Witcher et al, 2000)

In Northern Ireland, with no history of third-party payments, (Campbell, nd), initial progress was slower than in other parts of the UK. According to one commentator, the delay was because 'disabled people have shown little interest and health and social services boards are not ready' (Valios, 1997, p 3) – although which one of these perceived barriers may have caused the other remains an important issue to consider. Elsewhere, it has been suggested that low take-up in northern England and Scotland may be the result of a stronger culture of municipal welfare in traditional Labour areas (McCurry, 1999). One commentator has even suggested that such ideological concerns may be creating something of a 'north–south divide' (Pearson, 2000, p 463), with northern English and Scottish authorities perceiving direct payments as a means of eroding public sector service provision, and Conservative-led authorities in southern England promoting direct payments as a means of encouraging individual choice and cost-efficiency.

The progression of implementation

Those new to direct payments might be surprised by how difficult it is to get access to meaningful data in this area. Often the way that information is collected has changed over time, making comparisons difficult – and compiling overall summaries of the experience across the UK can sometimes require going back to the original statistical sources (which are different in each country). However, looking at the available data, we can see a slow but steady increase in the overall take-up of direct payments (see Table 3.1 in Chapter Three and Tables 4.1–4.3). In particular, these figures show a significant increase during the period that direct payments became mandatory in 2003/04 and when additional resources were being provided to set up information and support schemes for direct payments (see Chapter Three). Based on the available data, there are now no local authorities or trusts in the UK that provide *no* direct payments,[1] although there is still a wide variation in take-up. While some of the early research speculated about the reasons for this, there was no UK-wide research until the Direct Payments Survey in 2004 (a postal questionnaire sent to all local authorities in the UK and another sent to 234 support organisations to gather information on all aspects of direct payments implementation and arrangements for support; Davey et al, 2007a-b).

Table 4.1: Estimated number of people receiving direct payments in Scotland, 2000/01 to 2005/06

Year	Number	Increase on previous year (%)
2000/01	207	n/a
2001/02	292	41
2002/03	534	83
2003/04	912	71
2004/05	1,438	58
2005/06	1,829	27

Adapted from Scottish Executive, 2006, p 6, Table 1.

Table 4.2: Estimated number of people receiving direct payments in Wales, 2004–06

Year	Number	Increase on previous year (%)
2004	563	n/a
2005	853	52
2006	1,113	30

Adapted from Social Services Improvement Agency (n.d.) – for more detailed discussion of the implementation of direct payments in Wales, see Social Interface (2007).

Table 4.3: Estimated number of people receiving direct payments in Northern Ireland, 2004–08

Year (March)	Number	Increase on previous year (%)
2004	117	n/a
2005	248	112
2006	450	81
2007	660	47
2008	1,144	73

Adapted from DHSSPS, 2007, 2008.

The survey was a collaborative project that combined the work of three separate research teams who were all involved in national studies of direct payments:

• *Disabled people and direct payments: a UK comparative study* (Riddell et al, 2006; see also Priestley et al, 2007) combines the results of the two questionnaires with a review of official statistics, interviews with 21 key people involved in policy development and implementation, and a telephone survey of 102 officers responsible for direct payments.
• *An evaluation of the impact of the Social Care Modernisation Programme on the implementation of direct payments* (Vick et al, 2006) is a study to identify the key factors that led to the varied implementation of direct payments in England. The two postal questionnaires were supplemented by interviews with four policy makers, telephone interviews with lead officers in 43 local authorities and a support organisation coordinator in the same authority, and six case studies to provide a more in-depth profile of direct payments schemes.
• *Evaluation of the Direct Payments Development Fund implementation* is a study funded by the Department of Health, focusing specifically on how national policies have been implemented locally and on the support made available by the DPDF. Data was gathered from the two postal questionnaires described above and the results are contained within two reports (Davey et al, 2007a-b).

Emerging issues

The comparative study of the four countries showed that, despite having the lowest proportion of people in the UK with long-term illness or disability: 'By 2003, England had established twice the rate of take-up per 100,000 adult population compared with other parts of the UK. Whilst there have been rapid increases in all parts of the UK since then, this differential was still evident in 2005' (Riddell et al, 2006, p 7). The same study showed a similar regional pattern of direct payments in England as described earlier, with nine of the ten local authorities with the highest numbers of direct payments recipients located in the south or east of England (Riddell et al, 2005, p 80). This study revealed a complex interplay of factors that influenced the implementation of direct payments but concluded with three main themes:

- *The politics of devolution*: direct payments have been most strongly supported by central government within England and promoted there by Conservative-led local authorities. There has been scepticism in other parts of the UK by local politicians and trade unions about direct payments aiding the privatisation of social care.
- *Local cultures of welfare*: the flexibility or otherwise of existing purchasing arrangements and the ease with which they can be changed are important factors that have influenced local implementation.
- *The influence of the disability movement*: in the early days of implementation there was a strong correlation between those areas with a high take-up of direct payments and active user-led advocacy and support schemes. The need for effective support for direct payment users remains critical, but this study identified some concerns about the move of some user-led organisations away from advocacy and campaigning towards direct service provision (Riddell et al, 2006, p 16).

As part of the DH Modernising Adult Social Care research initiative (MASC), Vick et al (2006) explored the impact of four aspects of legislation that influenced the implementation of direct payments in England and found:

- The statutory requirement to offer direct payments was important and had been perceived as positive by local authorities. However, there was evidence of tension between the policy of increasing the uptake of direct payments and other policy initiatives (for example, to ration access to care).
- Inspection and performance monitoring was regarded as less important and there was concern that performance indicators may encourage some local authorities to focus on quantity rather than quality.
- The change in regulations about the employment of close relatives (see Chapter Three) was generally regarded as positive, particularly for those user groups who might find it difficult to access other assistance. However, there were also concerns about a range of difficulties that might arise through the payment of informal carers.
- The DPDF was seen as an important initiative, particularly in helping to target specific groups of service users, but there was no clear evidence whether it had directly led to an increased take-up of direct payments.

Finally, the Direct Payments Survey sought the views of local authorities on the extent to which a number of variables had helped or hindered them in the implementation of direct payments (see Box 4.2; see also Chapters Six and Seven). However, in addition to key differences between the four countries of the UK, the evidence to date also reveals a range of different experiences among different user groups (see below for further discussion).

Box 4.2: Factors influencing implementation in England

Top seven critical aiding factors:
- effective support scheme;
- training and support for front-line staff;
- leadership within the local authority;
- positive attitude to direct payments among staff;
- national legislation, policy and guidance;
- accessible information on direct payments for service users and carers;
- demand from service users and carers.

Top three critical hindering factors:
- concern about managing direct payments among service users and carers;
- resistance to direct payments among staff;
- difficulties with the availability of personal assistants.

(Davey et al, 2007b, pp 101-3)

The experience of different user groups

From the beginning, the strongest calls for reform came from people with physical impairments, and there is ongoing evidence to suggest that this group makes up the bulk of direct payments recipients. According to the Direct Payments Survey (Davey et al, 2007b, p 15):

- People with physical or sensory impairments are more likely to receive direct payments than any other service user group.
- The top five regions providing direct payments to this group had all had experience of early forms of indirect payments.
- The regional pattern of take-up by older people mirrored that of people with a physical or sensory impairment, albeit on a smaller scale.
- There were more people with learning difficulties receiving direct payments in the north-west of England than elsewhere, but the promotion of direct payments to this user group may have slowed as the focus turned to other groups.
- People with mental health problems are less likely to receive direct payments than any other group.

More recent figures show a similar picture (see Tables 4.4–4.7). Essentially, younger people with physical impairments are the largest group receiving direct payments

(42% in England, 45% in Scotland, 41% in Wales and 42% in Northern Ireland) and people with mental health problems the smallest (8% in England, 3% in Scotland, 5% in Wales and 3% in Northern Ireland). Against this background, this chapter now looks briefly at the experiences of various user groups, considering some of the issues that have contributed to this uneven pattern of take-up.

People with physical impairments

In many ways, the predominance of people with physical impairments receiving direct payments is unsurprising, since they have traditionally formed user groups that have been more powerful and politically active than those of other service users (M. Barnes, 1997). As a result, it was often people with physical impairments who were at the forefront of the campaign for direct payments, with early research suggesting that staff working with people with physical impairments were much more familiar with the concepts of independent living and direct payments than their colleagues in other settings (see, for example, Dawson, 2000). More recently, the MASC study (Vick et al, 2006, p 70) found little evidence of champions of direct payments for any user groups *other* than people with physical impairments.

Table 4.4: Breakdown of adults receiving direct payments in England, 2006/07

Service user group	18–64	65 and over	All ages	%
Physical disability /frailty	20,000	15,000	36,000*	75
Learning disability	7,300	200	7,500	16
Mental health	2,600	1,300	3,900	8
Substance misuse	60	–	70*	0.1
Vulnerable people	400	400	800	2
TOTAL	31,000	17,000	48,000*	100*

* Figures may not add up because of rounding.

Adapted from Health and Social Care Information Centre, 2008, p 69, Table, P2f.1a; p 70, P2f.1b and p 71, P2f.1c.[2]

Table 4.5: Breakdown of people receiving direct payments in Scotland, 2006

Service user group	0–15	16–17	18–64	65+	All ages	%
Physical disability	67	7	707	169	950	52
Learning disability	95	3	304	9	424	23
Mental health	6	2	42	12	62	3
Other	56	6	37	294	393	2
TOTAL	224	31	1,090	484	1,829	100

Adapted from Scottish Executive, 2006, p 7, Table 4 – tallying errors are taken direct from the original.

Table 4.6: Breakdown of people receiving direct payments in Wales, 31 March 2008

Service user group	No	%
Older people 65+ (excluding those with mental ill health)	269	14
Older people 65+ (with mental ill health)	25	1
Adults with a learning difficulty	354	18
Adults with a physical and/or sensory impairment	813	41
Adults with mental health problem	84	4
Others	422	21
TOTAL	1,967	100*

* Figures may not add up because of rounding.
Adapted from Cochrane, 2008.

Table 4.7: Breakdown of people receiving direct payments in Northern Ireland, 31 December 2007

Service user group	Number	%
Elderly	281	30
Mental health (under 21)	0	0
Mental health (21 and over)	28	3
Learning disability (under 21)	92	10
Learning disability (21 and over)	109	12
Physical disability (under 21)	96	10
Physical disability (21 and over)	294	32
Young carers	1	0
Carers (18 and over)	21	2
TOTAL	922	100*

* Figures may not add up because of rounding.
Adapted from DHSSPS, 2007.

Throughout the literature, it is the choice and control that direct payments enable that people with physical impairments seem to value the most (see, for example, the personal testimonies cited by Leece and Bornat, 2006). Thus, a study by SCOPE interviewed 38 people and found the majority of them identified independence as the key reason for applying for direct payments (McMullen, 2003). Similar sentiments were expressed by the 15 young people interviewed as part of a Joseph Rowntree Foundation study undertaken in the light of the extension of direct payments to 16- and 17-year-old young disabled people (Abbott, 2003). More recently, a report by the national user-controlled organisation Shaping Our Lives reflected the views of 112 service users as part of a government consultation for developing a new vision of the future of adult social care. People identified direct payments as a key route to independent living saying:

> "It's given me my life back. Now I control who's helping me and when they come in. It's also given me a social life and I can do things I want to do."

> "When you employ your own personal assistants, you have more say and know what you're going to get, when."
> (Beresford et al, 2005, pp 24–5)

However, this does not change the fact that the number of direct payment recipients remains low compared to the number of people receiving directly provided services (Fernandez et al, 2007, p 100) and that, for some people, access is still difficult (Glynn and Beresford et al, 2008). As an example, a key group whose needs are often overlooked is disabled parents, who may require additional hours as part of a direct payments care package for the physical aspects of parenting. In 1998/99, a Social Services Inspectorate report into services to support disabled parents found that this user group was sometimes excluded from direct payment schemes (Goodinge, 2000). Similarly, a SCIE study (Morris and Wates, 2006) identified a lack of focus on the experiences of disabled adults as *parents* rather than as people using services, but highlighted the potential for direct payments to meet support needs better. The study found that funding for direct payments could also be difficult, sometimes falling between the remit of children's services and adult services (see also Morris and Wates, 2007).

People with learning difficulties

When direct payments legislation was being debated, the government's initial intention was to exclude people with learning difficulties until the new scheme could be tested in practice (DH/Scottish Office, Welsh Office/Northern Ireland Office, 1996; see Chapter Three). This restriction was eventually overturned following concerted lobbying by organisations such as People First, and subsequent policy and practice guidance emphasised that local authorities should avoid blanket assumptions that whole groups of people are unable to manage payments (DH, 1997, 2000a, 2003a). In practice, however, the number of people with learning difficulties receiving direct payments was initially small, with many people denied access (Fruin, 1998, 2000; Gardner, 1999) and a widespread assumption that direct payments would not work for people with learning difficulties (Dawson, 2000). Information about direct payments was also often unavailable in accessible formats and members of staff working with people with learning difficulties were frequently unaware of this way of working (Holman and Bewley, 1999; Maglajlic et al, 2000).

By 2001, the government recognised that 'the small number of people with learning difficulties receiving direct payments is unacceptable' (DH, 2001f, p 48). Since then the Department of Health has produced extensive information both for local authorities and for people with learning difficulties to explain the concept of direct payments (see, for example, DH, 2004a-b, 2007). Produced in conjunction with key advocacy organisations such as Values into Action and Swindon People First, these easy guides are written in large print, in an accessible style, sometimes with an accompanying tape and CD (DH, 2004b).

Meanwhile, the number of people with learning difficulties receiving direct payments has been rising slowly. By March 2007, the number had risen to 7,500 out of a total of 48,000 (16%) (Information Centre, 2008, p 69), compared to 216 out of a total of over 3,700 (less than 6%) in the autumn of 2000 (DH, 2001f, p 48). The economic case for direct payments is compelling – the Direct Payments Survey found that despite the average hourly rate for personal assistants for people with learning difficulties being higher than for other user groups, the average weekly live-in rates for people with learning difficulties were considerably lower than for weekly costs of residential care (Davey et al, 2007b, pp 58-61). Even so, despite active encouragement by the government, the evidence suggests that people with learning difficulties continue to face a number of barriers. Over time, a recurring theme has been the issue of consent, with many local authorities concerned and/or confused about the extent to which people with learning difficulties are able to consent to and manage direct payments (see Bewley, 1998; Ryan and Holman, 1998a-c; Holman and Bewley, 1999; Williams and Holman, 2006 for a more detailed discussion). Although guidance is clear that people can receive as much support as they want/need in order to manage a direct payment, concerns about whether people with learning difficulties are 'willing and able' to receive direct payments still remain (Williams and Holman, 2006). In Scotland, this issue was overcome to a certain extent by the 2003 regulations extending direct payments to attorneys and guardians for people unable to manage their own payments (SSI 2003/243). In England, we are yet to see how the 2008 Health and Social Care Act, and the opportunity to appoint a 'suitable person' to act on behalf of someone defined as lacking capacity, will affect the availability of direct payments to people with learning difficulties (see Chapter Three).

In addressing issues of consent and capacity, several commentators have suggested ways forward for service users and practitioners alike – one solution, for example, is for money to be paid via an independent living trust (see Holman and Bewley, 2001). However, in addition to assistance in managing money, many people with learning difficulties (like all direct payment recipients) also need ongoing support. An innovative project that explored this issue was undertaken by Swindon People First and the Norah Fry Research Centre from 1999 to 2002. Entitled 'Journey to Independence', the project employed three researchers with learning difficulties to go around the country and talk with direct payments users and other key players involved in the design or delivery of direct payment schemes (Williams and Holman, 2006). While support was provided by a range of sources (including advocacy organisations, informal networks, family and friends), one of the main messages was that support needs to be ongoing and should not be withdrawn once direct payments are set up (Williams and Holman, 2006, p 75). Another study of independent support organisations found that peer support in particular can be very effective in inspiring other people with learning difficulties to see the potential opportunities that direct payments can bring (Bewley and McCulloch, 2004). Since these studies were completed, the government has offered finance through DPDF to voluntary organisations to run support schemes (see Chapter Three). However, evidence to date suggests that many support schemes focus more on the take-up and setting up of direct payments, rather than on maintenance and ongoing management (which are often left to the recipient themselves – see Davey et al, 2007a).

Mental health

Earlier discussion has already shown that very few people with mental health problems receive direct payments, and a mere 0.4% of the direct payments budget in England is spent on mental health service users (Riddell et al, 2006, p 8). The Department of Health admits that the current situation is unacceptable (in 2005, almost a quarter of local authorities in England were making no direct payments to people with mental health problems, and a further half were making between one and five). According to the National Institute for Mental Health in England (NIMHE) (2006, p 3): '*it is time for action*' (emphasis in the original). The initial neglect of mental health issues was apparent from the early stages of implementation – indeed, as the Direct Payments Bill was being debated in Parliament, there were specific attempts to *exclude* all service users with mental health problems (Beresford, 1996). In the early policy and practice guidance that was issued (DH, 1997, 2000a), there were very few references to people with mental health problems and little recognition that they might face additional barriers. In light of this, it is perhaps unsurprising that people with mental health problems have often found it difficult to access direct payments. Although it is difficult to be specific, it has been estimated that throughout the UK at one stage only ten people with mental problems were receiving direct payments (Maglajlic, 1999; Revans, 2000; Heslop, 2001), with no direct payment recipients with mental health problems in Scotland at all (Witcher et al, 2000). As a result, the Scottish Executive commissioned new research to investigate the barriers to direct payments for people with mental health problems (Ridley and Jones, 2003; Ridley, 2006). By 30 September 1998, the number of mental health service users receiving direct payments in England had risen to 13, spread over seven social services departments (Auld, 1999). With four such direct payment recipients, Essex was identified as one of the leading authorities, placing Britain ahead of many of its European neighbours (Brandon, 1998). Although there was then very little literature on direct payments and mental health, research undertaken by Anglia Polytechnic University (Brandon, 1998; Maglajlic et al, 1998, 2000; Maglajlic,

1999) and a number of important commentaries/testimonies (NCIL, ndb; Irish, 1998; Luckhurst, 2000; Revans, 2000) began to identify some key issues that were obstacles to more people accessing direct payments. These included (Maglajlic et al, 1998; Maglajlic, 1999):

- a lack of knowledge about direct payments among service users, staff and carers;
- low expectations of social services as a result of previous poor experiences;
- high eligibility criteria, with some service users feeling that they had to be almost 'sectionable' before they received any support – this is sometimes described as a 'Catch 22 situation' where you have to be so ill to receive support that you are then seen as too ill to manage a direct payment;
- difficulties managing money when ill and an awareness of being perceived as people not trusted to take care of themselves. For direct payments to be successful, all users and carers felt that they would need support, particularly when handling money and recruiting staff;
- the lack of other mental health service users using direct payments elsewhere.

The research commissioned by the Scottish Executive to explore the potential of direct payments was carried out in 2001 and included a telephone survey of all Scottish local authorities, focus groups with users and carers and 23 interviews with mental health service providers and service users. The study echoed many of the findings of previous research but particularly highlighted unfavourable staff attitudes and misunderstandings about eligibility for direct payments as 'formidable barrier[s] to access for mental health service users' (Ridley and Jones, 2003, p 650).

Aware of the situation in England, the government funded projects in five local authorities to promote independent living via direct payments for people with mental health problems (Spandler and Vick, 2006; see also Davidson and Luckhurst, 2002). At the start of the project there were no mental health service users in the pilot sites and by the end there were 58. In the evaluation the recipients reported significant benefits that direct payments offered in relation to increased opportunities and greater independence. However, despite this, 'only a very small number of mental health professionals had really grasped the principles of direct payments and independent living and were generally promoting it as a positive option to service users' (Spandler and Vick, 2006, p 112). Professionals were both selective in whom they offered direct payments to and also what they agreed they should be used for.

Based on this work, the Health and Social Care Advisory Service (HASCAS) undertook a project, 'New Directions', to promote the use of direct payments by people with mental health problems, including those from black and minority ethnic communities (Newbigging with Lowe, 2005). The project conducted telephone interviews and developed four focus groups, bringing together service users, practitioners, senior managers and voluntary groups with service users recruited to facilitate the groups. The practical and organisational barriers identified by the participants confirmed those outlined above, but the study highlighted additional obstacles faced by mental health service users from black and minority ethnic groups. These included language and cultural issues, inconsistency and inequality in the practices of different local authorities, and evidence that participants felt reflected 'institutional racism and notions about mental ill health and black people' (Newbigging with Lowe, 2005, p 19).

In addition to general barriers for all users, the Direct Payments Survey has identified specific issues for mental health service users:

- Particular difficulties were reported over the episodic nature of some people's mental ill health, and it may not always be appropriate to offer direct payments when people are in crisis (Vick et al, 2006, p 56). In this, and other studies, there was little evidence of advance directives being used to indicate what people wanted to happen at a time of crisis (Spandler and Vick, 2006).
- Lack of resources can limit how people go about meeting needs. Indeed, the Direct Payments Survey found that, generally, care packages were smaller for mental health service users than for other service user groups, with less than half of mental health users getting more than ten hours per week (Davey et al, 2007b, p 45). However, for some people such a short time *can* make a difference: 'I used to attend a day centre five days a week, but this was not stimulating and my five hours now are more valuable than five days used to be' (Newbigging with Lowe, 2005, p 23).
- There were difficulties meeting needs that fell within the boundaries of both health and social care and with agreeing financial responsibilities (Vick et al, 2006, p 69; see also Taylor, 2008).
- Appropriate support from people who had detailed knowledge, understanding and expertise in mental health issues was not readily available to recipients in either setting up or managing direct payments (Vick et al, 2006, p 66; see also Newbigging with Lowe, 2005).

Following the identification of the 'very poor' take-up of direct payments (Social Exclusion Unit, 2004, p 43), the government commissioned new guidance for a range of key stakeholders (NIMHE, 2006). How this will affect the take-up of direct payments for mental health service users has yet to be seen. However, the concerns of some professionals expressed in the research above are in stark contrast to accounts by service users of the ability of direct payments to transform the lives of people who have previously been disempowered and who have not been able to obtain a satisfactory response to their needs from directly provided statutory services (Davidson and Luckhurst, 2002; Newbigging with Lowe, 2005; Spandler and Vick, 2006; see also Chapter Five for more positive results with regards to individual budgets).

Older people

When direct payments were first implemented, they were initially prohibited for people aged 65 or over (unless the person had been receiving payments before the age of 65). Since older people are by far the biggest user group, this was widely interpreted as an attempt to prevent the 'floodgates' from opening in terms of public expenditure. However, from the very beginning, there was widespread concern from disabled people's and older people's organisations about the discriminatory nature of this approach and sustained pressure to remove the 65 age limit (NCIL, ndc, 1999; Age Concern, 1998). As a result, in 2000, the New Labour government announced its intention to extend direct payments to people aged 65 and over (DH, 1998b), a decision also welcomed by the Royal Commission on Long-Term Care (1999).

Since then, the take-up of direct payments by older people has been relatively low. In 2004, English local authorities spent only 0.8% of their community care budget on direct payments for older people, compared to 15.5% for people with physical impairments (Riddell et al, 2006, p 8). By 2006/07, however, there were 17,000 people over the age of 65 receiving direct payments (just over a third of all adult recipients), with direct payments to older people increasing at a faster rate than for any other service user group (a 37% increase from 2005/06 compared to an increase of 25% for younger adults) (Health and Social Care Information Centre, 2008, p 17).

To date, research specifically focused on the implementation of direct payments to older people has been limited. A study commissioned by Help the Aged before implementation found that most older people knew very little about direct payments, initially found the concept confusing and alarming, and were suspicious that direct payments might be a cost-cutting exercise by government (C. Barnes, 1997). Early experience of direct payments also suggested that older people could be put off direct payments by some of the difficulties (both real and perceived) of administering them, in particular the responsibilities of becoming an employer (Zarb and Oliver, 1993; C. Barnes, 1997; Hasler et al, 1999). In 2004, a key study that explored how direct payments were operating for older people was undertaken by Clark et al (2004) in three local authorities. Typically at that time, providing direct payments was not part of care managers' usual way of working. While some were enthusiastic about the prospect, others identified major difficulties that related to the workload and tight eligibility criteria, but primarily the 'nature of the client group' – with many older people felt by workers to be too frail to manage direct payments (Clark et al, 2004, p 40). Some of the main findings include:

- The majority of people chose direct payments in preference to directly provided services in order to have more choice and control over support arrangements or because it was the only way they could get what they needed.
- All the older people reported positive benefits to their physical health or sense of well-being.

- Having someone speak their own language and understand their cultural needs was important for older people from minority ethnic communities.
- Handling the relationship with their PA was the key to managing direct payments well and having access to an effective support scheme was crucial.

These issues are similar to those from other studies (for example, Glendinning et al, 2000a; CSCI, 2004; Poole, 2006; Vick et al, 2006), and key barriers seem to include:

- the haphazard nature of initial information (as well as delayed information);
- difficulties recruiting PAs;
- concerns about becoming an employer and meeting audit and administrative demands;
- difficulties accessing appropriate support schemes;
- rules on employing close relatives (prior to these being relaxed – see Chapter Three);
- the small care packages that some older people receive – leaving little to 'play with' when making alternative choices.

A smaller study in Cambridgeshire carried out among care managers and older people echoed many of these findings (Scourfield, 2005b), but raised an additional issue about the timing of the introduction of direct payments. Care managers in this study said that they often met older people for the first time at a point of crisis, when people wanted immediate help and when direct payments may not be the best option. Of course, the implication here is that the system as a whole needs a way of raising the possibility of direct payments with older people at an appropriate time – if not on first contact with services then at a suitable time when older people are best placed to consider such an option. Without this, there is a danger that direct payments are not mentioned on initial contact, and that the issue does not resurface later on either, once again emphasising the powerful 'gatekeeping' role that care managers hold (see Chapter Seven for further discussion; see also Chapter Five for discussion of older people and individual budgets).

Carers

Following changes in legislation, there were 7,700 carers receiving direct payments on 31 March 2007 (CSCI, 2008). Although these numbers have doubled in just under two years, still only 4% of the people receiving a service in their own right as carers receive direct payments. The take-up is also very varied between local authorities and, in 2006, 43 English councils reported that they still made *no* direct payments to carers (with only 17 councils making more than 100) (CSCI, 2008, p 100). However, these figures should be treated with caution as there may be some confusion about the classification of direct payments in some areas – for example, the MASC study reported: 'In one apparently high performing authority, over 90% of payments to people with mental health needs were actually one-off payments to provide respite for carers. Hence the figures for service users can appear inflated whilst carer figures are undercounted' (Vick et al, 2006, p 37). The same study found that, while direct payments were small in numbers, there were a higher proportion of one-off payments to carers, which included personal assistance and support within the home, sitting services, complementary therapies (Vick et al, 2006), the funding of a travel pass and the purchase of household equipment (CSCI, 2008). Moreover, while the 2004 Carers (Equal Opportunities) Act has now extended the range of support available to carers (including meeting needs in relation to work, education and leisure), few councils report using direct payments for these purposes: 'overall, the emphasis is on using direct payments to support carers to continue caring, rather than to support their fulfilment as citizens' (CSCI, 2008, p 100).

While barriers for carers are often similar to those for service users, a small online consultation by the Princess Royal Trust for Carers identified three key issues for councils to consider (Fletcher, 2006):

- ensuring that carers who are eligible for an assessment receive one;
- ensuring that carers receive appropriate information;
- ensuring that there is an adequate support structure in place (since employment and administrative issues can involve additional worry and stress for carers) – this issue is a recurrent theme from all research findings on direct payments and carers (Seddon et al, nd; Fletcher, 2006; SCIE, 2007; CSCI, 2008), and councils have responded in a variety of ways (see Box 4.3).

Box 4.3: Support for carers

- In the Birmingham area there is a large Somali population. Members of this community, although offered payments to purchase care, have had difficulty purchasing culturally appropriate care. Birmingham Crossroads is offering support by training two members of the community to become NVQ assessors and by employing staff from the community to work at the scheme and become professional carer-support workers (SCIE, 2007, p 43).
- Northamptonshire Carers Centre received funding from their county council to employ a direct payments advisor to support parent carers (Fletcher, 2006, p 181).
- Carers Buckinghamshire received funding from the county council to offer one-off grants to carers of up to £500. Purchases included essential household equipment, holiday for the carer and a series of massage and reflexology courses (Fletcher, 2006, p 182).

In addition, the opportunity to employ family members has proved useful for some carers. While there are mixed views about this (see Chapter Seven), many carers would echo the words of this woman: "My husband will not be looked after by anyone he doesn't know ... Hence I have really never had a break ... My daughter can be the carer so that is good as she knows my husband's illness so well" (Fletcher, 2006, p 182). Against this background, the potential opportunity from the 2008 Health and Social Care Act to extend direct payments to people with dementia may well give support to carers of older people with dementia who will only accept care from close relatives.

In practice, very few direct payments are made to 16- and 17-year-old carers (Fletcher, 2006). With the separation of adult and children's services, there is likely to be increased discussion between managers about whose responsibility a direct payment for a young carer would be (Leece, 2002). Managers in children's services might argue that payments would not be necessary if appropriate services were provided for the disabled adult, while adult services may argue that in reality there are many young people offering care who are not known to local authorities and any service that can potentially support those who are identified is beneficial. Where young carers positively choose to take on the role of caring they need to be supported to try and ensure it is a good experience; the provision of a direct payment may offer the opportunity for greater independence and choice for the young person and their family (albeit probably only in a small number of cases).

Parents of disabled children

When direct payments were extended to the parents of disabled children, the issue had received little attention from local authority children's services. Christine Lenehan, director of the Council for Disabled Children, believes this is because direct payments 'were an adult-based concept plonked on children, and it took quite a while to untangle what they meant for children' (quoted in Vevers, 2007). Despite this, there were 4,200 parents receiving direct payments by March 2006 (CSCI, 2008), compared to 2,265 a year earlier. Even so, the numbers are low and the government has made a commitment to increase the number of disabled children receiving direct payments (HM Treasury and DfES, 2007), producing and updating a parent's guide to direct payments (DfES, 2006).

To date, particular barriers in children's services appear to include the relatively underdeveloped nature of the 'market', with seemingly fewer alternatives to directly provided services. There is also some evidence to suggest that demand for assessments has increased as a result of direct payments, although it is not clear whether this is because of the reduced stigma attached to direct payments, dissatisfaction with current services or an expectation that direct payments will meet needs more appropriately (Carlin and Lenehan, 2004). However, for those parents who have accessed direct payments successfully, studies show that many have benefited. In one study in the north-west, key benefits included:

- *Flexibility*: "I can use support money in different ways. I can find different styles of care … I am able to select the carer and the types of care."
- *Appropriate type of care*: for example, recruiting a carer of the same sex to pursue the child's interest in football.
- *Effective use of a small amount of money*: over three-quarters of the sample were only receiving between £20 and £50, but had been able to utilise it in innovative ways that had both given the family a break and given the child a chance to get involved in local community activities.
- *Less involvement with a range of professionals*: one respondent commented, "I don't want a social worker; I just need some money to help us have an ordinary family life" (Blyth and Gardner, 2007, pp 238–9).

Similarly, a father interviewed for a SCIE knowledge review of the social care needs of children with complex health care needs and their families said:

> "The direct payment scheme has really transformed our family. Previously it was a struggle getting the help we needed but since direct payments we have been able to employ people who are fit, warm-natured, happy to be trained by us and willing to work with our schedules, for example, starting late on some mornings or accompanying us on holidays." (Marchant et al, 2007, p 22)

A different view was put forward in a study evaluating a small pilot project in Staffordshire (Leece et al, 2003). In the study the researchers compared the experiences of 13 families accessing direct payments with the same number of families using services arranged by social services. They found there were no greater benefits reported by the first group in terms of satisfaction with care or the degree of control they experienced over the way it was delivered. The study was undertaken in the early days of direct payments for this service user group and the researchers speculate that the reasons for their findings may be related to 'teething problems' in the setting-up and managing of direct payments, in particular recruiting and employing suitable staff (Leece et al, 2003). However, these practical problems, which have been well rehearsed throughout the literature, appear still to be an obstacle that prevents more parents accessing direct payments (Carlin and Lenehan, 2004; Blyth and Gardner, 2007; Marchant et al, 2007).

Overall, Blyth and Gardner (2007) identify five key messages for local authorities who are seeking to increase the take-up of direct payments by parents of disabled children:

- Arrange for independently managed direct payment support services to help with practical and emotional support.
- Direct payments need 'champions' – a senior manager who will develop a clear authority-wide strategy and drive it forward, and also at practitioner level to inspire confidence in other staff.

- Recruit 'recipient champions' who can promote direct payments and help share their experiences with others.
- Recipients in this study found the ability to employ close relatives very positive and an empowering experience for parents of disabled children to be managing rather than receiving services.
- Setting up an effective direct payments scheme needs *additional* resources in order to cope with a potential increase in demand for services, set up a suitable support scheme and train staff appropriately. Only then can a sustainable scheme be established.

However, a hint of warning remains from Carlin and Lenehan's study: 'Direct payments represent a significant change to the philosophy or underlying ethos of children's services. This barrier is key and councils are going to need significant reassurance that they can really let go and trust parents with direct payments' (2006, p 121).

Young people

Although the 2000 Carers and Disabled Children Act extended direct payments to 16- and 17-year-old disabled young people, a national ADSS survey in England and Wales showed that only 25 of the 104 authorities that responded offered direct payments to this group (Cozens, 2002, cited in Leece et al, 2003). In the same year there were no young people receiving a direct payment in Scotland (Leece et al, 2003). By March 2005, 492 young people in England (CSCI, 2006c) and 31 young people in Scotland (Scottish Executive, 2006) received a direct payment. Perhaps as a result of this, young disabled people have received little attention in the literature. A study by SCOPE interviewed 38 people, five of whom were young people, and found that the majority of them identified independence as the key reason for applying for direct payments (McMullen, 2003). In another study funded by the JRF, young people interested in direct payments saw a number of obstacles, including practical difficulties in accessing and managing direct payments (for example, whether their views would be taken seriously, and handling their relationship with a PA). However, they also saw having direct payments as an exciting opportunity to achieve more independence and freedom and thought it could possibly make them less reliant upon their parents, even if they remained living at home. Parents and professionals also interviewed as part of the study expressed concerns about whether young people would be able to manage their direct payments and how it would affect their relationship with their families (Abbott, 2003).

Seldom-heard groups

In addition to the main client groups above, the development of direct payments holds out the potential to reach a range of people excluded from or treated less favourably by directly provided services. While these are often described as 'hard to reach', we prefer the term 'seldom heard' as it seems to us to reflect more accurately the difficulty the system sometimes has in engaging with and responding to the needs of these groups. By definition, the following overview is very brief, but it seems at least possible that direct payments could have a potential impact on four particular groups:

- *People with HIV/AIDS*: while there is little data on the number and experience of people with HIV/AIDS receiving direct payments, preliminary work undertaken by NCIL and the National AIDS Trust has suggested that direct payments may be a particularly positive option, leading to greater flexibility, improved continuity, more control and improved health as fluctuating needs are met more effectively (Grimshaw and Fletcher, nd). One social work team in the MASC study reported that direct payments were particularly useful for black African service users with HIV (Vick et al, 2006, p 64). What was important here was the flexibility and choice for the individual to employ someone of their choosing. For some, this was a trusted friend or relative, while others preferred someone outside their immediate community as a result of concerns about privacy and confidentiality.

- *Gay men and lesbians*: although neglected by the majority of commentators, there are some accounts that suggest that direct payments may bring some positives to gay men and lesbians (although this raises a series of additional issues). In an early paper on 'Independent living, personal assistance, disabled lesbians and disabled gay men', Killin (1993) sets out some of the practical issues faced by gay and lesbian PA users, including discriminatory attitudes by PAs and the difficulty of knowing when to disclose their sexuality to their PA. Many of these issues have since been reiterated in PSI/NCIL guidance to local authorities (Hasler et al, 1999, pp 32–3), emphasising the need to consider the importance of peer support, maintaining confidentiality and specific measures to consult disabled lesbians and gay men seeking to live independently. Additional issues are also raised by the NCIL's *Rough guide to managing personal assistants*, which recounts some of the complexities of employing PAs for gay men and lesbians, including needing to be clear about the parameters of the job (Vasey, 2000).

- *People living in rural areas*: opinion is currently divided on the implications of direct payments for people in rural areas. While some believe that the flexibility of direct payments may be a positive way of trying to meet needs in places poorly served by directly provided services, others point to the complexities of recruiting staff and the cost of travelling to and from people's homes. However, it does appear as though the relaxation of rules on employing close relatives has been helpful for older people in rural areas who might want to employ family members living near to them (Vick et al, 2006, p 37). Similar findings have also been reported by a recent Commission for Rural Communities study (2008) into the implications of personalisation for rural older people, which also stresses the importance of contingency planning when arranging home-based services in rural areas – 'Plan B' must be ready to put into place if a PA is sick or unable to work. While the evidence is limited, our view is that many of the barriers cited in the literature apply equally to both direct payments and to directly provided services, but that direct payments may provide additional flexibility when seeking ways of overcoming some of these issues.

- *Black and minority ethnic communities*: experience to date suggests that direct payments may be a good way of meeting the needs of people from minority ethnic groups and may compare favourably with direct services (Hasler et al, 1999; Clark et al, 2004; Stuart, 2006; Vick et al, 2006; Davey et al, 2007b). Despite this, there is also evidence to suggest that people from minority ethnic groups may face additional barriers to accessing direct payments and remain under-represented (Butt and Box, 1997; Bignall and Butt, 2000; Butt et al, 2000; Maglajlic et al, 2000; Witcher et al, 2000; Stuart, 2006). In particular, research by SCIE (Stuart, 2006, p ix) identifies a range of issues, including:

  – assessment processes not taking account of black and minority ethnic service users' backgrounds and requirements;
  – service users being unaware of how to access or use information on direct payments;
  – difficulty in recruiting PAs;
  – shortage of appropriate advocacy and support services;
  – variable levels of commitment to direct payments among local authorities.

Within the broader literature there is much debate about the role of the family, and in particular the relaxation of the rule on employing close relatives. Some people argue that black and Asian people may wish to employ family members as PAs in order to obtain a more culturally sensitive service, while others feel that this would blur the role of family members and reduce the independence of the disabled person. However, a finding that is consistent throughout the literature is the importance of providing appropriate and adequate support for people from minority ethnic groups to find out about, access and manage direct payments (see Vick et al, 2006 for some positive examples).

International experience

Although this book focuses on the UK, it is easy to lose sight of the fact that the move towards forms of more individualised funding is something of an international trend. Although the following account cannot provide a detailed summary, the remainder of this chapter offers a brief flavour of the experience in some other countries, citing further references for those interested in following up specific examples in more detail. Thus, Box 4.4 shows the key features of direct payments schemes across Europe as far back as 1997, while Lundsgaard

(2005) provides a more recent overview in 12 OECD countries. Table 4.8 shows data from seven countries that Poole (2006, p 6) has reproduced from this study, illustrating the type of programme available, take-up and whether relatives may be employed.

Box 4.4: Key features of direct payment schemes, 1997

Belgium: Pilot independent living project from July 1997 for 15 people. The scope for employing PAs at unsocial times is limited due to strict legislation and a strong trade union movement.

The Netherlands: Direct payments were introduced in July 1995 for housekeeping, personal care and registered nursing services provided in the home, although there was strong opposition from trade unions and government concerns about the potential for abuse.

Austria: Direct payments were available from July 1993, although payments are low and it is expected that people needing more than four hours of care a day will live in an institution.

Germany: The German direct payments system is very medicalised. Disabled people receive less money if they choose to receive money directly rather than selecting support from approved providers.

Finland: Personal assistance is available, although there have been calls to promote this option further as a means of reducing the unemployment level within the disabled community. Payments are made directly to the PA, not through the individual disabled person.

The Czech Republic: Personal assistance was introduced in 1991 and a Centre for Independent Living was established in 1993.

Norway: Personal assistance can be claimed through the social security system (with payments made via local government, via the user or via cooperatives).

Sweden: Personal assistance has been a right in Sweden since 1994. Users can receive such personal assistance in a range of ways, including as an individual, through a cooperative, with an assistance company and through the municipal services.

Bratislava: Direct payments were introduced in January 1997 for an initial group of 21 users.

(ENIL, 1997)

Table 4.8: Take-up of individualised funding

Country	Type of programme	Employment of relatives?	Percentage of 65+ population in receipt of social care who have direct payments or a personal budget
Austria	Cash allowance	Yes	100*
Germany	Option of cash allowance or care-in-kind or a combination of the two	Yes	80 (including those who choose a care package that combines cash and services)
Luxembourg	Option of a cash allowance to cover first 7hrs/week of care	Yes	91 (including those who choose a care package that combines cash and services)
Sweden	Cash payment; minimum need of 17hrs/week	Yes	1
Netherlands	Personal budget – since April 2003 available to all those qualifying for long-term home-based care	Yes (but not in the same home)	7
Norway	Personal budget for care assistants when local authority considers this a better option than formal agency care	Yes	2
United States	Medicaid pay for a specified number of hours of a user-hired personal assistant	Yes (but not spouses)	18

Source: Poole, 2006, p 6.

*The Austrian system is closer to the UK equivalent of Attendance Allowance than direct payments/personal budgets.

In the Netherlands, older people are permitted to receive personal budgets with which to purchase care (Pijl, 1997, 2000; Coolen and Weekers, 1998; Weekers and Pijl, 1998). These were piloted on an experimental basis in 1991, evaluated and formally introduced in 1995. Despite pressure from service users, implementation was initially slow but, by 2003, 54,000 people in the Netherlands were in receipt of personal budgets, of whom a third were older people (Lundsgaard, 2005, p 18). However, the system here is heavily regulated and, according to a recent review, 'service providers are essentially still employed by the state, to the dismay of some users' (SCIE, 2007, p 9). In seeking to introduce personal budgets, a number of barriers were identified (Coolen and Weekers, 1998, pp 54, 58):

- financial barriers (the concern to contain costs);
- social barriers (problems relating to the employment rights of care-givers);
- implementation barriers (difficulty of matching personal budgets to assessments);
- professional opposition (from trade unions and formal service providers).

While the form and scope of direct payments vary considerably, research commissioned by the European Association for Care and Help at Home has found that the same key questions have been asked in most countries:

- Will more people apply for cash than for services?
- Should allowances become part of a social insurance system or should it be social assistance?
- What is the best way to assess an applicant and to determine the amount to be paid?
- Will the recipients of cash use it properly?
- Will the quality of services bought with the cash be adequate?
- Will PAs be treated well by their employers? (Pijl, 2000, pp 56-7)

In the US and Canada the context of direct funding for people receiving social care services is rather different (for full discussion, see Lord and Hutchinson, 2003; Hutchinson et al, 2006). Direct payments had a much earlier inception than in Europe, and Hutchinson et al (2006, p 49) describe 'individualised planning and direct funding as [having] evolved as cornerstones of a new paradigm of disability supports for citizenship and inclusion'. Unlike in the UK, the movement in North America has been driven by piecemeal local initiatives (Hutchinson et al, 2006, p 52). In reviewing the lessons learnt from this experience, Hutchinson et al (2006, pp 56–60) identify a number of key factors:

- the importance of values and principles that reflect self-determination and community participation in driving any direct funding initiative;
- policy frameworks are key to guiding change but are currently limited in North America;
- the power of independent planning support to build and sustain capacity for self-funding initiatives;
- non-bureaucratic, simple funding approaches that ideally can move between areas are important;
- small-scale change informs system change – the challenge is how to reproduce and maintain the values and principles evident in small-scale projects in building a larger, more comprehensive service system that addresses individualised planning and direct funding.

Finally, SCIE (2007) has produced a research briefing that gives a helpful overview of the UK and international literature on consumer–directed payments. Key issues include:

- the different models of support that different countries have found most useful – for example, a review of ten initiatives in Canada, Australia and the US found that support systems independent from service delivery were most helpful;
- the huge increase in demand for PAs has been apparent in all countries; in Belgium, for example, there has been a growth of private personal assistant temping agencies;
- issues of low wages for PAs and an unregulated market are common throughout;
- almost all countries have underestimated the costs of schemes and many have had to contain the rising demand for cash payments.

However, the concluding observation of the review is that: 'Consumer satisfaction and reported growth in autonomy have been the most frequently reported outcomes of consumer–directed care' (SCIE, 2007, p 9).

SUMMARY

In the early stages of implementation, the progress of direct payments was uneven, with more rapid implementation in the south of England than in the north, Wales, Northern Ireland and many parts of Scotland. Key barriers appear to include fears about the erosion of public services, a lack of awareness among social workers, financial concerns, a lack of accessible information and the absence of pump-priming to establish appropriate support mechanisms. When direct payments became mandatory and the number of people eligible for direct payments increased, the pace of change quickened. However, direct payments have sometimes been conceptualised from the perspective of people with physical impairments, and people from other service user groups have sometimes been excluded from, or found it difficult to access, payment schemes. Although different groups face different obstacles, recurring themes include a lack of appropriate information and support, unsupportive professionals, bureaucratic procedures and concerns about becoming an employer. Despite these barriers, forms of individualised funding have also been introduced in a number of developed countries (with the UK implementing payments much later than some of its neighbours). While a variety of approaches have been adopted and while many countries are working through obstacles to further progress, the fact that payments are available in so many different countries suggests at the very least that the concept of individualised funding may well be an idea whose time has come.

IMPLICATIONS FOR POLICY AND PRACTICE

- Direct payments have spread unevenly across different geographical areas and among different user groups. Often this seems to be to do with the way in which direct payments have been operationalised, and the history and culture of specific services.
- A key role is played by frontline workers, who act as gatekeepers to this system. This is explored in more detail in Chapter Seven, but the attitude and approach of individual practitioners may well be crucial to whether the option of direct payments is raised in a constructive way (or even raised at all).
- The role of support services is crucial (see also Chapter Seven) – the role of peer support, accessible information, ongoing support over time and positive role models can be particularly important.
- A senior 'champion' can be helpful in securing resources and maintaining profile. At the level of frontline practice, a practice 'champion' can inspire and encourage staff who may be uncertain or ambivalent about their role in helping people access direct payments.
- Although this chapter has tended to focus on overall numbers and trends, direct payments are only a means to an end; the quality of people's individual experience is more important than quantity per se.

Recommended reading and useful websites

For a national overview of the spread and impact of direct payments, see:

- Riddell et al's (2006) Economics and Social Research Council-funded comparative study of direct payments in the four countries of the UK;
- Vick et al's (2006) national study on the implementation of direct payments;
- Davey et al's (2007a–b) national surveys of direct payments policy and practice.

For a summary of all three studies and associated reports, see www.pssru.ac.uk/dps/dps_projects.htm.

The Care Services Improvement Partnership has produced a self-assessment and action–planning guide for local authorities (Murray et al, 2006), while the Social Care Institute for Excellence has published a series of answers to frequently asked questions (SCIE, 2005).

For an overview of the experience of different user groups, see:

- Abbott (2003) (for younger disabled people);
- Williams and Holman (2006) (for people with learning difficulties);
- Taylor (2008) (for people with mental health problems);
- Poole (2006) (for older people);
- Fletcher (2006) (for carers);

- Carlin and Lenehan (2004) (for parents of disabled children);
- Stuart (2006) (for black and minority ethnic communities);
- Commission for Rural Communities (2008) (for rural communities).

For international lessons, see:

- Lundsgaard's (2005) OECD review;
- SCIE's (2007) review of the international literature on direct payments;
- Lord and Hutchinson's (2003) discussion of 'individualised support and funding'.

Reflective exercises

1. Do you know anyone who receives direct payments? Talk to them and see how they found out about direct payments and how easy it was to get access to this way of working. Did they have assistance from support organisations and was this tailored to their specific situation? What were the key issues in terms of managing their direct payments? How does their experience compare to some of the opportunities and barriers discussed in this chapter?
2. If you work or are on placement in a local authority, look at the policies on direct payments in your organisation. Are they clear about who is eligible for direct payments, what the restrictions are and what your obligations are in relation to direct payments?
3. Talk to people within the team or elsewhere who have had experience of direct payments. What did they find were the things that helped or hindered the successful implementation of direct payments?
4. What other measures do you think need to be in place to encourage more people from seldom-heard groups to access direct payments?

Notes
[1] The Isles of Scilly and the City of London were excluded from official data as their eligible population was less than 100.

[2]

Data supplied by

The organisation that puts information
at the heart of decision making
in health and social care

The
Information
Centre
knowledge for care

NHS

FIVE

Personal budgets – where they came from and why they matter

This chapter explores:
- the history and evolution of personal budgets;
- key features, concepts and values;
- emerging evidence about impact;
- the potential implications for wider public services.

Although direct payments and personal budgets are often seen as two sides of the same coin, they are actually entirely separate ways of working (albeit with much in common). As explained in previous chapters, direct payments involve the payment of the cash equivalent of a directly provided service to a person eligible for social care, who then uses this to design their own support. They are the result of a longstanding campaign by disabled people and their organisations, and now have a long track record (with indirect payments in place for many years and direct payments formally in place since 1996 legislation). While personal budgets build on such history, they are very recent in their introduction (from 2003) and originated from allies of the disabled people's movement working within services for people with learning difficulties, rather than from disabled people themselves.

At its most simple, a personal budget involves being clear with the person at the start how much money is available to meet their needs, then allowing them maximum choice over how this money is spent on their behalf and over how much control they want over the money itself. While this could result in the person taking the full personal budget as a direct payment, there are several other ways of organising support (which can include a social worker managing the full amount on the person's behalf). Thus, the money need not actually change hands – the key is that the person knows immediately how much is likely to be spent on their needs, and can then be more creative in thinking of new ways to meet these needs. For all the debate that personal budgets have generated, this seems to us to be little more than 'sensible delegation' (personal communication, in Control) – ensuring that the person with the biggest vested interest in making a support package work as effectively as possible is able to control how that support is organised and delivered. Another key difference is that personal budgets can be spent on anything that can be shown to be meeting a person's assessed needs – and this can include a combination of public, private and voluntary sector services (including things that do not look like traditional 'services' at all). As explained in previous chapters, this differs significantly from direct payments, which cannot be spent on public sector services (and which arguably led to some local authorities adopting a 'well if you don't like what we offer, do it yourself' approach).

Perhaps most importantly of all, direct payments have sometimes felt like a very empowering way of working bolted on to traditional and unresponsive systems. While direct payments can transform the way in which people receive support, they have not yet changed the way in which people access services, the way they are assessed, the prevailing culture or the way in which the bulk of the social care budget is spent. In contrast, personal budgets seem to offer all of the advantages of direct payments, while also holding out the potential for transforming the system as a whole. It is for a combination of these reasons – because they are so new, because they derive from different sources to direct payments, because they are easy to confuse with direct payments and because they aim at broader system change – that personal budgets have attracted such strong responses, both positive and negative.

History and evolution

Although direct payments and personal budgets have a different history and focus, both have been greeted with high expectations from people using services and their allies. Following on from the high hopes that many people had for direct payments (see the quotation at the start of Chapter One from Oliver and Sapey, 1999), personal budgets and self-directed support have been described as 'potentially the biggest change to the provision of social care in England in 60 years' (Browning, 2007, p 3). Beginning initially within services for people with learning difficulties, the advent of personal budgets was closely linked to the aspirations of *Valuing People*, the government's strategy for learning disability services (DH, 2001f). Unlike many other policy documents, *Valuing People* does not focus on health and social care as an end in themselves, but on a broader vision for people's lives (with health and social care merely as a means to these ends). As set out in Box 5.1, the central focus was on four key principles: rights, choice, independence and inclusion. Given the history of social care summarised in Chapter Two, the commitment to such principles was always likely to lead to tension with the traditional social care system (which contained very few formal rights and relatively little choice, with rather a mixed track record with regards to independence and inclusion). While *Valuing People* brought a helpful focus to these debates, however, the history of personal budgets is inextricably linked with a group of people and calls for reform that might be described as an 'inclusion movement'. Although this approach receives much less attention than the more well-known concept of independent living set out earlier in this book, it draws many of its ideas from concepts such as supported living, person–centred planning and self-advocacy. It is thus very much against this background that *Valuing People*, personal budgets, self-directed support and in Control must be viewed.

Against this background, the concept of personal budgets was first developed by a small group of individuals meeting in 2003 to discuss ways of working within

Box 5.1: *Valuing People*

In 2001, the government's *Valuing People* (DH, 2001f) set out a new vision for learning disability services in the twenty-first century. The first such policy document since 1971, *Valuing People* emphasised the importance of four key principles:

- rights
- choice
- independence
- control

Individual chapters of the strategy then focused on topics such as disabled children and young people; choice and control; supporting carers; improving health; housing, fulfilling lives and employment; quality services; partnership working; and making change happen.

In particular, *Valuing People* argued that current services are characterised by variable quality; shortfalls of provision of particular services; varying degrees of commitment by local authorities and the NHS; and widespread isolation and social exclusion. Instead, the strategy proposed a series of radical changes to a broad range of services designed to improve the lives of people with learning difficulties and their families; promote choice, social inclusion and independence; and recognise people's rights as citizens.

the current social care system to bring about the biggest possible change for people with learning difficulties. While this process and the key people involved is described in more detail in Box 5.2, many of these early pioneers had a long track record of working to support people with learning difficulties to leave long-stay hospitals and live independently in the community. Throughout this previous work, a key frustration had been that the barrier to further progress always seemed to be the fact that so much of the money available was tied up in existing buildings and in pre-paid services, rather than available to use flexibly and creatively to support people in the community. In this way, in Control began life as an unusual mix of high principle and very down-to-earth pragmatism – essentially an attempt to think creatively how it might be possible to work within the current system to free up more resources to do things differently. In many ways, this is a mix that has continued throughout the life of in Control and become something of a defining feature. In the same way, the nature of in Control's origins has been important in terms of the design of personal budgets and the broader system of self-directed support, both of which were developed to be fully compatible with the current policy and legal framework.

From these initial discussions came a new way of organising social care (self-directed support), based on a new way of allocating resources and on a new way of enabling the individual to be in control of their support. As Box 5.3 suggests,

Box 5.2: The origins of in Control

In 2003 discussions [about how to transform the social care system] ... took place between Steve Jones, then Chief Executive of Wigan Metropolitan Borough Council, Martin Routledge of the Valuing People Support Team (VPST) and Julie Stansfield of the North West Training and Development Team. The emerging project gained strong support from Rob Greig, then leader of the VPST, and Jo Williams, Chief Executive of Mencap.

The group also included Helen Sanderson, one of the leading thinkers and practitioners of person-centred planning, and Simon Duffy of Paradigm (a leading consultancy agency). Simon Duffy had been working on practical systems for individualising funding so that individuals had more control of money for their support since the early 1990s. During this time he worked with service providers like Southwark Consortium and Inclusion Glasgow, and latterly with North Lanarkshire Council.

Carl Poll also joined the team. He was the founder of KeyRing, an innovative community support organisation ...

By late 2003, under the joint leadership of Mencap and VPST, the in Control Partnership was born ...

Aided by the sponsorship of the VPST and Mencap (each contributed £60,000), in Control was able to invite local authorities to participate in testing and further developing the model. Essex, Gateshead, Redcar and Cleveland, South Gloucestershire, West Sussex and Wigan came forward as the pilot authorities. Each authority contributed both funding (£20,000 each) and a commitment to building a new system of social care in their areas.

(Poll et al, 2006, p 8)

self-directed support is based on a series of seven steps. While the principles and concepts associated with personal budgets are explored in more detail below, the main point here is that the personal budget, so often the focus of discussion, is only part of a much broader attempt to transform the social care system as a whole – it is not an end in itself. Borrowing language and concepts from the manufacture of computer software, in Control describes this as a new 'operating system' that is 'open-source' in nature (that is, in Control makes new versions of its tools and models available to all members to implement as they are developed, constantly seeking feedback and developing new, improved versions – much the same as IT companies issue new versions of their software). Also crucial to understanding the work of in Control are concepts taken from the field of social enterprise and social networks. Essentially, in Control describes itself as a social innovation network that seeks to:

- *Connect:* in Control creates and sustains active membership networks for people to work together to find solutions to problems that frustrate citizenship.
- *Understand:* in Control tries to understand and measure the impact of the welfare system and new practices on the real outcomes that are valued by citizens, sharing information, analysis and intelligence across its networks.
- *Innovate:* in Control develops and tests new approaches to welfare reform, extending the boundaries of self-directed support and promoting other reforms to enhance citizenship.

Another more shorthand way of describing in Control is as 'the think tank that does' (personal communication), developing new bottom-up approaches that build on the realities of the lives of service users and frontline staff.

Box 5.3: Seven steps to self-directed support

Step 1 – set a personal budget: using in Control's resource allocation system (RAS), everyone is told their financial allocation – their personal budget – and they decide what level of control they wish to take over their budget.

Step 2 – plan support: people plan how they will use their personal budget to get the help that is best for them; if they need help to plan, then advocates, brokers or others can support them.

Step 3 – agree plan: the local authority helps people to create good support plans, checks they are safe and makes sure that people have any necessary representation.

Step 4 – manage personal budget: people control their personal budget to the extent they want (there are currently six distinct degrees of control: ranging from direct payments at one extreme to local authority control at the other).

Step 5 – organise support: people can use their personal budget flexibly (including for statutory services). Indeed, the only real restriction is that the budget must be used for needs the state recognises as legitimate and must be spent on something legal.

Step 6 – live life: people use their personal budget to achieve the outcomes that are important to them in the context of their whole life and their role and contribution within the wider community.

Step 7 – review and learn: the authority continues to check that people are okay, shares what is being learned and can change things if people are not achieving the outcomes they need to achieve.

(Adapted from www.in-control.org.uk; *see also Poll et al, 2006, pp 26-37)*

From here, it is harder to explain how the initial concept of personal budgets came to be taken up by government and promoted with such enthusiasm. Although it is beyond the scope of this book, the broader literature on policy making suggests that the way in which ideas are developed, announced and implemented can often be a form of 'muddling through' (Lindblom, 1959), based on an interaction between multiple and often competing interests. Certainly this seems to have been the case with the increasing policy interest in personal budgets. At this time, adult social care services were facing increasing pressure as a result of demographic and social changes, medical and technological advances and rising public expectations. Moreover, different interest groups appeared to have different motivations, with some interested in the potential of personal budgets to improve choice and control, and others seemingly interested more in whether this way of working could lead to cost savings (or at the very least make existing scarce resources go farther). In many ways, this seems similar to the history of direct payments, with different supporters potentially motivated by a desire to promote citizenship and independence on the one hand, or by a desire to roll back the boundaries of the welfare state on the other. While these two groups are often uneasy bedfellows in the long term, they tend to create a momentum for change in the short term when their interests and ideas begin to coalesce.

While the exact factors that contributed to an expansion of personal budgets are likely to be unclear for some time, the fact remains that this was a new idea that looked good, that fitted with current policy aspirations and that seemed to work. Despite the muddle that often surrounds policy, therefore, the fact that personal budgets were taken up so quickly and with such enthusiasm is in one sense a triumph of common sense. Even if the odds sometimes appear to be stacked against you, this seemed to demonstrate that the right people with the right ideas at the right time and with the right tactics really can make a difference. Thus, in 2005, official support for personal budgets came in three separate (albeit partially linked) government reports: the Department of Health's adult social care Green Paper, *Independence, Well-being and Choice*; a report from the Prime Minister's Strategy Unit on *Improving the Life Chances of Disabled People*; and a report from the Department for Work and Pensions, *Opportunity Age*, on the government's strategy for older people (see Box 5.4 for extracts). Following this, a commitment to piloting personal budgets also appeared in the 2005 Labour Party manifesto. As explained below, however, the government often adopted the term 'individual budget' to refer to a broader, but less well-defined, notion of a personal budget made up with money from diverse funding sources.

Box 5.4: Official interest in personal budgets

In 2005, the Department of Health's adult social care Green Paper, *Independence, Well-being and Choice*, proposed a series of pilots to develop the evidence base. Working with a number of different adult user groups and including a series of different budgets (including adult social care, equipment and adaptations, Independent Living Funds, Access to Work and Family Funds), the pilots (if successful) were expected to lead to the more widespread roll-out of personal budgets by 2012.

Also in 2005, the Prime Minister's Strategy Unit report on *Improving the Life Chances of Disabled People* argued that 'different sources of funding should be brought together in the form of individual budgets – while giving individuals the choice whether to take these budgets as cash or as services' (p 93). With national roll-out by 2012, this was to be based on a simplified resource allocation system, 'one-stop' assessment, greater self-assessment and access to advocacy.

This was supplemented by the Department for Work and Pensions report, *Opportunity Age*, which stated that 'we want to achieve a society where increasingly diverse older people are active consumers of public services, exercising choice and control, not passive recipients of them ... Over the next years, we will test out services which implement this model ..., including giving those who want them individual budgets which they can use to select their own care packages' (DWP, 2005, p xviii).

Finally, in 2005, the Labour Party manifesto pledged to 'give older people greater choice over their care. For every older person receiving care or other support, we want to offer transparent, individual budgets which bring funding for a range of services ... together in one place. We will pilot individual budgets for older people by the end of this year' (p 72).

Arising out of this, the government began a two-year pilot in 13 sites (see Table 5.1). Despite good intentions, this process seems to have struggled from something of an initial lack of clarity and from confusion over the key differences between the approaches being tested by in Control and the Department of Health. That this was the case seems to be demonstrated in a number of key early developments:

- The terminology used was confusing, with in Control and the Department of Health using the same term (which the former had invented) to refer to different concepts (see Box 5.5 for further discussion). While in Control initially used the term 'individual budget' to refer to its work in adult social care, the Department used the same language to refer to a more integrated approach in which local pilots experimented with bringing together a series of different funding streams. In a later attempt to resolve this issue, the Department of Health began to refer to 'personal budgets' for approaches that involve adult social care only, and 'individual budgets' for approaches that seek to integrate multiple funding sources. Given the confusion that occurred when the Department for Work and Pensions developed a new policy for the 'direct payment' of social security benefits (see Chapter Three), this seemed an unfortunate case of history repeating itself. Perhaps more importantly, it also meant that the national IBSEN evaluation of individual budgets described in more detail below was actually exploring something different to the model of self-directed support developed by in Control, and results therefore need to be interpreted with caution.

- After their initial pilot work in six local authorities, in Control began a second phase of work in late 2005 – within three months they had some 60 local authorities sign up as members. However, several of the Department of Health's 13 pilot sites were also in Control members (and indeed a small number of authorities were members of the original in Control six, the Phase 2 60 and Department of Health pilots).

- Policy explanations of personal budgets have sometimes been confusing, and it is still relatively rare to find the concept of personal budgets and their key features explained well (outside the work of in Control).

- The focus of the initial Department of Health approach was on integrating locally a series of relatively small-scale but very bureaucratic funding sources. While some progress was made, this seemed to set local pilots up to fail by asking them to tackle systemic issues that needed national attention (and perhaps even new legislation). Arguably, this was the wrong tactic to be adopting; perhaps greater progress could have been made by focusing on the much larger adult social care budget, rather than diluting the in Control model by taking on too many different funding sources at once.

- With the benefit of hindsight, the Department of Health pilots seemed to suffer early on from a lack of clarity about the nature of the intervention that was being tested, tight timescales, strong political interest and the difficulty of establishing cross-government pilots.

In spite of their very promising start and fairly unpromising national adoption, current policy has remained committed to the potential of personal budgets. That this was the case seems, at least in part, to owe something to the personal contribution of Ivan Lewis, then the care services minister, who became very much a champion of in Control and personal budgets. Thus, in late 2007, the government's *Putting People First* manifesto (HM Government, 2007) was signed by six government departments and a series of national health, social care and local government organisations (see Box 5.6). Although the self-proclaimed 'shared vision and commitment to the transformation of adult social care' set out a number of different approaches, the document pledged a further increase in the number of direct payment recipients as well as 'personal budgets for everyone eligible for publicly funded adult social care support other than in circumstances where people require emergency access to provision' (HM Government, 2007, p 3). At the same time, there was also a suggestion that 'in the future personal budgets for people with long-term conditions could include NHS resources' (HM Government, 2007, p 3). In early 2008, this was followed by a more detailed circular that focused more on implementation and support, including a new three-year £520 million grant to help councils make the necessary changes (DH, 2008a). Increasingly, recent reforms have been described in terms of a 'personalisation agenda', which is a relatively new phrase used to describe an overall approach in which 'every person across the spectrum of need [has] choice and control over the shape of his or her support, in the most appropriate setting' (DH, 2008a, p 2). While on one hand this seems like a reasonable shorthand for a more complex and important series of changes, it arguably lacks much of the clarity and practical focus of in Control's notion of 'self-directed support'.

As a result of these developments, personal budgets seem set to transform the nature of current adult social care, and the numbers of people involved are increasing rapidly. Across the UK, over 9,000 people are receiving personal budgets of one form or another (all figures in this paragraph are personal communications from in Control unless otherwise stated). From six pilots and 60 people receiving personal budgets from late 2003, in Control had achieved a membership of 60 local authorities by late 2005 and of 108 by late 2008. In addition, 19 sites had committed to a rapid and widespread implementation of personal budgets known as 'total transformation' (committing to 50 per cent of all service users receiving a personal budget within three years), while additional projects around 'Taking Control' (in children's services) and 'Staying in Control' (in health) have 27 children's departments and 37 PCT members respectively.

Table 5.1: Department of Health individual budget pilot sites

Site	Main focus
Gateshead	People with learning difficulties, people with physical/sensory impairments and people with mental health problems at times of transition from children's services to adult services, and from adult services to older people's services
Coventry	People with learning difficulties, people with physical/sensory impairments and people who use mental health services. They will all be people who are going through changes in their lives – e.g. growing up, moving from education to employment, leaving a family or other 'supervised' home to live more independently, moving from hospital or rehab to living in the community or at home, and people who are coming home from living in an 'out of city' placement.
West Sussex	Older people
Manchester	Older people, people with neurological illness, renal patients
Oldham	All adults
Barnsley	All adults, including young people in transition
Lincolnshire	Starting with older people, but later to include all adults
Barking and Dagenham	Older people, people with learning difficulties, people with physical impairments and people who use mental health services
Kensington and Chelsea	Older people and people with physical impairments
Leicester	People with learning difficulties, people with physical/sensory impairments. May include other people later in the pilot
Bath and North East Somerset	People with learning difficulties, older people and younger people with a physical/sensory impairment
Essex	People with learning difficulties, people with physical impairments, family carers
Norfolk	People with mental health problems

Source: Care Services Improvement Partnership individual budget website (http://individualbudgets.csip.org.uk/dynamic/dohpage2.jsp, accessed 20 June 2008).

Box 5.5: Changing language

Over time, the language used to describe this area of policy and practice has changed – and not always helpfully. Risking complicating matters yet further, a brief history is set out below:

When the initial group of people met in 2003 to share ideas, the term initially used was 'self-directed services'. However, it very quickly became apparent that this was not quite right (because it focused too much on formal services), and so the shorthand term changed to 'self-directed support'. Also at this time, the individuals involved decided that they needed a name and a brand for what they were starting to try to create, and chose 'in Control'.

By 2004, members of in Control were talking about the importance of an 'indicative resource allocation' (which, for some reason, never caught on!). Initially it is believed to have been a government minister who started using the term 'individual budget' to provide a more helpful summary of the concept (and certainly one that flows off the tongue better).

Following government interest in using this model to integrate different funding streams, the Department of Health and others began to reserve the term 'individual budget' to refer to the range of different models that they were piloting (see Table 5.1). in Control was therefore asked to find another term for its work in adult social care, deciding upon 'personal budgets' as an appropriate compromise. They therefore had to rewrite all their material, replacing 'individual budgets' with 'personal budgets'.

In response to these complexities, this book tries to use the term 'personal budget' to refer to the work of in Control and to changes in adult social care, reserving the term 'individual budget' for initial Department of Health pilots involving the integration of multiple funding sources. However, it is possible that current language will evolve further by the time this book appears!

Box 5.6: *Putting People First*

Ensuring older people, people with chronic conditions, disabled people and people with mental health problems have the best possible quality of life and the equality of independent living is fundamental to a socially just society. For many, social care is the support which helps make this a reality ... The time has now come to build on best practice and replace paternalistic, reactive care of variable quality with a mainstream system focused on prevention, early intervention, enablement, and high quality personally tailored services. In the future, we want people to have the maximum choice, control and power over the support services they receive.
(HM Government, 2007, p 2)

Key features, concepts and values

Given criticisms about the poorly explained nature of personal budgets at national level, it is important to be clear about the key features of this way of working. As personal budgets have become something of a hot topic, the biggest danger is that they get hijacked by people who do not understand them or who have other motives, allowing the old system to pay lip-service to the concept while essentially recreating itself. To guard against this, in Control sets out seven key principles (see www.in-control.org.uk):

- *The right to independent living*: if someone has an impairment that means they need help to fulfil their needs as a citizen, they should get the help they need.
- *Right to a personal budget*: if someone needs ongoing paid help as part of their life, they should be able to decide how the money that pays for that help is used.
- *Right to self-determination*: if someone needs help to make decisions, then decision making should be made as close to the person as possible, reflecting the person's own interests and preferences.
- *Right to accessibility*: the system of rules within which people have to work must be clear and open in order to maximise the ability of people to take control of their own support.
- *Right to flexible funding*: when someone is using their personal budget they should be free to spend their funds in the way that makes best sense to them, without unnecessary restrictions.
- *Accountability principle*: the person and the government both have a responsibility to each other to explain their decisions and to share what they have learnt.
- *Capacity principle*: people, their families and communities must not be assumed to be incapable of managing their own support, learning skills or making a contribution.

Building on this, in Control characterises its approach as shifting from a 'professional gift' model (in which the state uses the money it receives from taxes to slot people into pre-paid services through the work of professional assessors and gatekeepers) to a 'citizenship model' (in which the disabled person is at the centre of the process, is part of the community and organises the support they need and want; see Figures 5.1 and 5.2). While personal budgets are important, therefore, it is this shift in the relationship between the state and the individual that lies at the heart of self-directed support. This is also helpfully captured by Rummery (2006, pp 646-7), who argues that:

> The problem is that community care policy has never been framed within a discourse of citizenship ... New Labour has left largely unchallenged a system of providing care and support for disabled

Figure 5.1: Professional gift model of social care

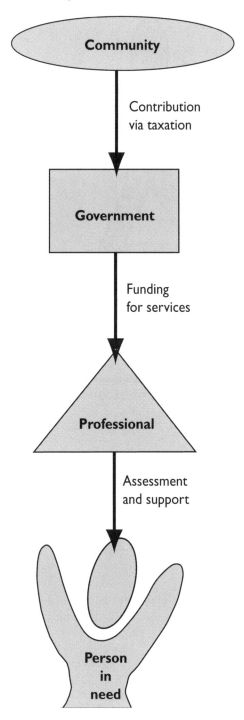

Reproduced with permission from Duffy, 2005a, p 153; see also Duffy, 1996.

Figure 5.2: Citizenship model

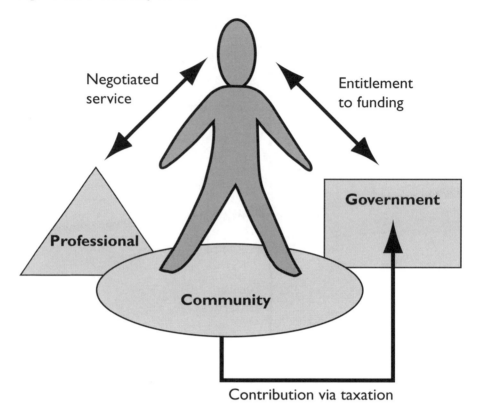

Reproduced with permission from Duffy, 2005a, p 155; see also Duffy, 1996.

people that was designed by the Conservative government to curb the spiralling cost of residential care provision and marketise the delivery of welfare. The fundamental aims and discourse of community care policy need to be challenged. We need to stop talking about 'the cost of care' and start talking about supporting citizenship and challenging social exclusion.

In developing this further, in Control has summarised some of the key differences between traditional approaches to social care and the new system of self-directed support (see Table 5.2).

Table 5.2: Social care versus self-directed support

Beliefs for social care	Beliefs for self-directed support
Disabled people are vulnerable and should be taken care of by trained professionals	Every adult should be in control of their life, even if they need help with decisions
Existing services suit people well – the challenge is to assess people and decide which service suits them	Everybody needs support that is tailored to their situation to help them sustain and build their place in the community
Money is not abused if it is controlled by large organisations or statutory authorities	Money is most likely to be used well when it is controlled by the person or by people who really care about the person
Family and friends are unreliable allies for disabled people and where possible should be replaced by independent professionals	Family and friends can be the most important allies for disabled people and make a positive contribution to their lives

Source: Duffy, 2005b, p 10.

Once a system of self-directed support is in place, it should include the seven steps set out previously in Box 5.3 (p 79). While these are relatively self-explanatory, five particular issues are worthy of further exploration:

- Philosophically, personal budgets and self-directed support link naturally to notions of self-assessment and person-centred planning. These are complex and important issues, and further details and resources are available via www.in-control.org.uk.
- Following an assessment, the person is effectively placed in a funding bracket according to the level of their needs using a Resource Allocation System (RAS). While this is an issue that often concerns local authorities, in Control has done significant work developing and improving the RAS process (see Box 5.7 for a brief summary). Crucially, the RAS ensures that people receive a fair and transparent allocation of funds according to their needs. As a by-product, in Control has found that 'some very high-cost services have proved to be entirely unnecessary and resources can be redistributed to those who need them'. Equally, 'people with lower levels of need are starting to receive appropriate modest levels of funding for the first time, thus avoiding a path towards crisis and costly services' (Hatton et al, 2008, p 36).
- Next is the centrality of the Support Plan, which should be done wherever possible by the person themselves and anyone else they wish to be involved (often friends and family). However, there are many other forms of support that should be available, including different forms of advice and brokerage (see Tables 5.3 and 5.4). A particularly helpful overview is provided by Senker (2008), who summarises the tasks or functions that underpin the notion of 'support brokerage' and sets out practical examples and ideas to help develop

this. In some ways, this broader notion of brokerage may contrast with the strong emphasis on Centres for Independent Living in the development of direct payments. Although support for personal budgets may well come from a CIL, there is no assumption that this is necessarily the optimal solution. Indeed, in an era when we no longer block-purchase care on people's behalf, it seems ironic to be block-purchasing support for people.

- After this, the management of a personal budget can be undertaken by a range of different people, depending on the needs and wishes of the person concerned (see Table 5.3). This again seems different from direct payments, where some local authorities seemed to adopt a 'take it or leave it approach': if you were perceived as not liking what the local authority was offering, then you were on your own (see, for example, Sapey and Pearson, 2004).

- In contrast to traditional social care, the emphasis shifts from the initial assessment (which often dominates much of current practice) to support planning and review (which are often neglected when workloads are heavy). In many ways, this reverses current practice, and is arguably a better place to focus in order to ensure the best possible support arrangements and the maximum possible learning.

Table 5.3: Different types of support

Source of support	
The person themselves, their friends and family	Wherever possible, this should be the main source of support
Support brokers	Help from an independent source – someone who is not involved in either arranging or providing support
Service providers	Help from a service provider the person trusts
Care managers	Some people may still need help from care managers – but a system of self-directed support should free them up from doing this for everyone in order to concentrate on those with the most complex needs and without access to other support
People in the community	Brokerage consists of a set of functions that could be carried out by many other people – including individuals, family members and community organisations

Source: Poll et al, 2006, p 31.

Box 5.7: The history of the RAS

RAS Version 1 – The first version of the RAS was developed by Simon Duffy before the beginning of in Control and it involved setting the budget in the light of three criteria: need, complexity, and community support ...

RAS Version 2 – At the beginning of in Control's early work in Wigan in 2003, Simon worked with colleagues to develop a more sophisticated system. This system set personal budget levels by correlating them to the cost of typical existing service packages ...

RAS Version 3 – In 2005, John Walters joined in Control as its technical director and brought with him a more sophisticated model of needs analysis that allowed the model to put a numeric value on different domains of need ...

RAS Version 4 – In 2006, more authorities wanted a system that could cope with much higher numbers of people from different care groups. John developed a new approach that allowed authorities to apply a 'price point' that would be multiplied by the figure that represented the level of need ...

RAS Version 5 – In 2007, John began work with [in Control's] partner organisation, Symmetric SD, to develop a further version of the RAS that could be delivered through the internet. This is called e-RAS. The key innovation here has been that in Control is finally able to go beyond setting the personal budget level by reference to the cost profile of the past. Instead, it is possible to use the data that is coming from the field to set the budget level. (Hatton et al, 2008, p 35)

Although very technical in nature, this brief discussion aims to show how different resource allocation approaches already exist and how in Control has developed and improved its methodology in constant dialogue with partners in the field.

Table 5.4: Managing a personal budget

Disabled person	The person manages their own money and support
Representative	A representative manages on the person's behalf
Trust	A trust is established to receive and control the money on the person's behalf (similar to a trust that might be set up for a child who inherits money)
Broker	Some people choose to pay an individual or organisation to act as their broker
Service provider	The service provider manages the person's money, but keeps it separate in an Individual Service Fund and spends it on behalf of/with the individual
Care manager	Some people may still want or need their care manager to manage their personal budget on their behalf

Source: Poll et al, 2006, p 33.

Emerging evidence about impact

From the relatively humble origins described above, in Control conducted a brief evaluation of the impact of self-directed support on the lives of a very small sample of people (31) in the first six pilot sites (see Poll et al, 2006 for all findings quoted in this and the next two paragraphs). Overseen by Professor Chris Hatton from the University of Lancaster, the evaluation involved before and after questionnaires completed by the individuals concerned (with an average of 46 weeks between the first and second questionnaires, range 18–61 weeks). Although only based on a very small group of people, the findings from this process were so encouraging that they generated debate and enthusiasm above and beyond the numbers involved. At the same time, it should be remembered that this sample was not necessarily representative and that many people who volunteer for pilots can sometimes be those who are the most dissatisfied with current arrangements and/or with the most motivation to make the new approach work. In addition, we have no information on what would have happened to these individuals anyway without the pilot, and so the relationship between the outcomes below and the concept of a personal budget is not necessarily causal. That said, the results are so promising that they remain worthy of further study.

As Table 5.5 suggests, at the second questionnaire more people felt that they made the important decisions over their own lives and were in control of their money. Satisfaction with support also increased (from 48% to 100%). Perhaps most importantly of all, many of the people involved were able to make significant changes in their lives (see Tables 5.6 and 5.7), shifting away from more institutional forms of support to more community-based, personalised ways of meeting need. In particular, the ten people living in residential care at the start of the process were all able to move into alternative accommodation in under a year. More generally, people made greater use of personal assistants and community support, with less use of services such as day care.

Also significant was the impact on the cost of current support packages. While all the above caveats about the size and limitations of the sample still apply, work in five other local authorities resulted in significant savings (the smallest amount saved was 12% of the cost of support before in Control; see Table 5.8). In the view of in Control, this was largely due to a more transparent allocation system that cut out expensive outlying cases and to a natural tendency for block-purchased services to over-provide even for people with lower levels of need (that is, once a service is block-purchased, it tends to get used, irrespective of whether the individual really needs it or not). Although this issue is explored in more detail in Chapter Six, these early findings clearly made an important impact on some policy makers and local authority leaders: based on the initial evaluation (albeit very small and limited), personal budgets seemed to hold out the possibility of achieving much better outcomes for less money, and few could ignore such a potential holy grail.

Table 5.5: The impact of personal budgets (2006)

Impact of personal budgets	Number of people (at Time 1 and Time 2) (total n = 31)
Making important decisions about your life	Doubled (from 6 to 12)
Control over your life	Increased from no one really happy to 17 really happy
Person-centred plan	Numbers with a plan increased from 12 to 27
Satisfaction with support	Went from 6 really unhappy and 9 unhappy to no one really unhappy or unhappy
Satisfaction with the money you have	From 9 really unhappy/7 unhappy/12 quite happy/2 really happy to 1/1/15/13 respectively
Happy with your home	From 10 really happy to 23 really happy
Happy with relationships	Most were at least fairly happy before, but there was still an improvement

Adapted from Poll et al, 2006.

Table 5.6 Changes in people's lives

Desired change	% achieved
Where I live	76%
Who I live with	81%
What I do with my time	69%
Who supports me	89%

Source: Poll et al, 2006, p 52.

Table 5.7: Type of support

Type of support	Before	After
Support at home	20	22
Employing PAs	8	22
Using day centre	12	11
Hours in day centre	4.5 days	3.5 days
Using family support	21	21
Using community support	8	15

Source: Poll et al, 2006, p 81.

Table 5.8: The impact of personal budgets on costs

Authority	Sum of support pre-in Control (£)	Sum of personal budgets (£)	Difference (%)
I	600,000	525,000	12
2 (desk exercise)	5,625,000	4,500,000	20
3 (in cases where there was a difference)	194,000	107,000	45
4	187,305	152,300	19
5	594,000	397,000	33

Source: Poll et al, 2006, p 67.

Also included in Poll et al's (2006) evaluation report is a brief description of the Small Sparks programme. Building on a community development project of the same name in Seattle, this small grant-giving programme sought to supplement the work of in Control with an additional approach for people with lower-level needs. As Box 5.8 explains, this was essentially an attempt to pump-prime innovative ways of boosting community involvement of people with learning difficulties via a series of small grants, matched either directly or in kind by people with learning difficulties themselves. At a time when the national trend was towards focusing on people with more and more intensive needs, this more bottom-up, community development approach was very much in keeping with the emphasis of the 2005 social care Green Paper (DH, 2005a) on preventative approaches for people with low-level needs.

In 2007, Henwood and Hudson (2007b) published findings from a Department of Health-funded review of early progress with self-directed support in three case study localities. These were deliberately chosen to include a spectrum of experiences, with one site an in Control pilot, one aiming to move towards large-scale transformation and one having had little engagement with self-directed support. Although at this stage there was little evidence about the impact of self-directed support on people's lives, the review provided a helpful snapshot of the implementation of this new way of working and identified a series of practical and cultural issues that will need to be overcome (see Chapters Six and Seven).

By 2008, Poll et al's (2006) evaluation was supplemented by more detailed research based on interviews with 196 people using self-directed support in 17 local authorities across England (Hatton et al, 2008). Again overseen by Professor Chris Hatton, the evaluation was at pains to stress the potential limitations of the study (for example, it was an incomplete and not necessarily representative sample, and people with learning difficulties and with physical impairments were more likely to report improvements than the small number of older people who took part). However, the fact remains that self-directed support again seemed to lead to positive outcomes (see Box 5.9), including significant improvements in some people's health and well-being, time spent with people they liked, quality of life, choice and control, contributions to community life and personal dignity.

Box 5.8: Small Sparks

'[In addition to developing personal budgets, in Control] also tested a small grants programme – Small Sparks – as a practical, inexpensive means of helping people to get involved… Four of the pilots each received £2,500 from in Control to distribute as grants of up to £250 on a match-funded basis. Small Sparkers could provide their contribution in funding …, in materials or in volunteer labour.'

In Wigan, Joe used the money to print a flyer for a sponsored bike ride. 200 people came and £7,000 was raised for Wigan Scope.

In Redcar, people at a day centre had an allotment, and used their grant to hold a BBQ to meet and socialise with other allotment-holders.

In West Sussex, some people had found it hard to open a bank account, and used their grant to run a display explaining 'easy steps to banking'.

In West Sussex and in South Gloucestershire, people used their grant to promote the work of a local toy library.
(Poll et al, 2006, pp 93–6)

Box 5.9: Outcomes of self-directed support (2008)

Participants reported improvement in:

- Quality of life (76%)
- Choice and control (72%)
- Taking part in and contributing to the community (64%)
- Personal dignity (59%)
- Spending time with people you like (55%)
- Health and well-being (47%)
- Economic well-being (36%)
- Feeling safe and secure at home (29%)

Of the 196 participants, 58% were people with learning difficulties, 20% were people with physical impairments and 13% were older people. 89% were White, 8% Asian and 4% Black. For some outcomes, people with learning difficulties and people with physical impairments were more likely to report improvement than older people (although this may be because the small numbers of older people involved were less likely to have been using services before the introduction of self-directed support and had, on average, used self-directed support for a shorter period of time).
(Hatton et al, 2008)

As part of a separate process, the Department of Health commissioned researchers from the universities of York, Manchester, Kent, King's College London and the London School of Economics and Political Science to carry out an independent evaluation of the 13 Department of Health pilot sites (that is, sites integrating other funding streams above and beyond adult social care). Published in the autumn of 2008, the final report (known as the IBSEN study) weighed in at some 305 pages, and provided an important insight into the early impact of individual budgets. Reiterating a point made earlier in this chapter, however, the Department of Health pilots were very different in origin and focus from the concept of self-directed support developed and evaluated by in Control – although many of the findings from IBSEN are relevant to both Department of Health pilots and in Control. Given the scale and breadth of IBSEN, moreover, a more complex and nuanced picture was always likely to emerge than was the case in earlier and more pragmatic evaluations. As suggested above, the advent of self-directed support has the potential to change the whole of the adult social care system, and any national evaluation was always likely to find a mix of positives, negatives, enablers and barriers. Indeed, if we carried out a national evaluation of the current system, the result would probably be equally complex, mixed and difficult to interpret. Finally, any national evaluation was always bound to struggle with trying to unpick which barriers and challenges are inherent to the concept of individual budgets, and which were more to do with the nature of pilot projects more generally. As a result, there was always likely to be a risk of mixed messages when the final IBSEN evaluation was published, and supporters and critics alike are likely to find much in the final report to debate and to reflect on in more detail.

With these caveats in mind, IBSEN remains crucial. Conducted by a series of leading social policy and social work researchers, the final study is detailed, rigorous and extremely rich in terms of the data it provides. Although key messages are summarised in Box 5.10, the research is so in depth that it deserves careful study in its own right (and the very brief overview provided here cannot do justice to such a complex evaluation). The study was also conducted in tight timescales with significant political interest and a number of policy changes and delays – so much so that the researchers are to be congratulated for being able to produce such a detailed insight in such difficult circumstances. Running from April 2006 to March 2008, the research focused on the outcomes of individual budgets, the experience of different user groups, factors aiding/hindering implementation and issues of effectiveness and cost-effectiveness. While the exact approach adopted is summarised in detail in the report itself, the research was based on a range of methods, including interviews with service users, frontline staff, local managers and individual budget leads, as well as a randomised controlled trial (an approach that allowed the researchers to compare costs and outcomes for people receiving an individual budget with those of a comparison group).

Box 5.10: The national IBSEN evaluation

- Overall, the study found 'encouraging indications of the impact of IBs [individual budgets] on individuals' lives, particularly the fact that those receiving IBs felt more in control of their lives than the comparison group' (p 236).
- Individual budgets are at least cost neutral – indeed they seem to cost on average £279 per week compared to £296 for standard services (although this difference was not statistically significant).
- In the short term at least, there was evidence to suggest that supporting people to access individual budgets may take additional staff time – and it remains to be seen whether this will reduce in future as the pilots are mainstreamed.
- Individual budgets had particular benefits for people with mental health problems and younger disabled people, with mixed results for people with learning difficulties.
- However, results were much less positive for older people, with the researchers pointing to a number of potential contributing factors (such as anxiety about potential changes to established support, fears about the burden of greater control, a tendency to approach services only in a crisis, the focus of older people's services on meeting personal care needs rather than broader elements of well-being, and the tendency for older people to receive smaller care packages compared to younger disabled people).
- Despite support for the potential to integrate different funding sources, this was a major source of frustration at a local level with only limited progress (as many of the funding streams arguably require national action if they are to be successfully integrated).

For further discussion of key enablers and barriers (including the impact on frontline staff; issues of eligibility, assessment and resource allocation; support planning and brokerage; risk; the experience of providers and commissioners; and the relationship with the NHS), see the full report (Glendinning et al, 2008). The final study also contains a wealth of information on people's hopes and aspirations, how they spent their budgets and the views of frontline staff.

Given its complexity, IBSEN was accompanied by a Department of Health summary (2008f), setting out key findings and providing an overview of the Department's response. Essentially, the Department has interpreted IBSEN as demonstrating that individual budgets can lead to better outcomes and higher perceived levels of control, with particular benefits for people with mental health problems (see Box 5.11 for a summary of outcomes for different user groups). Perhaps unsurprisingly, the Department's response spends significant time on the barriers that seem to exist within older people's services, and a linked report (DH, 2008g) summarises emerging lessons about good practice in this crucial area. Although some would see this as an attempt to put a positive gloss on a more nuanced set of findings, the Department's analysis of the current challenges in older people's services seems to us to be a helpful summary (DH, 2008g, p 1):

Previous experience with direct payments suggested that there would be significant challenges in making individual budgets work well for older people, particularly given the timescales of the [DH pilots]. The personalised approach of self-directed support represents a profound shift in focus; instead of being passive recipients of services, older people become active participants in their care and support. The experience of implementing individualised funding is less developed for older people than for younger disabled adults. This meant there was less experience to build on for older people and professionals working with them.

Box 5.11: Outcomes for different user groups

- Mental health service users reported significantly higher quality of life.
- Physically disabled adults reported receiving higher quality care and were more satisfied with the help they received.
- People with learning disabilities were more likely to feel they had control over their daily lives.
- Older people reported lower psychological well-being with individual budgets, perhaps because they felt the processes of planning and managing their own support were burdens.

(IBSEN, 2008, p 2)

The nature of the evidence

While the findings of IBSEN are different from the results of earlier in Control monitoring, these studies point towards an underlying issue with regards to the nature of evidence that is seen as valid when seeking to develop so-called 'evidence-based practice'. While this is a broader issue than can be dealt with here, it has previously been argued that the current emphasis on 'evidence-based practice' has become too dominated by formal research in general and by medical and quantitative research in particular (Glasby and Beresford, 2006; Glasby et al, 2007). Instead, Glasby and Beresford (2006) have called for a new notion of 'knowledge-based practice', combining different types of research, the practice wisdom of frontline staff and the lived experience of people who use services. Given that policy and frontline practice are nearly always ahead of the research evidence, in Control's emphasis on learning by doing, reflecting and sharing lessons may well offer a positive model for the future. In one sense, therefore, this represents a potentially exciting shift away from traditional 'evidence-based practice' towards a form of 'practice-based evidence'.

This is in no way to deny that there are complexities to consider and barriers to overcome when implementing self-directed support. On the contrary, learning from in Control coupled with the more independent IBSEN study reveals considerable positives, but also numerous complexities. However, the overall message from research, policy and practice to date seems to be that, with the right approach, self-directed support and personal budgets just seem to work. To demonstrate this, there can be no stronger 'evidence' than the stories of people who have received personal budgets (see, for example, Box 5.12).

Box 5.12: Joe's story (told by his mother, Caroline)

Our first child, Joseph Robert Tomlinson, was born in October 1988 … Our life was ordinary until 6 months later when Joseph contracted meningococcal meningitis.

To cut a long story short, after numerous assessments and examinations it was evident that Joseph had severe developmental delay and we entered a world we never knew existed – Service Land.

And so our journey changed. We were suddenly parachuted into a very strange and scary place. In this world of Service Land lots of other people became involved in our daily lives, constantly making recommendations to do this or do that. And all the time we seemed to have to ask for permission just to live an ordinary life.

But our life was certainly not ordinary. To function as a family we needed lots of support from other people, especially when Joseph's sister Rosie and his brother Jacob were born. Joseph, you see, finds it really difficult to sit still. He doesn't use words to communicate and his body doesn't always do the things he wants it to. In fact many people have said he is 'extremely challenging'.

So, as a family, we have needed help. But the help we received was what I call conveyor belt care. This means that services put in help at the most crucial parts of the day based on their assessment of our needs. For example, home care was provided by the Local Authority to come into the home and assist with getting Joe bathed, dressed and eating his breakfast. Then there was more help again at tea time. At first it worked okay. But as the service increased because of Joe's support needs we needed two people to assist him. In the end it began to feel that we were being invaded every morning and every tea time by an army of home care assistants. Due to rotas, rest days and everything else, the number of different people coming through our door had gone from two to over 40 in six months. This was totally unacceptable for Joe and very intrusive for us as a family. But all the time we felt that we had to be eternally grateful for the 'gift' of professional services – services that didn't really work. Not only did Joe's home care not work but he was also being sent to a school that was over an hour's drive away. Joe wasn't happy there and his connection with his community was getting weaker by the day. And it was all at a phenomenal cost to the Education Department. Joseph didn't need specialist out of borough support. He just needed people to listen to what he was trying to say in his own unique way.

So when we heard about in Control we jumped at the chance of being involved. We had felt over the years that we were passive recipients of a service system that intruded in our lives and confused Joe. What he really needed was a person-centred approach to his support. In other words it was designed for Joe, by Joe – and the people who knew him best. He also needed to be recognised as an equal citizen, someone with rights who was entitled to his own life, someone who was prepared to take on some responsibilities too.

We started to help ourselves by organising a circle of friends for Joe. Basically the circle consisted of people who loved and cared about Joe and other people who were paid to be in his life. The social worker also came and used its meetings as a starting point for his assessment. At the circle meeting we discussed Joe's dreams and visions for the future, what his skills and gifts were, a step-by-step approach to how he was going to get there and who we needed to involve.

The social worker used the assessment to give Joe an allocation of money from Social Services and we considered a number of the other funding streams that might be available to Joe. In short we applied for funding from the Independent Living Fund and we maximised Joe's benefits. It is essential that the individual maximises their benefits, because, in order to get a life, you need money to spend – a disposable income. This first phase of money enabled Joe to employ four Personal Assistants who work on a rotational basis and enable Joe to access ordinary social and leisure opportunities. (We need four because he needs two people at any one time to support him).

He now attends a gym, goes on the treadmill and swims in the pool. So he uses an ordinary facility, meets new people, has some important exercise which helps him to sleep. We get an excellent package from the local gym, Total Fitness – they allow any of his PAs to go with him. He visits a lot of the National Trust Parks as he is interested in history and likes to walk round the gardens. He loves fairs and fast rides. So Alton Towers is a great favourite, as well as Blackpool. He also likes to ride his bike, which is a specialised tandem. His PAs need the right range of skills to support him in his varied life style and we also need the flexibility from the PAs so that if we go away for a weekend the PAs can carry on working together as a team and can stop over at our house to support Joe round the clock. The management for the staff works relatively easily. I do a monthly rota, the PAs fill in time sheets and they get paid on a monthly basis. I have a local company of accountants doing the PAYE and it all works quite smoothly. We have insurance for the PAs and have to deal with any staff management issues, which so far has worked fine for us all. Over the past few weeks we have started to break down the funding within the education system and have enabled Joe to attend the local college. We have considered how he can be in control of all of his week.

So, what do things look like now? He goes to college 4 days a week funded by the Learning and Skills Council. He has his own PAs working with him within the college, and they are now paid by the college for this element of their work. No more taxis and escorts to get to college. Instead, he catches the bus like other young people. His PAs come to the house and support him from here to college. The walk to and from the bus stops sets him up for a calmer day in college. This is funded by the LEA. After college he goes on to the gym which is funded from his original social and leisure resource allocation from ILF and SSD.

On his fifth day – when he's not in college – he does voluntary work. This has only just started and we are trying out a few different things. The support for this is currently being paid for by the LEA until Social Services do a reassessment.

His weekends and evenings are the same as they were and support is paid for by ILF and SSD. It sounds complicated but in the whole scheme of things it isn't. In comparison to the difficulties around the support in our lives before Joe was in control, it is so much better for the whole family. Joe has consistency with the people supporting him through his whole week – people he has chosen. The support is flexible and works around what Joe needs to do. So if he has a dental appointment he just fits it into his life – like the rest of us - instead of his Dad or I having to take a half day off work to travel over an hour each way to pick him up! There are also many times when Joe doesn't have paid support and we are really happy as a family to support him at this time. This is so much easier than before because he has been active and has had a fulfilling day.

So, how will it move on in the future? We are setting up a trust as Joe turns 18 and the trust will manage the staff team and will have the legal responsibility for managing the finances. The trust will be people who love and care about Joe, and it will be developed so it is sustainable, as we, his parents, get older.

After all I never wanted to be his care manager, his accountant or his director of services. All I ever wanted to be is Joe's mum, doing things that mums do for their growing children – like doing the washing!

Reproduced with permission from the in Control website (http://www.in-control.org.uk/stories/index.php?storyid=5, accessed 20 June 2008) (see also Tomlinson, 2006). For further personal stories, visit the in Control website or watch the *Living your life, your way* DVD (Department of Health/Care Services Improvement Partnership/in Control, 2008).

The wider impact

Although it is beyond the scope of this book, part of the excitement with which (some) policy makers have greeted personal budgets may lie in the broader impact they could have on other public services. As outlined above, personal budgets represent not just a change to the social care system but, potentially, a shift in the relationship between the state and the individual. In a period of demographic pressures, advances in medicine and technology, changes in family structures and rising public expectations, such a shift seems to offer a potential way forward for welfare services more generally. Thus, while the Department of Health pilots summarised above have struggled to integrate particular funding streams, there has been interest in several quarters in the idea of experimenting with personal budgets in other areas of the welfare state. As the think tank Demos has argued, possible areas where such an approach might work could include job search and employment, drug user and offender rehabilitation, young people not in education, employment or training, and supporting families at risk (Leadbeater et al, 2008). Similarly, Duffy (2008) has suggested that the principles of self-directed support could be applied in areas such as community development, services for people dependent on drugs or alcohol, education, employment and housing. Viewed from this angle, personal budgets – although originating in social care – could form a significant part of future welfare reform.

Although this book has so far tended to focus on the needs of adults, personal budgets have significant implications for disabled children, for young people with support needs and for children's services more generally. This is a complex area, but a chapter by Nic Crosby in the 2008 summary of in Control's second phase provides a helpful overview (see Box 5.13). Essentially, Crosby's chapter argues that self-directed support should start as soon as people need additional support, whether this is at birth, on going to school, on moving into secondary education or on entering adulthood. From early initiatives in this field, it appears as though there are significant potential benefits to families taking greater control over the support that is provided to young children with support needs and that such ways of working could also help to ease transition into adult life. At the time of writing, a series of government pilots for personal budgets for children and young people is about to be launched (see Carlin et al, 2006 for an initial scoping study), and this seems to be a key area of state support where personal budgets could make a substantial difference.

However, of all the areas where personal budgets could be extended, one of the most prominent and controversial seems to be health care. Despite the current emphasis on joint working in health and social care, both direct payments and personal budgets are being actively promoted in social care at the same time (until recently) as they were being actively ruled out in health care (DH, 2006, p 85). While an extension of direct payments to some forms of health care has periodically been suggested (see for example, Glendinning et al, 2000a–c; Glasby and Hasler, 2004; Glasby and Duffy, 2007), it was not until 2007–08 that the momentum for change seemed to gather pace (see Harding, 2005; Alakeson, 2007; Conservative Party, 2007; Le Grand, 2007; Milburn, 2007; Brown, 2008; Darzi, 2008; Glendinning et al, 2008; Leadbeater et al, 2008) – see Box 5.14.

Box 5.13: Children and families in control

As summarised by Crosby (2008, p 79), key initiatives include:

- *Dynamite*: a two-year programme led by Paradigm to develop a model of self-directed support for young people.
- *Person-centred transition review*: a series of Valuing People Support Team pilots.
- *Improving Choice*: a programme by the Eastern Region Learning and Skills Council to use 'transition brokers' to develop post-16 provision for young people with learning difficulties who would otherwise have to attend specialist residential colleges.
- *Budget-holding lead professionals*: government pilot to explore how lead professionals can hold a small budget on behalf of individual children and families (see also Office for Public Management, 2006).
- *Learning and Living Now*: Mencap project to support young people with learning difficulties. This includes a resource allocation system, learning and living support plans and personalised support.
- *Building Blocks*: a project in Devon and Cornwall to explain concepts of choice, decision-making and taking control.
- *Person-centred Curriculum*: to support children and young people to develop the skills and approaches for self-directed futures.
- *Taking Control*: in Control's programme for children and young people, beginning with eight children's services in Autumn 2007.

Box 5.14: Extending direct payments/personal budgets to health care

In the West Midlands, the strategic health authority has pledged to pilot individual patient budgets as part of its regional 'Investing for Health' strategy (see http://www.ifh.westmidlands.nhs.uk).

At the same time (2008), in Control and the Integrated Care Network launched their 'Staying in Control' project to support health and social care communities seeking to explore the implications of personal budgets in health care.

Also in 2008, the government's Care Services Improvement Partnership commissioned one of the current authors to run a national workshop with individual budget pilot sites to explore the implications of individual budgets for the health and social care interface (Glasby, 2008b). While the workshop made a series of recommendations with regard to future policy and practice, a key finding was that many sites were effectively making individual budgets for forms of health care already and were starting to develop a series of innovative approaches and service models to help them do so.

Building on all this, the 2008 Darzi review of the NHS pledged to pilot the concept of personal health budgets in early 2009 and to legislate to enable direct payments for health care (where appropriate).

As a result, personal budgets are potentially important, not just in their own right, but as an example of the way in which they enable policy makers to develop a new approach to meeting the needs of citizens. Elsewhere, personal budgets have been characterised as a form of Conditional Resource Enhancement (CRE), with Waters and Duffy (2007) suggesting that it is possible for governments to seek to meet the needs of their citizens via a combination of five different approaches (see Figure 5.3):

- *Create legal and social structures*: the legal system can impose obligations on people to act fairly and can punish those who might act in ways that damage well-being (e.g. disability discrimination legislation aims to protect disabled people from unfair treatment).
- *Adjust income*: the tax and benefit system enables government to alter the resources people can control directly and the incentives under which they operate (e.g. social security payments to disabled people or tax credits to ease transition back to work for people who are unemployed).
- *Direct service*: the government provides, directly or indirectly, a range of health, educational or other services that people either must or can use, subject to whatever criteria govern eligibility to that service.
- *Adapt physical environment*: the government can change the structure of the environment within which the person operates (e.g. increasingly buildings are designed so as to enable people who use wheelchairs full physical access).
- *Conditional Resource Enhancement*: the government can also target resources towards those individuals who are eligible, but with specific conditions attached (e.g. personal budgets).

Viewed from this angle, the advent of personal budgets might be seen as arising as the government finds that funding, currently committed to direct services, is better managed by people themselves. Shifting resources into the form of a CRE could therefore be a way of improving the management of those resources, while still achieving the same social objectives. While these ideas are complex and are still developing, in Control have suggested that this new concept of a CRE might involve:

- *Autonomy*: the CRE must be under the control of the individual or of someone who can properly represent their interests.
- *Flexibility*: the CRE must be able to be put to different uses by the person – it cannot be so inflexible that it cannot be shaped by the person.
- *Targeting*: the person receiving the CRE must be eligible in some way for receiving the CRE.
- *Support*: the person receiving the CRE may get some form of support, information or advice.

• *Conditionality*: there must be some conditions, the breach of which would enable the CRE to be constrained, withdrawn or managed in some different way.

Figure 5.3: Five different strategies for improving well-being

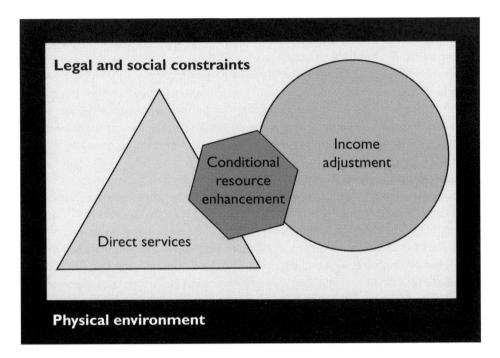

While this is discussed in more detail elsewhere (Waters and Duffy, 2007), a personal budget seems to be a particularly pure and strong form of CRE. Whereas other potential CREs (for example, wheelchair vouchers or Local Housing Allowance) tend to place heavy restrictions on *how* the CRE can be used, personal budgets focus on the purpose of the CRE and upon the *outcomes* that it is meant to achieve. This seems a particularly helpful approach if we are to assume that the individual citizen is best placed to decide how their needs should be met and that historical services are not necessarily the best guide as to what will be appropriate in the future. In addition, it is interesting to note that some previous CREs (for example, the notorious Individual Learning Account scheme) have been dogged by allegations of misuse, fraud and theft. In contrast, both direct payments and personal budgets (to date) seem to have been remarkably free of such abuse. While it is too early to know, one possible lesson here is that approaches that place resources under the control of those with the biggest vested interest in spending them effectively may be the safest way of managing resources.

Aside from being of intellectual interest, this discussion of the concept of a CRE is helpful insofar as it enables us to explore possible approaches to future welfare reform. It is probably too early to be clear, but at least three possibilities seem to exist (see Local Government Association, 2008 for an alternative view):

- Personal budgets may only be a transitional measure, allowing resources to shift from the state to the individual without completely disrupting social expectations about the state's duty to guarantee welfare for people who are perceived to be entitled to support by the general public. On this account, the CRE is a transitional state, and personal budgets may well become a form of income adjustment over time.
- It may be that the dynamic interaction or co-production now possible between professionals and the users of personal budgets is the optimal state for improving well-being and personal outcomes for the people who currently use social care. On this account, the CRE is the end-state and the extension of personal budgets will signify a significant new phase in the development of the welfare state.
- Against this, it is also possible that the development of personal budgets may lead to attempts to shift more private income or benefits into the framework of the CRE (although this is not advocated by the current authors). This is a very different strategic direction, reducing the level of resources over which the individual has autonomous control. For example, a possible option for the reform of English long-term care includes the notion of a 'partnership model' (Wanless, 2006) in which the state guarantees to pay a certain proportion of the cost of such support and the individual makes up the difference (either via personal savings/income or via the social security system for those on low incomes). In future, it would be perfectly possible for such a model to be implemented via a CRE. Similarly, there might be scope to shift some social security payments (such as current disability benefits) into the CRE framework. Thus, while personal budgets have been developed in the context of trying to shift control away from direct services and towards the individual, this is not the only possible direction – it is also possible to use CREs to make resources that were clearly under the control of the individual more conditional.

The link to direct payments

Perhaps most important of all is a key question that has been poorly addressed in much of the discussion to date: how do direct payments differ from personal budgets? As we have tried to set out in this chapter, personal budgets are only part of a broader movement towards self-directed support that is seeking to change every aspect of the social care system. Although direct payments fit with this approach, they are only one of the delivery mechanisms by which the personal budgets element of self-directed support might be achieved. Thus, they are both a separate issue and inextricably linked at the same time, but clearly have scope to develop in tandem. That this is the case is helpfully illustrated by an important joint statement by in Control and the National Centre for Independent Living, which sets out a jointly held view that the goal for disabled people is independent living, but that self-directed support is a key route to achieving this (see Appendix for the full text).

In addition to this, a powerful analogy has been provided by Julia Winter, a recipient of both direct payments and personal budgets and director of Liberation Partnership (a user-led social enterprise supporting people to access personal budgets). Speaking at Community Care Live 2008, she suggested that, with hindsight, receiving direct services felt very much like infancy (with no choice and control over your life). In contrast, direct payments felt like adolescence (because of the way they were sometimes operationalised, you could have the money to go to the shop, but you had to buy what was on the list and bring back the change with a receipt). In contrast, although it was initially very hard work, receiving a personal budget felt like adulthood (Winter, 2008).

SUMMARY

Having summarised the history, spread and key features of personal budgets, this chapter has set out the (impressive) results of early research and evaluation. Whilst recognising the very real limitations of these often small-scale and emerging findings, the positives that have been achieved seem so significant that the concept of a personal budget seems worthy of further exploration. Perhaps even more important than this is the practical evidence from people using personal budgets, their families and those who work with them – and this practice-based evidence is arguably more powerful and important than the inevitably limited research. Indeed, such has been the enthusiasm for personal budgets to date that the key issue seems to be not *whether* they are rolled out, but *how* and *how quickly*.

Above and beyond this, personal budgets also represent a shift in the relationship between the state and the individual. By framing personal budgets as a form of 'Conditional Resource Enhancement', there is scope to place this specific policy in the broader context of the different strategies available to government when seeking to improve the well-being of its citizens. Using this approach, it is possible to conceive of a future in which current CREs could become a form of income adjustment, could emerge as the optimal approach to meeting the needs of disabled people, or could even provide a mechanism for making (currently) individual resources more conditional. While the best way forward may well be a topic for another book, the key issue for present purposes is the way in which the concept of a Conditional Resource Enhancement may enable a deeper understanding of personal budgets and of possible strategies for future reform. Viewed from this angle, the widespread enthusiasm (but also the potential controversy) that has surrounded personal budgets becomes more readily understandable.

IMPLICATIONS FOR POLICY AND PRACTICE

- By being clear with people from the outset how much money is available to plan their support, there is scope for people to be much more innovative. They can also go about meeting these needs in a way that makes sense to them, given their individual circumstances and aspirations.
- Viewed from this angle, personal budgets are nothing more than sensible delegation, and the assumption is that the best person to make decisions about support is often the person with support needs themselves or someone as close to them as possible.
- Although there are practical and cultural issues to overcome, personal budgets seem to have had extremely positive results in terms of outcomes for people needing support and effective use of scarce public resources.
- Personal budgets give a greater sense of transparency and citizen entitlement. In this sense, they represent a shift in the relationship between the individual and the state that could have implications for a number of other public services.
- While the government is to be commended for recognising the benefits of personal budgets and committing to rolling them out, there is a very real risk that a lack of understanding of the underlying principles of self-directed support could significantly limit the impact of personal budgets.

Recommended reading and useful websites

For further details on the nature and impact of personal/individual budgets, see:

- the in Control evaluations (Poll et al, 2006; Hatton et al, 2008);
- Henwood and Hudson's (2007b) report on the implementation of self-directed support;
- the final report of IBSEN (Glendinning et al, 2008) – in addition to the full study, a series of early articles shed light on some of the emerging challenges (Manthorpe et al, 2008a–b; Rabiee et al, 2008), while two DH reports (2008f–g) explore next steps and emerging good practice in older people's services.

Useful introductions are also available in Simon Duffy's articles in *Journal of Integrated Care* (e.g. Duffy, 2004, 2005c, 2006, 2007), while Demos provide an overview that is free to download (Leadbeater et al, 2008 – see www.demos.co.uk).

Official policy aspirations are set out *Putting People First* (2007) and the more detailed local authority circular on *Transforming Social Care* (DH, 2008a). Earlier documents such as the social care Green Paper (DH, 2005a) and *Improving the Life Chances of Disabled People* (Prime Minister's Strategy Unit, 2005) are also useful. For an overview, SCIE (2008) publishes a 'rough guide' to personalisation.

For personal accounts, good practice examples and access to relevant documents, processes and templates, see the in Control website (www.in-control.org.uk). Other helpful sites include the Care Services Improvement Partnership (www. individualbudgets.csip.org.uk) and the National Centre for Independent Living (www.ncil.org.uk).

In particular, the *Living your life, your way* DVD (Department of Health/Care Services Improvement Partnership/in Control, 2008) is an excellent resource with a series of personal accounts of the practicalities, the power and the potential impact of personal budgets.

An official 'personalisation toolkit' is also available via www.personalisation. org.uk, with a series of useful tools, guides, examples and frameworks to help councils implement self-directed support.

While much of this book tends to focus on the implications for disabled people and for frontline staff, there are clearly significant implications for current commissioners and service providers (see, for example, Tyson, nd; OPM, 2007; Baxter et al, 2008; Bennett, 2008; CSIP, 2008; Glendinning et al, 2008).

For further discussion of the concept of CREs, see Waters and Duffy (2007).

Discussion of the potential extension to health care can be found in reports by Glasby and Duffy (2007) and Alakeson (2008). For discussion of the implications for other areas of state welfare, see Leadbeater et al (2008) and Le Grand (2007).

Reflective exercises

1. In a group, take turns to describe what you understand by the term 'personal budgets' and how this differs from direct payments. To what extent do your definitions agree with each other, and are you clear about the differences and similarities between direct payments and personal budgets?
2. We often demand higher standards of proof for new ways of working than we do for previous approaches, and place new ideas under greater scrutiny than the status quo. Imagine that the social care system has always been based around a system of personal budgets. If a new policy maker proposed abolishing personal budgets and returning to the social care system as it currently exists, what arguments would you put forward to justify this approach?
3. Think of someone with social care needs whom you have worked with or read about. Could personal budgets have helped to achieve different outcomes for the person? What barriers might have prevented this?
4. Find and read the personal budgets policy of your department or of the local authority where you live. To what extent does the model stay true to the principles and values set out in this chapter?
5. If you needed to access social care services, what outcomes might you want to achieve for yourself and your family and what would your priorities be? From your knowledge of current approaches, how easy would it be to meet these outcomes via traditional services? How might you use a personal budget to meet these needs in different ways?

6. What impact could direct payments and personal budgets have in health care, and what would some of the barriers be?
7. Reflecting on the concept of a CRE set out above, how helpful do you find this as a way of understanding the potential options open to policy makers for public service reform? What other CREs can you think of, and how do they differ from personal budgets in terms of principles of autonomy, flexibility, targeting, support and conditionality?

SIX

The advantages of direct payments and personal budgets

This chapter explores the impact of direct payments and personal budgets in terms of:

- choice and control;
- morale and well-being;
- positive changes in people's lives;
- use of resources.

Although many people talk enthusiastically about the advantages of direct payments and personal budgets, it is important to return to the research evidence in order to examine and confirm current understandings and to overcome continued resistance, constantly making and remaking the case for new ways of working. In particular, many of the early debates around the merits of direct payments either predated the 1996 Community Care (Direct Payments) Act, or were published in the early days of the new approach. As a result, there is a need to revisit this initial material and supplement it with more recent research – especially for students or for workers who have qualified more recently. Since personal budgets are new for everyone, summarising the key benefits is particularly important. However, the positive aspects of direct payments and individual budgets have also been highlighted in earlier chapters, so the following account is very much a summary of material presented throughout the whole book.

Choice and control

In the early 1990s, research into the ILF revealed that making cash payments directly to service users gave a sense of control and choice that could not be achieved via statutory services (see Box 6.1; Kestenbaum, 1993b; Lakey, 1994). While respondents found directly provided services to be inflexible, costly and severely limited in terms of the availability and level of service on offer, they valued the freedom that ILF payments provided. Receiving money with which to employ their own care assistants enabled them to choose staff that they felt had the right strengths and skills. The disabled person could also employ someone of a particular sex and could select carers who spoke the same language as they did. Above all, ILF recipients valued being able to hire staff with whom they felt able to develop a good relationship, choosing people with the right personality to make the care package work. As a result, the disabled people were able to establish and maintain longer-lasting relationships with their staff and enjoyed greater continuity of personnel. At the same time, they were also able to create flexible support arrangements to meet often-fluctuating needs. Throughout a number of research studies, respondents repeatedly emphasised the control that ILF payments gave them and the self-respect that they felt as a result of their status as an employer. Rather than being dependent on others to determine and meet their care needs, the disabled people themselves could determine what Kestenbaum (1993b, p 38) describes as 'the what, how, who and when of care arrangements'.

Box 6.1: Choice and control

For many applicants, the ILF was not just about making up for unavailable statutory services. It was the preferred option. From a disabled person's point of view, the provision of cash makes the important difference between having one's personal life controlled by others and exercising choices and control for oneself. Money has enabled ILF clients not only to avoid going into residential care, but also to determine for themselves the help they require, and how and when they want it to be provided. In many cases, where that freedom and corresponding self-respect are not central components, care in the community may be no better than institutional care.
(Kestenbaum, 1993a, p 35)

In 1993, respondents in Morris's study of disabled people's experiences of community care emphasised the many advantages that employing PAs could bring:

> "I'm a husband, a father and a breadwinner. And ten years ago I was in an institution where I couldn't even decide when I would go to the toilet."

> "It means that I can get up in the morning when I want to, and lead the kind of life that I want to ... To not be reliant on my family and friends ... to keep all that separate [so that] to them I'm me rather than someone who needs help."

> "It means exercising choice and control, having the right to choose who gets me up and who puts me to bed."

> "I'm living on my own, living in the way I like. I can come and go as I like."

> "I employ people ..., which allows me to have the life style that I choose."
> (quoted in Morris, 1993a, pp 125–6)

In 1994, similar findings emerged from Zarb and Nadash's study for BCODP. For many respondents, indirect/direct payments were crucial in enabling recipients to control the times when support was provided, who was employed, what sort of assistance was provided and how it was provided, thereby enhancing quality of life and personal dignity. Overall, the most important aspect of a payments scheme was found to be having choice and control over one's own support arrangements. This in turn led to more reliable and flexible services that enabled needs to be more fully met:

> "I am in control. I can decide when I want help. The way help is delivered – I feel it is *my* life, not someone else's. You are not fitted in to other people's time table. Freedom – you can choose *who* you have. If you don't like them you can have someone else. You can choose the manner in which a task is performed, unlike when home care staff are used. It releases me to have family as family and friends as friends." (quoted in Zarb and Nadash, 1994, p 90)

Following the 1996 Community Care (Direct Payments) Act, further research has emphasised the centrality of choice and control. For Peter Brawley, then chair of Glasgow's Centre for Independent Living, direct payments were a major step forward for disabled people:

> "For people such as myself, for whom the traditional option would have been institutionalised care, being able to choose a personal assistant has made a great difference. I am living with my wife in the community, going out to work every day. It gives us the chance to maximise our potential and take our proper place in a changed world." (quoted in Hunter, 1999, p 10)

Similar sentiments are echoed by other commentators, who point out that future generations will take direct payments for granted and will not be able to believe that there was ever a time when such payments were not available:

> The direct payment issue is a prime example of the sort of thing that will astound future generations. It will amaze people to think that there was a time when disabled people were thought unable or untrustworthy to receive, without hesitation, the finance they need for the purchase and organisation of their own assistance. (Mason, quoted in Morris, 1993a, p 164)

In 1999, a study carried out by the Social Services Inspectorate found that direct payments recipients were more satisfied with their care arrangements than people receiving direct services, citing feelings of control as a key factor (Fruin, 2000, pp 15-16). For one service user in particular, a direct payments scheme had "just turned everything around – it has given me self-respect" (quoted in Fruin, 2000, p 16 and DH/SSI, 1999c, p 19). In Norfolk, all respondents in an evaluation of a local direct payments project saw the scheme as a means of gaining more choice and control in their daily lives (Dawson, 2000, p 17). This was also the case in Scotland, where direct payments recipients valued the opportunity to exercise choice and control, contrasting this with previous disempowering experiences of direct services:

> "Things couldn't be better now. It's given me much more freedom and control and I play a more active role in family life. Choice, freedom and control sums it up for me. It has been amazing, my life has completely changed." (quoted in Witcher et al, 2000, para 6.10)

In Staffordshire, service users also saw direct payments as a means of enhancing their choice, power and control (Leece, 2000), while in Birmingham, direct payments gave recipients greater control over their care arrangements, increasing their independence, quality of life and power over their own situation (Riley, 1999). These were also important issues in a study funded by the Department of Health into direct payments and the health and social care divide (Glendinning et al, 2000a-c). By being able to exercise control over the support they received, direct payment recipients were able to tailor care to their individual needs and personal preferences, ensure continuity of care, develop flexible packages of care that encompassed a greater range of tasks and enhance their own independence.

The importance of choice and control has also emerged as a key issue from publications produced by organisations of disabled people such as NCIL. In 1999, PSI/NCIL guidance for local authorities began by stressing that direct payments are a means to an end and a way of achieving independent living:

> Of all the advice given by disabled people who use payment schemes, people who run support schemes for payment users and those who commission payments schemes, one starting point emerges clearly and firmly: it's about independent living. Every aspect of a direct payment system needs to be geared to enabling disabled people to achieve maximum choice and control in their everyday lives. (Hasler et al, 1999, p 5)

A similar message also emerges from NCIL's *Rough guide to managing personal assistants* (Vasey, 2000), which highlights many of the difficulties of employing PAs, but ultimately reiterates the centrality of the increased choice and control:

> Disabled people are forever being cast as vulnerable, hence the services that support us tend to be overprotective. Direct Payments are about the right to take risks, to learn, like everyone else does,

from our mistakes and to develop into wiser, stronger people. That is independent living.

> "Having PAs enabled me to find out who I am and now enables me to be who I am." (Vasey, 2000, pp 129-30)

More recently, Stainton and Boyce's (2004) study of users' experiences of direct payments in two Welsh local authorities emphasises once again the centrality of choice and control. Having previously had negative experiences of directly provided services, people valued being able to choose their own staff, the greater familiarity and empathy in the relationship between disabled person and PA, and being able to control the timing and pattern of support. As one person remarked: "it really is the best thing since sliced bread. I am totally in control" (Stainton and Boyce, 2004, p 449). CSCI (2004) has also identified flexibility, choice and control as central features of direct payments (see Box 6.2), as has research commissioned by Skills for Care and the General Social Care Council (IFF Research, 2008; see Table 6.1). As one participant in a service user-controlled review of direct payments in Wiltshire suggested:

> "There are times when I just put my head in my hands and wonder why on earth I am putting myself through all the hassle of employing people when I could theoretically receive an equivalent service ... Yet I then remember starting out on a service and know that I could never go back to that, although at the time I thought the service was good. The quality and flexibility I now have is because I have an individually designed package to suit not just myself but also my family and lifestyle and it is worth every second of any stress." (quoted in Carmichael and Brown, 2002, p 800)

Box 6.2: People's experiences of direct payments

"Direct payments give me independence and control over my life."

"Direct payments give me control. I now have a say in what I eat and drink, when I have a bath, what I do and when I do it. I can choose carers that can help me to live my life. I can have continuity instead of a different carer every day"

"I live alone and I wouldn't be able to do this without the direct payments scheme."

(CSCI, 2004, p 9)

With the advent of personal budgets, both research and practice have continued to stress the importance of choice and control. Thus, Poll et al's (2006) evaluation of the first six in Control case study sites found that the number of people satisfied with the amount of control they had over their lives increased from 42% to 97% as a result of receiving a personal budget (p 41). This was confirmed in 2008, when monitoring suggested that 72% of participants reported improvements in choice and control, with 27% reporting no change and only 1% saying that things had got worse since starting self-directed support (Hatton et al, 2008, p 20). At a local level, service user accounts suggest that personal budgets allow the individual to 'set the agenda', giving them increased choice and control over how their needs are met (see, for example, Daly and Roebuck, 2008).

Table 6.1: Attitudes towards direct payments

Impact of direct payments	% of people (n = 526) agreeing strongly
Support better suits my individual needs	81
I have more choice over who supports me	78
I can now have the same person supporting me all the time	77
I can get help at times when a council care worker would not be willing to work	64
I can get help with tasks and activities not provided by the local authority	63
I now rely less on family and friends	55

Source: IFF Research, 2008, p 39.

Despite this, a similar but slightly more nuanced finding has emerged from Henwood and Hudson's (2007b) review of the implementation of self-directed support. While there was once again a strong sense that some of the main benefits of personal budgets are their impact on choice and control, there were subtly different views about the extent of such choice and control. In particular, Henwood and Hudson identify three different perspectives, each of which may have implications for the impact of self-directed support, with participants adopting either weak, medium or strong formulations (see Box 6.3). As set out in Chapter Five, this may reflect the fact that the concept of self-directed support has not always been articulated clearly and coherently, and so may be interpreted differently at local level.

Box 6.3: Different degrees of choice and control

'Weak' interpretations occurred where participants saw self-directed support as a way of 'putting people at the centre' of things and tweaking existing direct payment approaches.

'Medium' interpretations involved recognition that control over the money was a key way of ensuring that the service user took centre stage.

In 'strong' formulations, participants emphasised the need to transfer power from professionals and from the social care system to individuals, with the money more of an enabling mechanism to allow this broader shift to take place.

(Henwood and Hudson, 2007b, pp 9–10)

Morale and well-being

For direct payment and personal budget recipients, feeling in control of their own lives seems to have important implications for health and well-being. There is a large literature in the field of psychology to suggest that control is essential to well-being and an important element in shaping people's lives and their susceptibility to stress. Often, psychologists distinguish between people who have an internal or an external 'locus of control'. Whereas 'internals' feel in control of what happens to them and that they have the power to influence their lives, 'externals' tend to believe that they have little control over what happens to them since this is the result of outside factors beyond their command (Thompson et al, 1994, pp 54-5). This can be crucial, since research suggests that 'internals' are more successful than 'externals' at work in terms of pay, promotion and job satisfaction, and that they are better able to cope with stress (Andrisani and Nestel, 1976). This has been supported by Kobasa (1979), who suggests that people with a greater sense of control over what happens to them will remain healthier than those who feel powerless in the face of external forces. Another key contribution has been made by Seligman (1975), who believes that 'externals' are more likely to experience 'learned helplessness' (where people who constantly find that they have little power to influence their own destiny lose motivation and give up trying).

With regard to social care, evidence is beginning to emerge that the increased sense of control which receiving direct payments and personal budgets entails can enhance well-being and morale. Certainly, this was one of the early findings to emerge from research into the ILF, which suggested that receiving cash payments enabled some disabled people to remain in the community rather than enter hospital or residential care (Kestenbaum, 1993b). For one service user, Mr R, ILF payments gave him the confidence to do other things, safe in the knowledge that the physical side of his care was under control and that his support arrangements were keeping pressure sores at bay (Kestenbaum, 1993b, p 39). As the government was considering the potential of direct payments in the mid-1990s, John Evans, then chair of BCODP's Independent Living Committee, was clear that direct payments would have a direct effect on people's quality of life:

> Direct payments allow disabled people to be less dependent, to have real choices about how we live our lives … They have a real impact on quality of life – on health, wellbeing, psychological development, and relationships with others. (quoted in George, 1994, p 14)

After the introduction of direct payments in 1996/97, research conducted by the PSI/NCIL suggested that replacing directly provided services with cash payments may not only be more cost efficient, but might also bring a range of additional social and economic benefits:

> Savings may come from a reduction in demand for acute and/or long-term health care on the basis that full independence may well be associated with higher levels of quality of life and the associated benefits in terms of general well-being. (Zarb, 1998, pp 8-9)

Improved mental and physical health was also a key outcome for disabled people during research into direct payments and the health and social care divide (Glendinning et al, 2000a, 2000c). For many direct payment recipients, enhanced choice and control increased their self-confidence, morale and emotional and psychological health in a range of areas. For some respondents, the depth of their relationship with their PA was a crucial source of support and helped to prevent feelings of isolation. For others, the quality of care that they were able to arrange for themselves had a knock-on effect on their attitude to their impairments and symptoms. This was particularly the case for people with mental health problems, who felt that direct payments gave them the confidence and support they needed to recover from their illness.

More recently, Stainton and Boyce (2004) found that direct payments can bring significant psychological benefits, increasing people's confidence, making them feel more optimistic about their lives and motivating them to explore new avenues (p 451):

> "It's built up my self-esteem, given me a lot more confidence, made me feel I'm part of the real world, not just a drag on it physically and financially … I feel now my horizons are limitless."

> "I have got my life back … I have got choice. I can do things … No such word as can't or no or you shouldn't."

With the advent of personal budgets, the impact on health and well-being appears to be even more pronounced. In one sense, this is to be expected from the international evidence, with a summary of US research (Alakeson, 2007) suggesting that outcomes could well improve under self-directed support, with self-direction believed to promote prevention and early intervention to a greater extent than traditional services (which focus more on intervening after a crisis). Certainly, in the UK, 47% of the 196 people involved in Hatton et al's 2008 evaluation reported improvements in their health and well-being (with only 5% reporting that things had got worse, p 17). Given that this is an area where self-directed support might not be expected to have an immediate impact, these initial findings seem very positive. In particular, those most likely to report improvements tended to have been using self-directed support for over a year rather than for a shorter period, had assistance to plan their support from friends or family and had support to plan from a wider range of sources. While it is important not to read too much into early data, this might suggest that self-directed support has the potential to impact significantly on health and well-being, but that it will be important for the social care system to focus on the needs of those with the least access to support in order to ensure maximum benefits for all (see Chapter Seven for further discussion).

Outcomes and positive change

While choice and control are important ends in themselves, the practical upshot seems to be the increased ability for people to make changes in their lives and to achieve outcomes that are meaningful to them. In one sense, this is a theme that runs throughout this book, and almost all of the case studies and research findings cited in other chapters illustrate the potential of direct payments and personal budgets to transform people's lives. In many ways, both direct payments and personal budgets seem to operate very much like pebbles thrown into a pond, with ripples that spread out much further than their initial impact (both in terms of the life of the individual and throughout the social care system more generally). Certainly, this was one of the findings from Stainton and Boyce's (2004) review of direct payments in two Welsh local authorities, with the authors noting how direct payments had 'permeated aspects of the lives of many users well beyond the direct influence of their care package' (p 449). Interestingly, the greater choice and control experienced by direct payment recipients in this study was also felt to help them live lifestyles less constrained by externally imposed routines, and a number of participants in the study were engaged in voluntary work, were attending vocational courses or were using personal assistance when at work. Given the national emphasis that is now being placed on lifelong learning, on voluntary work and on supporting disabled people to engage in paid employment, the potential impact of direct payments in this area seems worthy of further exploration.

In addition, the findings of early in Control evaluations illustrate the way in which self-directed support can enable people to make desired changes to their lives and achieve a range of outcomes that matter to them. Thus, as Chapter Five demonstrated, many early personal budget holders were able to design support that enabled them to reduce their use of institutional forms of service provision, make more use of community supports and play a greater role in their communities – all within a relatively short period of time and for either the same or less money than their original support package (see Box 6.4 for further examples). However, behind these findings there seems to be a more fundamental point about the nature of direct payments and personal budgets. While previous approaches have often been very service-led (essentially slotting people into pre-existing and pre-purchased services), direct payments and personal budgets have the potential to focus on assessed needs, allowing individuals and their networks to be more creative in terms of how they go about meeting these needs (and to do so in a way that achieves outcomes that make sense to the individual in the context of their own lives, communities and aspirations). Viewed from this angle, direct payments and personal budgets are less about money changing hands than they are about freeing people up to make much better and more meaningful decisions

Box 6.4: Achieving desired outcomes

Julia, a disabled parent, has used her individual budget to enable her to run a disabled people's organisation, to install air conditioning (which has prevented two hospital admissions) and to organise regular support to pick her son up from school.

Cyril and Beryl, both in their 80s, have used an individual budget to remain living in their own home. Instead of going into a care home for 'respite', they have been able to go to a hotel in Bournemouth and arrange support there (which was also cheaper than respite care).

Kate has a learning difficulty, and has used an individual budget to enable her to live independently and to access an IT course.

Frank is 91 and has used an individual budget to remain living in his own home. Although his family arranged support from a live-in care agency, the organisation concerned did not have a contract with the local social services and so could not have provided this support through the local authority. The individual budget enabled this existing arrangement to continue and prosper.

Cindy is registered blind and uses an individual budget to enable her to look after her young children (including going to mother and toddlers, doing the school run, shopping, housework and attending appointments etc).

Florence employs her granddaughter (a trained care worker). While her previous carers encouraged her to stop walking (for fear of a fall), her granddaughter has enabled her to walk again. In the DVD, the family are going to Longleat for the day.

Evangelos is the former manager of a travel agency and plans to use his individual budget to enable him to meet his personal care needs, but in a way that enables him to get out of his flat and socialise.

Elsie is 83 and uses an individual budget to get a regular bath at a local Age Concern centre (since her bathroom is inaccessible).

George has mental health problems and has used his individual budget to stay well and out of hospital. Instead of 'respite care', he went on holiday with a friend to Tunisia. He has also bought some painting materials in order to develop his interest in art (which is very different to the art he might do at a traditional mental health day centre).

Bob uses his individual budget to pay for practical support that helps him meet his personal care needs, but which also helps him work for a local disabled people's organisation. It has always been his ambition to go up in a hot-air balloon – while he has not yet managed this, the DVD shows him flying an aeroplane for the first time.

Angela is 92 and pays for her own live-in support. Her individual budget is used to pay for additional assistance in the evenings. Her overall support enables her to continue her life-long commitment to teaching and lecturing.

All personal stories taken from the *Living your life, your way* DVD (DH/Care Services Improvement Partnership/in Control, 2008).

about meeting needs. As one individual budget holder in Coventry suggested to local evaluators (Daly and Roebuck, 2008, p 21):

> "The individual budget pilot has allowed [my] needs and aspirations to be understood in a way that a traditional assessment would not allow. In the past [my] ability to perform tasks would be the main focus of an assessment and the consequences of doing the task would not be considered."

In many ways, a similar message was to emerge from the national IBSEN evaluation (Glendinning et al, 2008, p 67), with 47% of people who accepted the offer of an individual budget suggesting that this had changed their view of what could be achieved in their lives 'a lot' (19% said 'a little').

Use of resources

Throughout the implementation of direct payments and personal budgets, issues of cost and of cost-efficiency have been paramount. While the possibility of direct payments legislation was being debated in Parliament, initial government opposition was based at least in part on fears about the cost implications of making payments to individuals instead of providing services (see Chapter Three). When direct payments were formally introduced, therefore, the accompanying guidance emphasised that:

> A local authority should not make direct payments unless they are at least as cost-effective as the services which it would otherwise arrange … Local authorities may, if they choose, make direct payments at a greater cost than the cost of arranging the equivalent service, provided they are satisfied that this is still at least as cost-effective as arranging services, ie that the increased cost can be justified by the greater effectiveness arising from enabling the person to manage his or her own services and live independently. (DH, 1997, p 16)

As a result, much of the research to date has included a consideration of value for money. In many cases, this has even happened in studies where the researchers do not appear to value cost-efficiency themselves, but feel the need to include a discussion of this issue because of its centrality to the government's agenda. For this reason, there is a substantial body of literature that suggests that direct payments are more cost-effective than directly provided services and, in some studies, may sometimes even be cheaper.

Certainly, this has been the case with the ILF, which has been found to be around 30% cheaper than direct services (quoted in Mandelstam, 1999, p 233). Prior to the implementation of direct payments, Morris wrote that 'enabling people to employ their own personal assistants is a more cost-effective way of meeting personal assistance needs than using local authority home care services' (Morris, 1993a, p 168). This assertion appeared to be based primarily on research conducted as part of an evaluation of the Personal Assistance Advisor post at Greenwich Association of Disabled People (Oliver and Zarb, 1992). Even when the cost of the support provided by the advisor was taken into account, the scheme still appeared to be cheaper than providing services directly. As Conservative minister, Nicholas Scott, wrote in his foreword to the evaluation: 'This report on Personal Assistance Schemes in Greenwich shows that as well as being cost effective, such schemes offer disabled people a greater degree of independence when compared with traditional forms of provision' (Oliver and Zarb, 1992, Foreword).

Perhaps the most influential study was carried out by Zarb and Nadash (1994), specifically seeking to address issues of cost-efficiency in response to the then Conservative government's reluctance to legalise direct payments (see also Evans and Hasler, 1996). In order to compare the care packages of service users receiving some form of payment with those of people receiving direct services, the study sought to calculate unit costs for both types of support, taking account of all the expenditure involved. Although the methodology for compiling and comparing this data was complex, the researchers concluded that care packages financed by direct/indirect payments were, on average, some 30–40% cheaper than directly provided services (see Table 6.2). In addition to this, the researchers also noted that the concept of 'cost-efficiency' should incorporate not only issues of cost, but also a consideration of quality. That direct payments resulted in higher-quality services had already been demonstrated earlier in the study, where payment recipients suggested that:

- Payment schemes met a wider range of needs than traditional services and led to fewer unmet needs.
- People receiving payments had more reliable support and experienced fewer problems with their care.
- Payment recipients expressed higher levels of satisfaction than people using directly provided services.

Overall, the researchers were adamant that:

> Every pound spent through a payments scheme not only goes further than a pound spent on services, but also purchases assistance of a higher quality ... Direct/indirect payments clearly represent better value for money than direct service provision. (Zarb and Nadash, 1994, p 143; see also Table 6.2 and Box 6.5).

Table 6.2: Average hourly unit costs

Type of care package	Average hourly unit costs of care
Direct/indirect payments	£5.18
Directly provided services	£8.52

Source: Zarb and Nadash, 1994, pp 117-43.

Box 6.5: Costs and benefits of direct payments

What the research evidence tells us is that direct payments have consistently been shown to be a cost-effective mechanism for enabling disabled people to access high-quality support that maximises choice and control at equivalent or, often, lower cost than other forms of community-based support. The most detailed study carried out in the UK, for example, showed that support packages based on direct payments were on average 30–40% cheaper than equivalent directly provided services. This study also highlighted very clearly that people receiving direct or indirect payments had higher overall levels of satisfaction with their support arrangements than service users. This was particularly noticeable in relation to reliability and flexibility and the degree of confidence that people had in their support arrangements being able to meet their needs.

Other smaller-scale studies have shown similar results. The evidence from this research demonstrates that user-controlled money goes further, so investing in independent living is a more cost-effective use of public finance.

(Zarb, 1998, p 1)

After the implementation of direct payments, research has continued to emphasise the cost-efficiency of paying money directly to disabled people. In West Sussex, a new direct payments scheme was reported to have made direct savings of £30,000 per year for just 15 recipients, while at the same time enabling them to purchase additional hours of care that would have cost £23,000 if delivered by in-house services (quoted in Hasler, 1999, p 7). In Scotland, research suggests that direct payments can lead to a more efficient use of human and financial resources, while also improving the quality and appropriateness of care (Witcher et al, 2000, para 7.8). In particular, the researchers found that time invested in setting up direct payments schemes can be recouped in the medium/long term, that direct payments can be cheaper than using agency care and that direct payments improve quality by enabling needs to be met more effectively. In Norfolk, it proved difficult to calculate some of the hidden costs associated with a direct payments scheme, but an evaluation still concluded that direct payments were a more cost-effective option than traditional services. This was despite the fact that the support arrangements in this particular scheme were extremely complex and that responsibility was split between two different agencies, thus duplicating a number of costs:

> Direct payments are a cheaper alternative than direct service provision or contracted agency services and become cheaper still comparatively over time ... It is difficult to envisage an alternative means of delivering a community care service ... which would be cheaper than a direct payments scheme. (Dawson, 2000, p 46)

Elsewhere, anecdotal evidence suggests that direct payments may *not* necessarily be cheaper than directly provided services, but *do* represent value for money. This is the opinion expressed by Roy Taylor, then director of community services for the Royal Borough of Kingston-upon-Thames and chair of the former ADSS Disabilities Committee. In a Department of Health (1998a) promotional video, Taylor warns against the assumption that direct payments will necessarily result in huge savings for local authorities, but does emphasise that:

- Disabled people have shown themselves to be very innovative in designing care.
- Disabled people are in control of their payments and want to use this money as effectively as possible.
- Disabled people can often make better use of their payments than the local authority.

More recently, the growing literature continues to suggest that direct payments enable a more effective use of scarce resources – with opinion divided as to whether or not this actually reduces overall costs. In evidence submitted to the Wanless Review on the funding of older people's services, for example, Poole's (2006) analysis of direct payments and older people cites local evidence of potential savings, with one case study local authority reducing costs by around 17% of direct service costs (p 11). Elsewhere, the Audit Commission (2006) has suggested that introducing choice can lead to higher-quality services, increased control and greater user satisfaction, but that there is a trade-off to be made between start-up costs and any longer-term efficiency gains. While direct payments can cost more to set up and administer, the benefits can include greater flexibility, more empowered users and more appropriate care for minority groups. Having explored a series of different scenarios, the Audit Commission concludes that direct payments are likely to add to the cost of providing social care where direct payment rates are no lower than the cost of in-house provision. However, where direct payment rates *are* lower than in-house unit costs, there is scope for savings (which range in size depending on how many direct payment recipients there are and how much lower direct payments are than in-house unit costs). While this is probably not surprising, it means that there is a crucial trade-off to be made between the rate of direct payments, any savings that might occur and the extent to which the rate enables people to meet their needs (see Chapter Seven for further discussion).

Since the advent of personal budgets, the emerging evidence suggests that this way of working may also be more cost-effective than the previous system, largely because it helps to unleash the creativity of people who have previously been passive recipients of services. In early in Control pilots, five case study authorities saved a minimum of 12% (see Poll et al, 2006). Elsewhere, Demos research in ten local authorities suggests a possible saving of around 10% (compared to the cost of traditional services). When excluding those people moved onto a personal budget because their needs and funding had both increased, the cost savings were closer to 15% (Leadbeater et al, 2008, pp 37-8). In the second phase of in Control (2005–07), detailed costings for 104 people who had previously used traditional social care prior to receiving a personal budget revealed a reduction in average costs by 9% (from £29,319 to £26,615) (Hatton et al, 2008, p 47). When people without prior experience of traditional social care were included, the figures fell further (by 15%, from £29,319 to £24,857). While these figures are often disputed by external commentators, a particularly helpful contribution to the debate comes from in Control's paper on 'The economics of self-directed support' (Duffy and Waters, 2008). Although this stresses that current data is incomplete, Duffy and Waters argue that the previous system is inherently inefficient because of the extent to which it is shaped by the pre-purchased services it has inherited from the past. This, it is claimed, leads to a potentially massive waste of resources, in a number of different ways (Duffy and Waters, 2008, pp 49–54):

• Resources are misdirected (as people have to have what there is rather than what they want or need).
• Multiple funding sources and assessment processes duplicate effort.
• The system forces people to inflate their needs in order to get help and to play down their strengths and family networks.
• The current system rarely innovates as decisions are taken too far away from the individuals they affect.
• There are very high transaction costs (perhaps as much as 30% of the current budget is spent in this way, including high spending on contracts and commissioning, care management and service management/administration etc). However, it remains too early to know how much of this infrastructure is necessary and how much resource could be freed up in an era of self-directed support.

Quite what this means in practice is currently impossible to know, but remains (quite literally) the billion-dollar question. For some, self-directed support offers the opportunity to free up significant wasted resource in order to reinvest this money in meeting the needs of an ageing population, providing support to people with lower-level needs and investing in prevention. For others, this money could be reinvested in other priorities (essentially reducing the overall social care budget as money is moved elsewhere). For a third group, however, there is a potential counter-trend. As Duffy and Waters (2008, p 54) have argued:

> At present, the unattractiveness of the current social care system acts as a vicious form of rationing – rationing by not offering appropriate services. For some people, this lack of confidence in the quality of services acts as a significant deterrent … If they can afford to stay away from services … they do. However, when Self-Directed Support is available and authorities offer people choice, flexibility and control,

'new' eligible people [may] come forward and claim their right to a service.

In many ways, this links back to the origins of social care (explored in Chapter Two), with 21st-century social care still operating a version of the principle of 'less eligibility' and 'the workhouse test'. While this raises questions that are beyond the scope of this book, the key issue is that the transparency of self-directed support holds out the potential for us to decide how much money to spend on adult social care as a society and how this is divided between people with support needs – irrespective of how much need and how much money there is out there, self-directed support allows us to take clear decisions about how best to respond to these challenges. Of course, a major irony here is that some supporters of self-directed support are so enthusiastic because of the financial transparency it brings, while some critics are hostile for exactly the same reason. Ultimately, perhaps, your view on whether or not transparency is a good thing probably depends on whether you think some of the rationing decisions we currently take should be open or hidden – and self-directed support goes right to the heart of this debate.

SUMMARY

Overall, direct payments and personal budgets seem to be two of the most powerful mechanisms available to transform the social care system, giving greater choice and control and delivering different and better outcomes for the same (or maybe even for less) money. While it remains early days, the emerging evidence is so positive that, at the very least, these are ways of working that seem worth exploring and developing further. Although Chapter Seven examines potential barriers, we nevertheless believe that many of these relate to the way in which direct payments and personal budgets have been implemented – not to the underlying concept of direct payments and personal budgets per se. While further research and testing will be required as these ideas develop, all the available evidence (from research, from policy and from practice) seems to suggest that direct payments and personal budgets *just work*. Although it will take some time for research and for the evidence base to catch up with practice, the lived reality of people's lives seems to suggest that both direct payments and personal budgets have something powerful to offer that the social care system, people who work in it and people who use services should not (and probably cannot any longer) ignore.

IMPLICATIONS FOR POLICY AND PRACTICE

- Direct payments and personal budgets offer greater choice and control to disabled people over their services and lives.
- This has the potential to improve morale and well-being.
- Being in control also enables people to make practical changes in their lives and to achieve outcomes that matter to them.
- Although opinion is divided, both direct payments and personal budgets seem to represent a more effective use of resources, since (at worst) they enable better outcomes to be achieved for the same amount of money.
- Outstanding issues include the extent to which a new system will encourage people with previously unidentified needs to come forward and/or the extent to which any direct savings can be reinvested in the system.

Recommended reading and useful websites

This chapter draws out key findings from more general material summarised in Chapters Three to Five, and so there are fewer further resources than in other chapters. As with Chapters Four and Five, some of the key overviews include:

- national direct payment studies such as those by Riddell et al (2006), Vick et al (2006) and Davey et al (2007a–b);
- in Control evaluations (Poll et al, 2006; Hatton et al, 2008);
- the national IBSEN evaluation (Glendinning et al, 2008).

Early insights into the limitations of directly provided services and the potential of individualised funding are available from user-focused accounts provided by Kestenbaum (1993a–b), Morris (1993a) and Zarb and Nadash (1994).

As in Chapter Five, the *Living your life, your way* DVD (DH/Care Services Improvement Partnership/in Control, 2008) is an excellent resource with a series of personal accounts of the practicalities, the power and the potential impact of personal budgets.

For discussion of the cost-effectiveness of direct payments, see Zarb and Nadash's (1994) crucial study. A particularly helpful summary of the issues surrounding costs is available via in Control's paper on 'The economics of self-directed support' (Duffy and Waters, 2008; see also Glendinning et al, 2008).

Reflective exercises

1. Think about your daily life and the practical tasks you need to carry out to get up, wash, get dressed, eat and get out of the house to work or study. If you had an impairment, how feasible would it be to continue your current daily routine with the support of directly provided services? How might this be different with direct payments or personal budgets?

2. What do you value most about your life? From your knowledge of directly provided services, what would you have to give up about your current life if you had to rely on directly provided services?

3. Talk to someone who has experience of living with an impairment (a service user, a neighbour, a family member). What did receiving direct services feel like, and how could this experience have been improved? Compare this with the experiences of direct payment recipients and personal budget holders in this chapter (see also Chapter Five).

4. Have you ever felt completely dependent on another person or organisation – and helpless to influence the outcome? (This needn't be to do with social care and could be from any walk of life). How did this make you feel and what impact did it have?

5. Reflect on a recent case (at work or on placement) – how much money was spent on the services provided and how effective were they in meeting the person's needs? Was this a good use of money? Could the same amount of money have been spent on something different in order to try to achieve the same ends?

6. For a recent person you have worked with, try to move away from the traditional service-led approach ('Mrs Smith needs home care'). Instead, try to identify the underlying need. Draw up a table with three columns (see below), listing the need, the way in which direct services might respond and the possibilities opened up by direct payments/individuals budgets.

   For example:

Assessed need	Direct service response	Options via direct payments/ personal budgets
Help having a bath	• Home care – can't guarantee what time or who will come; waiting list. • May be possible to install shower, but this isn't urgent and there's a very long waiting list.	• Employ own staff and decide who/what/when. • Support from family member (individual budget could pay their travel fare). • Install shower in bathroom. • Hire PA to go swimming and shower at pool etc.

SEVEN

Possible barriers

This chapter explores:
- the different motives of those supporting direct payments and personal budgets;
- the barriers that can be created by some frontline workers;
- the consequences of inadequate funding levels;
- the risk of exacerbating inequity;
- the impact on the workforce;
- the danger that local authorities use direct payments to 'offload troublemakers';
- practical barriers;
- staff recruitment.

As Chapter Six demonstrated, direct payments and personal budgets bring a range of benefits that can enhance the choice, control and well-being of recipients. However, we have also seen how pressure for direct payments built up over a long period (Chapters Two and Three) and how organisations of disabled people were able to mount a sustained campaign for the new legislation to be introduced. As a result, direct payments were initially nearly always viewed positively, and were arguably subjected to less critical reflection than should perhaps have been the case. While we believe that direct payments and personal budgets *do* bring a number of very real advantages, there have been a number of limitations and contradictions in practice that workers and service users need to consider. As Fernandez et al (2007) observe, many of these fall into one of two different categories:

- practical implementation barriers (which are capable, at least in principle, of being resolved by technical or management interventions);
- political, economic and social factors (which presumably require national and more fundamental change to resolve altogether).

While different accounts have tended to focus more on one or the other of these, the reality is that key barriers are likely to derive from a more complex mix of both factors. Against this background, this chapter seeks to explore a number of key questions, including:

- Are direct payments and personal budgets the product of a government seeking to restrict public spending and introduce a flawed notion of consumerism into community care services?
- Does the success of direct payments and personal budgets rely too heavily on the attitudes and training of frontline workers?

- Are direct payments and personal budgets adequately financed, and do recipients receive enough money to purchase sufficient care?
- Could direct payments and personal budgets introduce a two-tier system, leaving people who opt for direct services in a disadvantageous position and/or enabling those with the loudest voice/the greatest family support to get better outcomes?
- Might direct payments and personal budgets lead to the greater exploitation of care workers and of women?
- Could direct payments and personal budgets leave service users vulnerable to abuse or at risk of significant harm?
- Is there a risk that some authorities could use direct payments and personal budgets to distance themselves from service users they perceive as 'troublemakers'?
- Are the practicalities of managing direct payments and personal budgets prohibitive?
- Are the barriers to recruiting staff too difficult for some people to overcome?

Consumerism and public expenditure

Although direct payments offer increased choice and control, it is often forgotten that they were introduced by a Conservative government firmly committed to New Right or neoliberal social and economic policies. Building on the work of thinkers such as Hayek (1944), Friedman (1962) and, more recently, Murray (1984), the New Right approach has been summarised in terms of a belief in three key issues:

- the free market
- the minimal state
- individual liberty and responsibility. (Adams, 1998, p 85)

Within social policy, this has led to a neoliberal critique of state welfare that acquired increasing significance after the economic crises and political polarisation of the 1970s. As Alcock (1996, p 12) explains:

> [The New Right's] main argument was that state intervention to provide welfare services ... merely drove up the cost of public expenditure to a point where it began to interfere with the effective operation of a market economy. They claimed that this was a point that had already been reached in Britain in the 1970s as the high levels of taxation needed for welfare services had reduced profits, crippled investment and driven capital overseas. [At the same time] the New Right also challenged the desirability of state welfare in practice, arguing that free welfare services only encouraged feckless

people to become dependent upon them and provided no incentive for individuals and families to protect themselves through savings or insurance. Furthermore, right-wing theorists claimed that state monopoly over welfare services reduced the choices available to people to meet their needs in a variety of ways and merely perpetuated professionalism and bureaucracy.

After the election of Margaret Thatcher as prime minister in 1979, these ideas acquired increasing support at the heart of central government, culminating in a series of market-led reforms in traditional public sector services such as education, housing and the NHS. Within community care, such reforms were to transform social services departments from direct service providers into service purchasers, with an explicit brief to contract a significant amount of care from the independent sector (Lewis, 1996). These changes were presented as 'promoting choice and independence' and giving 'people a greater individual say in how they live their lives and the services they need to help them do so' (DH, 1989, p 4). This has been described by Means and Smith (1998a, p 83) as promoting a form of 'empowerment by exit':

> 'Exit' is essentially a market approach which seeks to empower consumers by giving them a choice between alternatives and the option of 'exit' from a service and/or provider, if dissatisfied. The consumer, in other words, will be able to change provider, and if a large number of them make the same decision about the same provider then that provider will be punished for their inefficiency by going out of 'business'.

Although neoliberal attempts to recast service users as consumers have led to greater emphasis on service quality, a consumerist approach to social policy has been criticised by a number of commentators (see, for example, Barnes and Walker, 1996; Means and Smith, 1998a). As Marian Barnes (1997, p 3) has suggested, empowerment by exit and the consumerist philosophy on which this is based both rely on a number of essential preconditions:

- Alternatives need to exist.
- The person concerned needs access to information not only about alternatives, but also about characteristics of alternatives that might suggest that they would overcome dissatisfaction with existing services, but also not substitute new for existing problems.
- Moving from one option to another should be practically possible.
- Moving from one option to another should not of itself generate damaging disruption.

As Barnes continues: 'If one considers the circumstances in which most people use health and social care services, it is clear that all these circumstances will rarely apply.'

In addition to promoting the notion of welfare recipients as consumers, the New Right also emphasised the need to curtail public spending on welfare. As we have seen in Chapter Two, the ILF introduced in 1988 was restricted in 1993 as a result of concerns about rapidly increasing costs. We have also seen in Chapters Two and Three how financial concerns thwarted previous attempts to introduce direct payments in the early 1990s and how government guidance emphasised the need for direct payments to be at least as cost-effective as the services that they replaced. Although the 1996 Community Care (Direct Payments) Act was introduced three years after the reform of the ILF, this was seen as less of a financial threat to the government since direct payments were to be operated by local authorities within their existing cash-limited budget 1998a, p 85). As the number of direct payments has increased ov there is evidence of a 'north–south divide' (Pearson, 2004, p 4), with Conservative strongholds in southern England more likely to adopt direct payments than areas associated more with 'Old' Labour politics. Indeed, of the ten 'top' local authorities that make the most direct payments, seven are Conservative-controlled, possibly reflecting the importance of local political histories in shaping reactions to direct payments (Riddell et al, 2006, p 7).

More recently, similar concern about financial risk seems to have accompanied debates about personal budgets, and at least some of the current policy enthusiasm seems to come from the perception that this may be a way of responding to the needs of a rapidly ageing population without investing what many would see as the necessary resources (see Chapters Five and Six for further discussion). Thus, as Henwood and Hudson (2007b) have demonstrated, some of the enthusiasm for personal budgets may have come from a range of different perspectives, with some keen to cut costs, some eager to transform the public perception of social care and others concerned about the role of social welfare in promoting or undermining independence. Described as 'a Holy Trinity of support', this prompted one respondent in the study to comment that, if so many apparently different people find the concept attractive, "then we may all be thinking it is something rather different" (Henwood and Hudson, 2007b, p 34).

Against this background, the introduction of direct payments and of personal budgets begins to take on a new and slightly more sinister appearance. While direct payments undoubtedly bring a number of very real benefits, it is also possible to see them as an attempt to promote a flawed notion of 'empowerment by exit' and to do so in a way that would not result in an escalation of public expenditure. In such a scenario, it would be left to local authorities to balance the books and reconcile the very real demand for direct payments with already stringent budget constraints. While this should not prevent service users from benefiting from the many advantages of direct payments and personal budgets, it does suggest that there may be conflicting agendas, with service users and central government each wanting different things from the reforms. This contradiction has been identified most forcefully by Pearson (2000, 2004), who has emphasised the tensions between the social justice discourse of the disability movement and the market discourse of government. In the same way, Askheim (2003) argues those apparently committed to the notion of 'empowerment' can support the concept either from a market-based consumer stance, or from a radical civil rights perspective. This is further developed by Spandler (2004, p 190), who describes direct payments as 'a complex confluence of new right, New Labour and welfare user movement ideologies and demands', with scope to mask a range of underlying tensions and conflicts. As Fernandez et al (2007, p 99) argue:

> The policy appeals across the political spectrum … Conservative commentators can applaud its market-like characteristics, while for New Labour the policy resonates neatly with the broader thrust of the choice in public services campaign … The policy also seems to be remarkably popular with those users who have secured access to it.

Whether or not this is a good or a bad thing probably depends on your point of view. However, as Spandler (2004) observes, what would be dangerous is to assume common interests and to deny the existence of conflict − this will only reduce the impact of direct payments and personal budgets, prompting polarised responses and undermining critical discussion of the underlying issues. For frontline workers, moreover, such tensions may ultimately lead to role conflict as they try to support direct payment and personal budget recipients, while working within a system and within financial constraints that are not always as emancipatory as the initial policy rhetoric may suggest. Elsewhere, we have developed these arguments further (Glasby, 2007), suggesting that the initial campaigns for change that surrounded direct payments and personal budgets involved some potentially very uneasy bedfellows coming together, often with very different motivations and expectations. While this created enough momentum to change policy, it remains to be seen what happens next if different groups with different values really do begin to diverge significantly. As Spandler (2004, p 202) suggests:

> Having explored some of the complexities … it seems clear that neither a simplistic pursuit of [direct payments] as empowerment, nor a kneejerk reaction against them as mere cost-cutting consumerism is an adequate response. [Direct payments] are not clearly a 'consumerist' or a 'democratic' approach to social policy …, but actually an example of the convergence of the two, a convergence that yields both problems and possibilities.

Similarly, as Sapey and Pearson (2004, p 65) suggest:

> Direct payments do make use of free market principles and there can be a contradiction between the individualism of this approach and the need for collectivity in the responsibility for welfare ... Direct payments need to be seen as an integral part of a collective approach to the provision of support. Implementing direct payment schemes provides a possibility of promoting independent living and access to mainstream economic and social life, but also could become a threat to collective responsibility for welfare and the notion of caring communities if it is interpreted within an individualist framework. The challenge is to do the first and not the second.

The 'gatekeeping' role of social workers

Time and time again, a major barrier to an extension of direct payments has been shown to be the attitudes and knowledge of frontline social workers. This was widely anticipated as the 1996 Act was being implemented (Oliver and Sapey, 1999), and subsequent events have tended to support those uncertain about the capacity of social services departments to embrace the significant changes implied by direct payments legislation. In Scotland, practitioners were deterred by perceived expenditure and workload implications, by a lack of understanding of direct payments, or by a fear of a loss of control (Witcher et al, 2000). Others feared that service users would misspend their payments on drugs or alcohol and there was a widespread suggestion that senior managers may be deliberately 'blocking' the implementation of the 1996 legislation. Overall, understanding of direct payments was limited, with some departments unsure of the differences between direct and indirect payments.

Elsewhere (Fruin, 2000, p 17), the Social Services Inspectorate has found evidence of an ambivalent attitude to direct payments among staff:

> "I am very worried about direct payments – vulnerable people managing their own services." (social worker in a multi-disciplinary team)

> "Can I risk [direct payments] ... on behalf of clients?" (adults' team social worker)

Some members of staff lacked knowledge about direct payments legislation and about local procedures, disadvantaging their service users. In the local inspections, direct payments sometimes had a low profile among non-specialist workers and might not be adequately publicised through fears that this would create additional demands on already stretched budgets. On one occasion, proposals for a direct payments scheme were hindered by the lack of a champion to drive forward the project and a lack of understanding about the role that direct payments could play in the range of services designed to support independent living (DH/SSI, 1999a-c). Similar findings were also to emerge from Norfolk (Dawson, 2000) and Staffordshire, where an evaluation of a direct payments pilot project emphasised the need to promote awareness not only among disabled people, but also among social workers (Leece, 2000, pp 39-40). In West Sussex, social workers were found to have very little knowledge of direct payments, with some practitioners claiming that people with learning difficulties could not receive direct payments but that disabled children could (quoted in Leece, 2000, p 39). Findings such as these supported previous research in London that suggested that people at all levels – users, carers and junior members of staff – have little knowledge of direct payments (Brandon et al, 2000; Maglajlic et al, 2000). In the case of people with learning difficulties, interviews with ten users, ten carers and ten members of staff found that only two members of staff out of the 30 people interviewed had even heard of direct payments (Maglajlic et al, 2000, pp 100-1). For older people, research carried out by Age Concern suggests that few staff within social services knew anything about direct payments (even in areas with a history of them), raising serious questions as to how service users were to be kept informed (Age Concern, 1998; see also Box 7.1).

Box 7.1: Lack of information

"The information that gets here is lousy. Sometimes they tell you something, like 'you can have this' … And then they say that it's going to be in two months, three months … and then you hear nothing else about it." (quoted in Maglajlic et al, 2000, p 101)

"My social worker had difficulty accessing relevant information. Her manager did not have the answers to her questions and could not tell her where to find the answer." (quoted in Leece, 2000, p 39)

Despite widespread information campaigns, many people with learning difficulties still know nothing about direct payments. (Bewley, 2000, p 14)

As the Direct Payments pilot project progressed, it became increasingly apparent that the single most significant factor in determining who became an employer through direct payments was the potential employer's social worker. (Dawson, 2000, p 22)

Elsewhere, it may not just be lack of knowledge that hinders implementation, but political and/or professional opposition. Depending on the political views of local councillors and social services managers, some authorities may view direct payments as a threat to their own in-house domiciliary and day care (George, 1996), representing a form of 'privatisation by the back door' (Hasler et al, 1999, p 7). At the same time, direct payments might be expected to lead to a change in social work practice, prompting a shift away from providing/purchasing services for disabled people to supporting them to purchase their own care. This feature of direct payments is particularly identified by Dawson (2000) in her evaluation of the Norfolk Independent Living Project. During the study, it became apparent that a significant majority of people without previous experience of indirect payment schemes heard of direct payments through their social worker, but that some practitioners were withholding this information. Whereas staff specialising in work with people with physical impairments were familiar with the concept of indirect payments, workers from mental health or learning difficulty teams had little knowledge of users purchasing their own care. As the evaluation progressed, it became clear that the introduction of direct payments involved 'a change of culture' in which individual workers were having to take on more of an enabling role (Dawson, 2000, p 53). While some staff relished this role, others were less enthusiastic, and the take-up of direct payments was directly linked to the approach of individual workers (see Box 7.2).

Box 7.2: The role of care management

My involvement in the promotion of direct payments does raise questions for me about the current state of play in care management. Care managers are extremely important gatekeepers in the whole direct payments story. I have a strong impression that people with learning difficulties who have been able to access direct payments have always had a champion on their side. This has often been a forward-thinking (and tenacious) family member, independent advisor, advocate or, sometimes, care manager. These care managers have been vital in the promotion of direct payments so far, but they are not the majority within social services. If direct payments are to become an easy mainstream option ... then enabling people to access them must become normal care management practice. For this to happen, significant change is required to individual, team and organisational practice around care management ... The care management system is under many pressures and the truth is that direct payments are not a daily priority for many care managers ... This is a shame because the ethos of direct payments is extremely exciting. Care managers now have the chance to actually give service users the money to buy their own services. This sharing of power, this chance to see individual lives flourish whilst practical support needs are met, is a fantastic opportunity for care managers to be inspired by their job. The opportunity is there.
(Bewley, 2000, pp 14-15)

In one sense, such barriers might have been expected (especially given the scale of the cultural challenge that direct payments imply). Unfortunately, this does not yet seem to be something that is going away; perceived resistance from frontline staff remains a key feature of the recent direct payments literature. According to a survey of direct payment support services, for example, resistance from staff was the second most frequently cited barrier to direct payments (Davey et al, 2007a, p 83), while CSCI (2004) has placed similar emphasis on the potentially negative impact that a lack of meaningful information and support from care managers can have. At local level, Clark and Spafford (2002) have demonstrated how many workers found it hard to take ownership of this new way of working due to time/work pressures, anxieties about how to offer direct payments in a meaningful way, concerns about interpreting the guidance on being 'willing and able', tensions between promoting empowerment and balancing risk, and concerns about flexibility for some versus equity for all. As some of the participants in the study commented:

> "We don't need this; we've already got enough hassle, do we need any more hassle?"

> "It's daunting to offer something that you don't fully understand yourself."

> "You lose your autonomy ... it's like the symbol of wearing a badge to say you're a professional and then suddenly the badge disappears, 'Ah, they won't know what I am'."

> (Clark and Spafford, 2002, pp 250, 252)

However, a particularly vivid description of the role of social workers in influencing people's access to direct payments comes from Ellis's (2007) study of assessment and care management practice in one English local authority. While Ellis argues that direct payments might be able to help social workers re-engage with the core values of the profession, the realities of frontline practice (especially time and financial constraints) meant that practitioners often rationed access to direct payments by a variety of informal means. These included introducing the concept in a defensive manner, restricting access to information, focusing on assessment and simply leaving a leaflet about direct payments, or making assumptions about the 'right sort of person' for a direct payment. Such tactics were justified in a range of ways (see Box 7.3), and Ellis's study provides a fascinating insight into the subconscious processes that can sometimes make us adopt particular critiques of a specific policy as a way of justifying how we respond to the pressures of the workplace. Interestingly, the language employed by many of the participants in this study also serves as confirmation of the continued dominance of Duffy's 'professional gift' model (see Chapters Two and Five), with workers often using words such as 'let', 'allow' and 'give' in relation to their role in working with service users (Ellis, 2007, p 418).

> ## Box 7.3: 'Justifications' for rationing access to direct payments
>
> In legitimising their rationing of access to direct payments, social workers put forward a number of 'justifications' (Ellis, 2007), including:
>
> - the perception that direct payments meet 'wants' rather than 'needs' – that they are optional extras above and beyond the core business of current social care;
> - the belief that direct payments enable people to meet their needs in non-traditional ways, and this could be inequitable for recipients of directly provided services;
> - concerns about financial abuse.
>
> While these are all potentially legitimate concerns (albeit ones to which we think there are very robust answers), Ellis's study is especially helpful as it highlights the way in which the pressures of frontline practice can hinder the offering of direct payments, with the practitioners concerned citing such factors not necessarily because there are genuine barriers, but in order to justify the stance they feel forced to take by practice realities.

In many ways, the crucial role of social workers in encouraging or preventing disabled people from accessing direct payments is hardly surprising. Previous research into the information provided by social services departments has suggested that inefficient distribution systems and poor targeting can prevent information from reaching the right people at the right time and in the right place. Although many authorities produce material in different formats and languages, most information has historically been in standard print (Fryer, 1998). Even where authorities make considerable efforts to produce accessible information for minority groups, the publicity and leaflets that do exist may not always find their way to the people who need them (DH/SSI, 1997). For disabled people trying to make sense of the complexities of social services bureaucracy, the difficulty of obtaining accessible information about the options open to them has been well documented (see Box 7.4; Beardshaw, 1988; Zarb and Oliver, 1993; Barnes, 1995; Davis et al, 1997). In one research project, two case study social services departments were not providing disabled people with the information and advice they needed, since frontline staff saw requests for information as potential demands on their services (Davis et al, 1997). Elsewhere, the Social Services Inspectorate found that information for disabled people could be out of date and repetitive, not specific to disabled people, inaccessible to people from minority ethnic groups and poorly distributed (DH/SSI, 1996). Even after direct payments became mandatory rather than discretionary, there is still a key role for frontline staff in communicating the different options as positively as possible, so as not to bias service users and artificially constrain choice. As one participant in a national study of the implementation of direct payments observed:

"What I am concerned about is *how* people are being offered it. If it's presented as a positive alternative, people are more likely to take it up, but if it is not sold to hard to reach client groups, they won't touch it ... Teams are becoming aware that it is mandatory, however it still comes down to the social worker and selling direct payments and there is a block here, they don't feel confident and are lacking info. Making it mandatory has helped a bit but it hasn't dealt with the problem." (Vick et al, 2006, p 33)

As the quote above begins to suggest, it has long been recognised that social workers occupy a crucial gatekeeping role and can work in a number of informal ways to limit the demands made upon them (Rees, 1978; Satyamurti, 1981). Described by Lipsky (1980) as 'street level bureaucrats', social workers have been shown to use their professional discretion in order to balance competing priorities and to protect themselves against the overwhelming pressures that they face (see Box 7.5). Often, they will seek to manage their workloads by making assumptions about their service users, categorising them and forming stereotypical responses to their needs, thereby adding a degree of stability and predictability to their work. Although the concept of street-level bureaucracy was initially applied to the reorganisation of social services departments in the 1970s, research funded by the JRF has demonstrated that frontline practitioners continue to behave in similar ways (Davis et al, 1997; Ellis et al, 1999). Based on observations of social work assessments and interviews with users and carers, the study found that workers used screening mechanisms, computer-based assessments and eligibility criteria to manage demand, thereby rationing their time and resources. Although the methods of rationing would appear to have changed since the 1970s, the gatekeeping role of social workers is just as real. Against this background, the success of direct payments is likely to continue to be closely linked to the attitudes and actions of frontline staff, and it will be important to ensure that practitioners receive sufficient information and training to be able to become forces for change rather than obstacles to progress.

Box 7.4: Access to information

Information is also a key pre-requisite to disabled people having genuine choice and control over how their needs are to be met. Without information about available resources, how to access services, or about their rights, it is impossible for people to make genuine choices or determine what kind of support is most appropriate to meet their self-defined needs. However, previous research has often highlighted information poverty as a major constraint on providing appropriate and adequate solutions to disabled people's support needs.
(Zarb and Oliver, 1993, p 9)

Box 7.5: Street-level bureaucracy

The decisions of street-level bureaucrats, the routines they establish, and the devices they invent to cope with uncertainties and work pressures, effectively become the public policies they carry out ... Public policy is not best understood as made in legislatures or top-floor suites of high-ranking administrators, because in important ways it is actually made in the crowded offices and daily encounters of street-level workers. (Lipsky, 1980, p xii)

With the advent of personal budgets, the issues at stake arguably become even more profound. While personal budgets start to overcome some of the practical concerns that frontline workers have raised about direct payments (for example, that some user groups would find administering their payments too onerous and that payments could not be used for public services), the move to a system of self-directed support requires a radical rethink of the nature of modern social work. Under self-directed support, the role of the local authority is to allocate a financial resource to the individual, then to check that the support plans they are making seem sensible and that the needs for which the personal budget is provided are being met. Thus, the focus shifts from the current very heavy emphasis on assessment, to support planning and review – almost reversing current practice. In addition, the role of social workers is to support those people without access to other forms of support or those who want a social worker to help manage their personal budget. While some see this as undermining the professional status of social workers, others see it very much as freeing up extremely skilled and experienced staff to concentrate on those people who need them most – essentially enabling social workers to do what they came into the job to do in the first place (see Glendinning et al, 2008, ch 12 for evidence of both views). Certainly, this is the line taken in recent government thinking, with a paper on the workforce implications of *Putting People First* stating that:

> Achieving [policy aspirations for adult social care] ... relies on the capacity, competency and commitment of the social care workforce ... to empower and support people who use services and supports to exercise that choice and control. It will mean a workforce assuming a more proactive and enabling role in how they respond to people's needs and preferences but having far less control over the details of the support that people receive – taking on roles which strongly focus on brokerage, information and service advocacy. It will mean less direct management control over people's lives by social care professionals, but still ensuring they carry out their duty to care. It will mean embracing new ways of working when it comes to identifying and responding to risk and becoming less risk averse. *This*

is not a relinquishing of responsibility: it is working in a true partnership between social care workers and people using services, their carers, those who volunteer and the wider community. Such partnership working is, we know, why so many people decided to become social care professionals in the first place. (DH, 2008h, pp 4–5, emphasis added)

While this is a stance with which we fully agree, the evidence from direct payments suggests that substantial training and development may be required in order to persuade frontline staff that this is indeed the case. Without this, personal budgets could struggle with the same cultural challenges as direct payments, and their impact could be weakened. Early on, moreover, there is evidence to suggest that the introduction of new ways of working can increase rather than reduce workloads, with staff having to operate old and the new systems at the same time (Glendinning et al, 2008, ch 12).

To date, the early signs are mixed. While there has been enthusiastic engagement with self-directed support in some areas, a number of barriers still remain (see Glendinning et al, 2008 for a summary; see also Mickel, 2008). Although this is very much an oversimplification, battlelines have often seemed to be drawn between personal budget recipients and their allies on the one hand, and some social care professional bodies and broader public service trade unions on the other (see Box 7.6 for examples). While some of the short-term tensions between these two groups have undoubtedly been increased by the scale and pace of reform, it seems a shame to us as external observers that all stakeholders involved in the delivery and receipt of social care do not currently seem able to find common ground and a shared value base. Although this is perhaps to be expected with such fundamental changes, social care workers and people who receive services both have very few allies, and it would be unfortunate if the whole of social care cannot unite behind the concept of self-directed support and work together to tackle some of the remaining complexities and barriers.

Box 7.6: Tensions in the social care workforce

As an example of those passionate about the potentially liberating impact of direct payments and personal budgets, Simon Stevens (an independent disability trainer and consultant, and regular columnist in *Community Care* magazine) has argued that:

> My attempts to quell my feelings about trade unions have not been successful. After realising that a system in which personal assistants are paid by disabled micro-employers is likely to be the way forward, they appear to have decided to abandon rational debate. Instead, they are beginning to spread 'caveman-style' propaganda that disabled people are naturally bad employers who will disobey their legal duties and abuse their staff ... This is an interesting opening standpoint in what is clearly going to be a long and bloody battle between the rights of service users and indeed their staff with the demands of an external self-appointed 'god', making judgements on highly complex issues about which they have little understanding. I strongly believe that if my staff were forced to join a trade union, I would be better off dead. (Stevens, 2008)

Shortly afterwards, a Scottish study by Unison was presented in the trade press as being critical of the workforce implications of self-directed support:

> Personalised support schemes are breaching the employment rights of care assistants, Unison has warned. A Scottish study by the union found that some employees were failing to benefit from the minimum wage, statutory leave or maternity pay. Evidence from self-directed support schemes in Scotland showed care assistants hired by disabled people using personal budgets worked under conditions which broke employment law. (Lombard, 2008)

Leaving aside the detail of these two stances, the way in which both were reported (and the reaction they generated) is probably more important than the original column and research study – what this suggests is that finding common ground in a way that brings people needing support together with those who provide it can be difficult, and that the issues can quickly become polarised if we do not focus sufficiently on the underlying principles and goals of self-directed support.

This is clearly complex and disputed territory, but a paper by in Control provides a helpful summary of many of the key issues (Duffy, 2007). In particular, Duffy identifies three limitations of current approaches to care management:

* *The inflexibility of the resources that are available to identify and meet need*: although the early advocates of care management envisaged significant flexibility, many care managers find that they have to rely heavily on existing block-contracted services and thus have little discretion to meet needs in other ways.

- *The disguised nature of the rationing system by which resources are assigned*: while the care management guidance required social workers to operate within appropriate budgets, the process of rationing has tended to lack transparency (with the result that workers can feel a conflict of interest between supporting the person and balancing the books, and that access to resources can often depend on the extent to which individual workers can advocate on behalf of 'their' client).
- *The professionally dominated process of planning and organising support*: at present, care managers are meant to assess, develop care plans and organise support for all – irrespective of the capacities, networks and gifts of the individuals concerned. Interestingly, when approximately 100 care managers were asked who was the best person to plan and organise support for people on their current caseloads (around 800 cases), they often chose other people (family, friends, service providers or the person themselves) rather than a care manager (see Duffy, 2007, p 7).

In contrast, Duffy argues, self-directed support makes the allocation of resources to meet need transparent, improves support planning and frees care managers up to focus their skills on those who need them most. As one personal budget project manager observed:

> "Generally speaking, the introduction of [personal budgets] has been met with considerable enthusiasm and commitment by practitioners ..., principally because of the focus on user empowerment and creativity in support planning. Many practitioners and team managers feel that this is 'what real social work is about ... it's what I trained for'." (quoted in Duffy, 2007, p 11)

In addition to in Control material on this issue, one of the most insightful commentaries on the scale of the cultural challenge that accompanies self-directed support comes from Henwood and Hudson's (2007b) review of progress in three case study local authorities. As the researchers conclude, 'If [self-directed support] is to become established there has to be an understanding of its professional and organisational ramifications, otherwise – rather like the history of direct payments – it will tend to be seen as a marginal activity bolted on to existing arrangements' (Henwood and Hudson, 2007b, p 14; see also Box 7.7). In particular, Henwood and Hudson identify a series of cultural challenges that will need to be overcome for self-directed support to be successfully implemented, including:

- the culturally conservative nature of social care, with many social care organisations seen as 'not well-suited to radical change' (p 15);
- the difficulties in supporting current care managers to take on new roles and become fully committed to the new system;

- a history of 'giving and doing' (p 20), with a workforce that measures itself by its ability to do things *for* people and give them services;
- fears that self-directed support could lead to an overly individual approach and threaten collective social welfare;
- concerns that self-directed support could end up meeting 'wants' rather than 'needs';
- a tendency for some frontline workers to mistrust service users and carers (with implicit assumptions that significant input from professionals is required to safeguard public money);
- assumptions that older people would not want the perceived complexities associated by some participants with self-directed support.

Box 7.7: The cultural challenges of self-directed support

"We are often tempted to change processes rather than behaviours. This is about changing a set of behaviours – process and legislation is a second-order issue. For me this is about a change in mindset."

"I am generalising, but I don't think the penny has dropped yet. People think they can do it as an add-on. Unless work is actively done quite soon we are going to struggle to implement this."

"There is sometimes resistance from social workers who aren't sure they came into social work to provide money to people."

"Most people totally agree with the principles but are wary that it will undermine their role. They are saying will there be a need for social workers and that 'we are professionally qualified for a reason'."

(Staff reactions, Henwood and Hudson, 2007b, pp 14-18)

As Henwood and Hudson (2007b, p 26) observe:

> What much of the above … reveals is a stark interpretation of [self-directed support] – an 'all or nothing' model in which the service user either takes the full package unaided or sticks with the current arrangements. It suggests that there needs to be a greater emphasis upon [self-directed support] as a continuum of options, as well as on the availability of personalisation support mechanisms.

Arising out of this analysis, Henwood and Hudson identify 'a variety of understandings and views' about self-directed support (2007b, p 27), dividing participants in their study into one of three different categories that may prove helpful when seeking to implement self-directed support locally:

- outright supporters – who fully understand and are committed to the principles of self-directed support;
- qualified supporters – who may support the overall principle but have some concerns;
- 'the confused and the critics' (p 29) – who either do not understand self-directed support or are hostile to it (or both).

Financial difficulties

The financial implications of making cash payments to disabled people are an issue that has continued to be debated throughout the campaign for direct payments and beyond (see Chapter Six for further discussion). We have also already seen how the motives of central government may have been influenced by a neoliberal belief in rolling back the welfare state and how concerns about public expenditure thwarted a series of early attempts to legalise direct payments in the early 1990s (Chapter Three). There is now a growing consensus that financial concerns may be a major obstacle to the success and progress of direct payments, preventing some local authorities from promoting their schemes and potentially leaving recipients with insufficient funds to purchase adequate care.

In the early days, a key barrier to the implementation of direct payments may have been a lack of pump-priming to establish schemes with an appropriate support infrastructure (Wellard, 1999). Direct payments may be more cost-effective than direct services when a successful scheme is up and running, but there are workload and cost implications in seeking to set up such a scheme in the first place. In Oxfordshire, for example, the Social Services Inspectorate found that the need to make budget reductions of £10 million over three years had a significant impact on its services for disabled people (DH/SSI, 1999d). In light of its financial difficulties, Oxfordshire Social Services decided that it would be too expensive to establish and support a direct payments scheme with a large infrastructure (such as a Centre for Independent Living), opting instead for a much smaller advice service. In Scotland, research has found that lack of resources can be a major barrier and that some workers can be discouraged by significant increases in their workload as schemes are in their infancy and in areas where support mechanisms for direct payment users are limited (Witcher et al, 2000). In many cases, direct schemes were financed from generic community care budgets, with no additional funding. For departments already struggling to manage overstretched budgets, this was often a major disincentive to promoting direct payments as an option for disabled people. As one director of social services commented: "There won't be any extra provision in the revenue support grant, and direct payments could in fact attract more people into community care and so create additional demand. This could lead to delays in community care assessments, which are already a problem in many places" (quoted in George, 1996, p 24). Unfortunately, this was an issue that was identified as a potential problem from the very beginning, but one that is still to be adequately addressed:

> Funding could also prove to be a problem ... The pump priming and on-going revenue we have asked for shows little sign of materialising. This is an issue on which we will need to pitch hard for during the expenditure round ... If the goal is to extend basic direct payments schemes on a widespread basis then pump priming will be necessary. If pressure for an even greater coverage becomes intense, then significant additional funds may be needed. (Taylor, 1996c, pp 9–10)

Elsewhere, there was evidence of considerable financial implications in an evaluation carried out in Norfolk (Dawson, 2000). Although direct payment packages were found to be cheaper than directly provided services, this comparison did not take account of a number of 'hidden costs' during the early stages of the direct payments scheme. In this particular case study, implementing direct payments required management time, a seconded worker to reassess people transferring from a previous third-party scheme and a range of consultative and team meetings (see Box 7.8). Negotiations were also extremely complex, requiring a commitment from senior management and considerable partnership working with a range of disability groups. Although the majority of these start-up costs were incurred early on in the scheme and might be expected to decrease as direct payments became more firmly established, the investment required to implement a direct payments scheme did have financial implications that may have concerned some local authorities.

Box 7.8: Hidden costs

Cost of direct payments, 1999–2000: £735,867

Estimated cost of equivalent services: £764,560

Hidden costs:
Management time
A seconded worker
Consultation
Team meetings
Negotiating and setting up support services
Establishing system for monitoring and payment

(*Adapted from* Dawson, 2000, pp 43-4)

If financial concerns can create difficulties for local authorities, they can also be detrimental to direct payment recipients. Prior to the implementation of direct payments, Morris (1993a) revealed how indirect payment schemes and ILF contributions often failed to take account of indirect costs (including extra expenditure on food, entertainment and transport when being accompanied by a PA, as well as the costs of being an employer). For many people, this not only meant that such expenses had to come out of other income, but also contributed to bad employment practices, such as employing assistants on a cash-in-hand basis and failing to take out appropriate insurance. Hardly surprisingly, such issues were of particular concern to organisations such as the United Kingdom Home Care Association, which expressed its fears that the subsequent introduction of direct payments might not take into account the full costs of overheads and the responsibilities incurred by becoming an employer: 'If direct payments are going to be extended through legislation, then we have to make sure that they are not merely a back door way of reducing the cost of care' (quoted in Bond, 1996, p 20).

Since direct payments were formally implemented in April 1997, there has been ongoing concern about the hidden costs that managing payments may entail. In Scotland, many direct payment calculations did not appear to include National Insurance, sickness pay and contingency money (Witcher et al, 2000). In Staffordshire, a start-up payment of £25 to cover advertising costs, stationery, postage, telephone and travel expenses was welcomed by some recipients, but criticised by others as being inadequate:

> "An initial newspaper advert was placed and £25 did not cover the costs."

> "The money allowed for advertising needs to be reassessed. You cannot advertise in the local press for less than £80. Supermarkets often refuse to put in what they consider to be job applications on their advertising boards." (Leece, 2000, p 40)

Another key concern is the level of payments that local authorities choose to make. Since this sum is discretionary, it tends to vary considerably from area to area, and the amount of support that direct payment users receive is very much a 'postcode lottery'. In a Scottish study, hourly payments for PAs ranged from £3.60 to £11.64, and some authorities had no mechanisms for paying enhanced rates for unsocial hours or for workers with additional skills (Witcher et al, 2000). More recently, Davey et al's (2007a) national survey has provided one of the most detailed overviews of the current state of play. Although the picture that emerged was incredibly complicated, there is evidence to suggest that some local authorities may be making insufficient payments and, in our view, setting direct payment recipients up to fail. While key findings are set out in Box 7.9, key areas for further analysis include significant variations across the UK, different levels of recognition of unsocial hours, the extent to which support services and start-up costs are fully funded and different approaches to dealing with any surpluses built up by direct payment recipients. Elsewhere, there is a tendency for eligibility criteria to get tighter and tighter, squeezing direct payment packages and allowing less and less time for specified activities (Hasler, 1999). Such tensions are also quickly picked up by frontline staff, who can sometimes feel trapped between the empowering rhetoric of direct payments and the severely financially constrained nature of current social care: "We're told one thing then another ... we're told there are no limits to direct payments, be creative one minute and told to watch our spending the next ... nobody knows what to expect" (Ellis, 2007, p 410).

Box 7.9: Direct payment rates

- Payment rates vary significantly across the UK, with Northern Ireland and Wales making lower payments than England and Scotland. However, rates can still vary even within regions.
- After deductions for tax and National Insurance, a direct payment recipient with a physical impairment can afford to pay on average £6.08 per hour.
- Different local authorities have different approaches to tax, National Insurance, holiday pay, sick pay, start-up costs, contingency funds and support costs.
- Most local authorities make direct payments at a rate lower than the average cost of preferred independent sector providers and than in-house domiciliary care.
- Some authorities pay a higher rate to service users who wish to use an agency.

(Davey et al, 2007a, ch 7)

Overall, NCIL's *Rough guide to managing personal assistants* (Vasey, 2000) is adamant that insufficient payments are a central obstacle to successful direct payment schemes:

> Some of the difficulties described in this book could be sorted out by a more substantial Direct Payment. Without enough money independent living becomes stressful and in some circumstances almost too stressful ... Money is one of the key factors in the crusade. It is both liberator and jailer and we have to resist all attempts to minimise care packages and maximise charging. If we fail then we will be in big trouble. We will have no money to pay for the other parts of our lives (mortgages, children, vehicles) or to pay for the other mammoth costs associated with significant impairment. (Vasey, 2000, p 10)

A further financial difficulty concerns local authority monitoring processes. Throughout the campaign for direct payments, there was widespread concern about the financial implications of making payments to individual disabled people (see Chapter Three), and subsequent direct payment schemes have included clearly defined monitoring procedures to ensure that money is spent appropriately and efficiently. In many ways, this attention to financial detail is to be commended because it enables the local authority to audit its expenditure effectively, and protects disabled people against accusations of misusing their payments. However, there is also a danger that monitoring processes can become overly bureaucratic, acting as a disincentive to take up direct payments. To prevent this from happening, PSI/NCIL recommend that monitoring should be proportionate to the minimum requirements to protect the liabilities both of the disabled person and of the local authority (Hasler et al, 1998). This should only include setting up a separate bank account and providing copies of time sheets and bank statements – anything more may be considered excessive.

As a result, organisations like NCIL were initially critical of financial guidance issued by the Chartered Institute of Public Finance and Accountancy (CIPFA) (1998), which was deemed to be unnecessarily complex and obtrusive, failing to take account of the expertise of disabled people who had been running their own payment schemes for many years (NCIL, ndd; see also Box 7.10). While most disabled people want to demonstrate that they have spent their payments correctly, this must also be balanced against the underlying feeling that some direct payment recipients have that social services staff do not trust them and that they have to account to others for everything they do (Hasler, 1999; Maglajlic et al, 2000). This has since been clarified in more recent CIPFA guidance, which is clear that 'monitoring arrangements should be light touch and proportionate to the level of risk involved' (CIPFA, 2007, p 17).

Box 7.10: CIPFA guidance

NCIL has great concerns over some of the guidance offered by CIPFA ... As this organisation's advice is viewed by [local authorities] as sacrosanct, any departure from their approach is met with almost total resistance. Direct Payment Support Schemes have contacted NCIL to complain that CIPFA monitoring and accounting arrangements are far too bureaucratic and complex for 'users' and social service practitioners to use practically on a day-to-day basis. The procedures are highly intrusive and burdensome, putting many people off the idea of managing a payment scheme ... Disabled people's established Independent Living Schemes have developed accounting and audit procedures for Direct or 'Third Party' Payments over a considerable number of years. They are therefore in a position to demonstrate highly 'workable' procedures which fully meet legal and public accountability requirements. Unfortunately CIPFA failed to involve such a body of expertise when they compiled their material. (NCIL, ndd, p 5; for more recent CIPFA guidance with a very different approach, see CIPFA, 2007)

A final financial barrier is the tendency of some local authorities to impose cost ceilings on direct payment packages. Highlighted by organisations such as Age Concern (1998), NCIL (ndd) and Values Into Action (Holman and Bewley, 1999), the practice of limiting care packages through cost ceilings has been criticised by the government, who feel that this may result in premature admissions to residential care (DH, 1998b). Cost ceilings have also been opposed by a number of disability campaigners, who have argued that limiting the amount of community-based care available to disabled people contradicts the fundamental tenets of the Independent Living Movement:

> We do not support the use of cash ceilings, as we feel that they are entirely incompatible with needs led assessment. (NCIL, ndd, p 6)

> Many local authorities operate a cost ceiling as a way of controlling their community care budget. In some this is a guideline to care managers, in others it is a straightjacket. In authorities operating a rigid cost ceiling, people whose care needs exceed a set amount are directed to residential care ... People in residential care lead 'unnecessarily isolated and restricted lives'. They are unable to take paid work and, in all but a few cases, are unable to contribute to their local communities. Within the disability movement, campaigners have been arguing that it is both inefficient and inhumane to force people into residential care because of lack of funds for community-based support. The resulting waste of human potential is a poor use of national resources, as well as personally damaging to the people concerned. (Hasler, 1997, p 13)

> People generally want to live in their own homes if they can, and admission to institutional care ... can lead to lower self-confidence and a decline in activity. Yet the evidence is that many authorities are setting a financial ceiling on their domiciliary care packages, ... which can lead to premature admissions to care homes when care at home would have been more suitable. (DH, 1998b, p 14)

These are controversial issues that are beyond the scope of this book. However, the advent of personal budgets arguably makes some of this situation easier (while still not resolving all of the underlying issues). By linking financial resources to individual need in a fully transparent process, personal budgets spell out clearly what money is available for individuals to spend on their needs. While this does not get around the fact that there may not be enough money in the system as a whole, it gives the individual a sense of what they have available to meet their needs as best they can ('how much they have to play with' in everyday language). By being transparent about this, personal budgets also increase the opportunity for lobbying central government over funding levels – whereas no one seemed to understand how much money was available or where it went under the old system, this now becomes much clearer.

The risk of inequity

Of all the concerns that have been raised about direct payments and personal budgets, the perceived risk of increasing inequity and creating a 'two-tier' system has been one of the most prevalent and profound. If you asked many people working in public services what values they uphold, equity is likely to emerge as a defining feature of the welfare state – although many people would acknowledge that it is often difficult to achieve in practice. As Leece and Leece (2006, p 1380) suggest:

> It has been suggested ... that direct payments may be offered to and taken up disproportionately by well educated, more affluent, middle-class people, who are seen and feel able to take advantage of the opportunities offered by arranging their own support as opposed to accepting traditional service provision (Spandler, 2004; Leece, 2004). If this is the case, then the system of cash payments currently in place could be creating a two-tiered system of social support.

Certainly, some of the early history of direct payments can be interpreted in this way. As Leece and Leece point out, several early studies highlighted a significant number of direct payment recipients at local level who had prior experience of management roles and/or of supervising staff (Clark et al, 2004; Leece, 2004). Moreover, as Chapter Four has demonstrated, direct payments have been uneven in their spread, with certain regions and particular user groups benefiting more than others (see also Riddell et al, 2005). Given this, is there not a danger that direct payments become the preserve only of the articulate and the rich (and even then, only in certain localities), leaving the less well off and the less educated to directly provided services that have become even less responsive as a result of such 'cream-skimming'?

This is clearly a powerful argument and something to guard against at all costs. However, our view of the evidence to date is that this rests on a series of mistaken assumptions. As Le Grand (2007, pp 32-3) has pointed out, current services already favour the middle classes, who have always tended to benefit most from state welfare: 'the better off have louder voices: they also have better contacts and sharper elbows'. That this may be the case in social care too is suggested by a comparison of the cost of care packages versus level of need – in one case study local authority, funding under the traditional care management system was allocated very unevenly (with, for example, two people with similar needs receiving services costing £3,000 or £30,000 – see Duffy, 2008 for further discussion and analysis). In contrast, a system of personal budgets brings financial transparency to what was previously an opaque process – helping to ensure that people with equal needs start to receive equal resources. Rather than reducing equity, therefore, it seems as though personal budgets may have the potential to increase it.

Turning to the specifics of direct payments and personal budgets, it is interesting to note that both have been criticised for benefiting different groups most. While direct payments have been taken up most enthusiastically by people with physical impairment, personal budgets developed out of the inclusion movement, and the majority of early budget holders were people with learning difficulties and their families (although interestingly the biggest user group is now older people). In one sense, this should be reassuring – given the very low base from which learning disability services have come from historically, something that can work for people with learning difficulties (given the discrimination and low expectations they often face) ought potentially to work well for everyone.

When it comes to the more detailed research findings, Leece and Leece (2004) provide a fascinating overview based on an initial sample of 5,000 people who received a financial assessment from a case study local authority between 2002 and 2005. While their conclusions are inevitably tentative, they suggest that there were no statistically significant differences between direct payment recipients and users of traditional services in terms of wealth. Building on such findings, a 2008 review by the think-tank Demos (Leadbeater et al, 2008) addresses the issue of equity head on. For Demos, the assumption that personal budgets rely on a marketised form of social care which risks creating inequity is fundamentally misplaced for four main reasons:

- The current system does not treat people in a fair and consistent way, and there is often a poor fit between need and resources. At present, the system 'rewards the most articulate at the expense of the less confident: those who are most confident in complaining or most able to work the rules of the system stand more of a chance of getting the services they want. Giving people the same budgets to spend puts people on a much more equal footing' (pp 47–8).
- Personal budgets create a much fairer, more transparent link between need and resources.
- A key current inequity exists between those who can fund their own care and those who cannot. Thus, personal budgets 'offer state-funded clients the choices currently available only to the middle classes outside the system' (p 48).
- Personal budgets can work for all groups – including seldom-heard groups. By tailoring support to meet individual needs and aspirations, there is scope for self-directed support to be much more inclusive than previous ways of working. As an example, minority ethnic communities in Oldham make up 20% of the population, but only 1% of people accessing traditional social services. With the introduction of personal budgets, the figure rose close to 10% (p 48).

Finally, for all the concerns that have been raised about the longer-term implications of direct payments and personal budgets, the reality is that the solution to a potential 'two-tier system' is not to reduce everyone to the 'lower tier', but to work hard to make sure that everyone has access to the same opportunities for choice and control (that is, to achieve equity by raising standards to the highest level rather than by reducing them to the lowest common denominator). As Sapey and Pearson (2004, p 63) observe:

> How social workers act in relation to concerns about equity is an important indicator of attitude. If an improved or superior service via a direct payment is a sign of the success of the scheme, this should encourage social workers to view it positively rather than as a problem. A constructive response would be to promote the raising of standards of all services rather than criticise direct payments.

The exploitation of care workers and of women?

Most personal care is provided by women, who are typically poorly paid and may have substantial family commitments (Balloch et al, 1999; Abbott, 2000). In terms of family/informal care, research suggests that there are 5.7 million carers in Britain, 58% of whom are women (DH, 2000b, p 15). While there are more male carers than was previously expected, women are more likely than men to carry the main responsibility for caring, provide more hours of care and are more likely to be assisting with personal care (Arber and Ginn, 1995a; Twigg, 1998; DH, 2000b). This is particularly the case in intergenerational caring, which is once again associated more with women than with men (Twigg, 1998).

There is now an extensive body of literature to suggest that caring may have major (and often negative) physical, financial, social and psychological consequences, not just in the short term, but also in the long run after the caring relationship has finished (see, for example, Goodman, 1986; McLaughlin and Ritchie, 1994; Arber and Ginn, 1995b; Drew, 1995; Hancock and Jarvis, 1995; Carmichael and Charles, 1998; Henwood, 1998; Hoffman and Mitchell, 1998; Barnes, 2006). Against this background, initial restrictions on using direct payments to employ close relatives (see Chapter Three) meant that women providing care for disabled family members continued to do so free of charge, without being able to receive a wage for their work via their family member's direct payments. This is a complex issue, but it is possible that the government's decision to prevent the employment of close relatives may have been motivated by the assumption that female family members should already be providing care free of charge and that paying them for their work would make direct payments far too expensive. By initially preventing family members from being employed by direct payment recipients, therefore, the government may have been contributing to the exploitation of women.

In terms of paid carers, gender issues are once again significant. During the 1970s, data collected by the Department of Health and Social Security suggested that women formed 64% of social workers, 70% of residential home care assistants and 83% of social work assistants, with most management positions falling to men (Howe, 1986, pp 23-4). By 1987, social services departments were identified as the most occupationally segregated area of the welfare state, with women comprising 87.2% of the social services workforce (Hallett, 1989, p 33). In addition to practising as social workers and social work assistants, women were thought to make up around three-quarters of the 'manual workforce', receiving low rates of pay and working as home helps, domestic staff and wardens of sheltered housing (Jones, 1989). By 1990, 86.5% of the social services workforce were women, with the majority employed as part-time workers (Davis, 1996, p 122). Once again, social services departments were found to be 'pyramid organisations in which women dominate the base and men outnumber women at the peak' – a feature of social work that had not changed significantly since the creation of local authority social services departments in 1971 (Davis, 1996, p 123).

During the 1990s, research carried out by the National Institute for Social Work suggested that women represented well over 80% of the social services workforce in England, Scotland and Northern Ireland, often combining their work with substantial family commitments (Balloch et al, 1999). Perhaps unsurprisingly, stress levels were higher for women with young children who worked full time than for their male colleagues (Ginn and Sandell, 1997), and women were more likely to be employed at lower grades and at lower management levels than men. By 2001, a Unison survey of 3,047 home carers found that more than 97% were women, receiving low pay, often working unsocial hours, suffering from back pain and finding their work increasingly stressful (Unison, 2001). By the early 21st century, 80% of whole-time equivalent social services department staff were women (National Statistics/Information Centre, 2007, p 3), while the figure for the domiciliary care workforce was 83% (UK Home Care Association, 2008, p 8). 'Care work', in short, is a gendered activity.

Against this background, it seems likely that the majority of PAs employed by direct payment recipients will be women (see also IFF Research, 2008). We have already seen how some direct payment schemes can create financial difficulties for disabled people due to their failure to take into account hidden costs. Viewed from this angle, could direct payments result in the greater exploitation of women? Certainly, this is the stance adopted by commentators such as Ungerson (1997), who argues that direct payments may generate hardship for poorly paid women and other vulnerable groups. Rather than an internal market or quasi-market, Ungerson likens direct payments to a 'flea market' in which everyone involved is on low incomes, the services delivered are not highly valued, some activity is illegal and where it is possible, in some situations, to find a particular 'bargain' or 'treasure' who will work well beyond market and contractual requirements. Underlying this is a clear gender issue that Ungerson (1997, p 50) is quick to highlight:

> Although we know next to nothing about the kinds of people that work as personal assistants – except anecdotally – one can begin to guess who will come forward. Many of them will be women wishing to fit casual work, at unsociable hours, around the calls of their domestic lives

and generate an income for themselves and their children. Some will be students in need of money to support their education, but will be able to work in flexible packets of time. Others will be seeking housing solutions to their accommodation problems; some will be on benefit looking to enhance their incomes, either legally up to the earnings disregard for their particular benefit, or illegally beyond their benefit rules. Although direct payments will be 'monitored' by local authorities to ensure they are being spent properly in care services, there is nothing to suggest ... that the market itself will be carefully policed. Hence, informal and illegal contractual arrangements, where the workers have no employment rights of any kind, are likely to develop.

Although Ungerson was writing before direct payments were formally implemented in April 1997, research findings do suggest that her concerns may have some weight. In 1993, a study of the experiences of disabled service users found that some payment recipients made cash-in-hand payments to PAs because of the inadequacy of the money they received (Morris, 1993a). Around the same time, Zarb and Nadash (1994) found that around 60% of respondents felt that the wages that they paid to PAs were too low. Many did not pay their workers holiday pay, and a few people made payments cash-in-hand. Should they receive any increase in funding, many people signalled their intention to increase their workers' wages and/or increase the number of hours worked (see Table 7.1). This led the researchers to the conclusion that 'although some people employing their own workers feel they have had to cut corners in the way they organise their support, this is invariably out of necessity rather than by choice' (Zarb and Nadash, 1994, p 42). Other studies have suggested that the rates of pay which direct payment recipients are able to offer do not reflect the types of work that PAs are expected to undertake nor the skills that they may require (Glendinning et al, 2000a-c). Similar concerns have also been raised elsewhere in Europe, as a French director of social services has acknowledged: "Disabled people are happier and more independent [receiving direct payments], but the position of employees is fragile, with less training, less security and irregular hours of work" (quoted in Wellard, 1999, p 23).

Table 7.1: How people would spend an increase in payments

	Number	%
Increase weekly hours	14	37
Increase workers' pay	13	34
Increase workers' hours and pay	6	16
Pay workers' tax/National Insurance	5	13
Total	38	100

Source: Zarb and Nadash, 1994, p 42

More recently, Ungerson has developed her initial contribution with further research at a local level as well as cross-national research in five EU countries (see, for example, Ungerson, 1999, 2003, 2004, 2006; Ungerson and Yeandle, 2007). While this is detailed and important material, the essential argument is that changes in the boundary between work and care have resulted in new forms of relationship between disabled people, their families and employees – what is often called a 'commodification of care'. As a result, it is argued, direct employees often have less clearly defined roles, which can lead to a decline in employee rights and working conditions, unregulated labour and difficulty for workers in leaving or exercising rights because of emotions such as guilt, friendship and feeling part of the family. Similar issues have also been raised by a range of other commentators, including some trade unions, who have voiced concerns about the potential for poor employment practices (see, for example, Lombard, 2008; see also Scourfield, 2005a for a broader discussion of possible workforce implications).

In response, disabled researchers such as Morris (1997) have emphasised that we should not be treating disabled people receiving direct payments any differently from other groups receiving state support. Thus, the majority of disabled employers probably do not pay cash-in-hand, and even those that do are probably no different from many non-disabled people who purchase services such as cleaning and childminding on an informal basis. In many ways, therefore, the receipt of direct payments is little different from the receipt of child benefit:

> How many people pay someone to do their housework, and how many pay cash in hand? Those of us who do so may think of ourselves as good employers: we may pay at or above the local 'going rate', some of us may pay sick pay, bank holidays and holidays (I suspect more will not), but most of us don't deduct tax and national insurance or pay the employers' national insurance contribution. In fact, most of us would find it hard to get a cleaner if we insisted on anything other than a 'cash in hand' relationship. Does this mean that we are exploiting these low-paid women? ... The child benefit system is ... a system of cash payments made to individuals. I wonder how many mothers spend their child benefit in parts of the informal economy or on goods and services in the formal economy made or delivered by low-paid workers. Yet presumably Clare Ungerson would not wish to use this to question the value of the child benefit system. (Morris, 1997, pp 58-60)

For Morris, direct payments represent an opportunity to break down the stereotypes that disabled people have traditionally faced and establish their status as citizens, able to use cash payments in order to do what they want rather than what professional workers think they want. As a result, Morris feels that social researchers have a moral responsibility to collaborate with what she sees as a civil rights movement concerned with people's right to choice and control over their own lives. While both arguments (Morris's and Ungerson's) are persuasive, a way forward would surely seem to lie in the findings of Zarb and Nadash (1994): that many disabled people would want to pay higher wages if they received higher payments. Ultimately, the risk of exploiting women may lie not so much in the concept of direct payments itself, as in the way that many schemes are operationalised, restrictions on employing family members and the inadequate levels of payments that may sometimes be made.

More recently, a fascinating study commissioned by Skills for Care has started to shed light on the employment conditions of personal assistants and the workforce implications of direct payments (IFF Research, 2008). Based on interviews with 526 direct payment employers, a survey of 486 PAs and a more detailed telephone survey with 100 of the participating PAs, the study provides an important overview of a long-neglected issue. However, the results were controversial (see Box 7.11). As in previous studies, direct payment recipients reported high levels of satisfaction, and those with experience of directly provided services were clear that direct payments were superior. When the study was reported in the trade press, however, the focus tended to be on a small section of the report to do with training – only 7% of direct payment recipients had organised formal training for their staff, and this prompted debates about the extent to which disabled people were acting as good employers. What is staggering about the research, however, was the level of satisfaction reported by PAs. Overall, 95% of PAs were satisfied with their role (with only 1% quite unhappy and the rest neither happy nor unhappy), and 90% felt appreciated in their role either most of the time or frequently (IFF Research, 2008, pp 93-5). While these figures seem high for any job, they seem astounding in a role that is often low paid, unglamorous and emotionally and physically difficult. Moreover, on closer inspection, there are similar themes from other (albeit very small) studies – including some of Ungerson's own work, where some PAs express significant satisfaction with their work (see also Leece, 2006b). Overall, it appears as though PAs may have worse terms and conditions than local authority home carers, but may be happier, less stressed and attracted at least in part by the flexibility of the role. Quite how we have managed as a system to turn this into bad news is, at first glance, unclear. While these issues are likely to remain controversial, we believe that direct payments offer the possibility of a more satisfying, meaningful and productive relationship between the employee and their employer, and that this may be behind the high levels of satisfaction reported above. While this way of working does blur boundaries and may be problematic if things go wrong, it still seems much more positive than negative to us.

Box 7.11: The experience of employers and PAs

In 2008, a study of the workforce implications of direct payments found that:

- 79% of direct payment recipients were very satisfied with the support they were receiving, and 89% trust their PA completely. Both results compare very favourably to people's experiences of directly provided services, which were sometimes very negative.
- Direct payments were felt by the researchers to lead to better-quality and more reliable support, with fewer problems and fewer incidences of potential abuse than with direct services.
- Although being an employer was daunting for some, the majority did not feel like this (and people were happier with being an employer the longer they had been doing it, suggesting that experience can help to build confidence).
- Most people (66%) could find an appropriate PA quickly – but those who reported problems cited issues such as a low number of applicants, poor attitudes, not being willing to work the hours needed and/or not having the right personality.
- There are an estimated 76,000 people working as PAs in England, 87% of whom are women. One-third of PAs had no previous paid employment providing social care, so it seems likely that direct payments have encouraged a significant number of new people into the social care workforce.
- 95% of PAs were happy with their role and 90% felt appreciated most of the time or frequently. However, some were concerned about low pay (32%) and working more hours than they would ideally like (18%).
- Only 7% of employers had paid or arranged for training for PAs, although 19% provided training on the job themselves. The researchers concluded that some of this may be to do with a potential underfunding of direct payments, and many direct payment recipients were prepared to arrange training if this was properly funded.
- Direct payment recipients tended to emphasise personal factors (such as having a friendly attitude, being willing to work the hours required, adapting to the employer's individual needs etc) more than previous skills and experience.
- 79% of employers would find a register of care workers useful, but only 46% thought it should be compulsory. When asked a second question, 71% would like to retain the right to employ someone not on the register. Among PAs, 87% thought registration was a good idea.

(IFF Research, 2008)

With the move to a new system of self-directed support, many of these issues are arguably easier to reconcile. In particular, there are two key issues:

- The resource allocation system developed by in Control provides something of a compromise. While the RAS does take the level of family support into account when allocating resources, it does not penalise people for having access to families in the same way as the old system. Thus, someone without any family support will get more resources than someone with the same needs and plenty of family support – but the latter will still be entitled to more assistance than they might have done under current eligibility criteria.

- By letting people know how much money is available to meet their needs, the individual can now decide how they want this money spent on their behalf, whether it be via private/voluntary/public services, via friends and family and/ or via something that does not look like 'services' or 'support' at all. While this does not totally remove some of the issues described above, it gives individuals and families much more space to decide upon the types of relationship they want to have with each other (and leaves social care workers and the state out of this complex and sensitive territory). Although social workers still have a role to play in ensuring needs are met and in ensuring people are safe in situations where adult protection concerns apply, the move to personal budgets seems to simplify much of the previous debate by leaving much more to individual choice, preference and circumstances.

Risk

As pressure for direct payments mounted, a key feature of the government's initial refusal to implement such a scheme was the argument that making cash payments to disabled service users would leave them at risk. This was rejected by disabled campaigners (who argued that they were already at risk from substandard local authority services), and ultimately defeated. However, even after the successful implementation of direct payments, concerns about risk have continued to surface (Burrows, 2001; George, 2001) and do raise doubts about direct payments as currently conceptualised.

In most of the literature, the issue of risk is either downplayed or rejected outright. In a Department of Health (1998a) promotional video, one commentator is adamant that the risk associated with direct payments is minimal and that taking risks is a central feature of being in control of one's own services. A similar argument is also put forward by NCIL, who emphasise that taking risks is an important citizen right and that the empowerment offered by direct payments can actually reduce risks by making people more in control of their lives (see Box 7.12). Elsewhere, there is evidence to suggest that some local authorities have responded to perceived risk by adopting very strict and rigid policies that deter potential direct payment recipients and undermine the flexibility that this way of working is meant to deliver (see, for example, CSCI, 2004). This seems to be particularly the case when designing audit and reporting processes, which can sometimes be over-prescriptive and disproportionate to risk (CSCI, 2004).

Box 7.12 Risk versus empowerment

Protection from abuse is linked to empowerment in that it is the common experience of disabled people that the more we are in control of our lives, and the support we need to lead them, the less likely we are to find ourselves in abusive situations. It must be recognised that historically, disabled people's freedom of movement, choice and control has been regularly denied or curtailed in the name of 'safety' ... Disabled people must be given the same rights to take risks as all citizens.

(NCIL, 1999, pp 4, 8)

Although risk should not undermine direct payments, this is an issue that needs to be addressed (particularly if frontline staff and the general public are to feel comfortable with this way of working). While organisations such as NCIL are correct to suggest that risk has traditionally been used to restrict disabled people's liberties, this does not mean that risk can be ignored or that action to increase safety should be overlooked. As a practical illustration of the risks which employing a PA can entail, Vasey's (2000) *Rough guide to managing personal assistants* describes a number of situations in which PA users have found themselves employing exploitative or dishonest workers (see also Box 7.13 for a more extreme example).

Box 7.13: Dialling 999

In the October 2000 edition of the BCODP *Personal Assistants Users' Newsletter*, one woman described how her PA arrived for an evening shift drunk. The PA had been in the woman's employment for 11 months without having a day off or being late once, and said that her drunkenness was due to domestic pressures. Although the woman wanted to give her PA the benefit of the doubt, it soon became apparent that the PA was so drunk that it would be dangerous for her to assist the woman. When the woman tried to send her away, however, the PA became abusive and refused to leave the woman's house. When the woman tried to phone a friend, the PA tried to wrestle the telephone off her. After the woman's friend had called the police the PA eventually left. Since the woman had placed a clause in her contract that PAs can be instantly dismissed if they arrive for work under the influence of alcohol or drugs, she was able to terminate the PA's employment immediately.

(Bailey, 2000)

As part of its modernisation programme for public services, the New Labour government issued a White Paper emphasising the need to protect 'vulnerable people' from abuse and to change the way that social services are provided and regulated:

The present regulatory arrangements are incomplete and patchy, and the Government will replace them with a system that is modern, independent and dependable. Taken together with the establishment of the General Social Care Council [to regulate the training and conduct of social care workers], these reforms will put in place new systems for ensuring that when people receive care it is safe and of high quality ... and that the staff on whom they rely have the training, skills and standards that are necessary for the work they do. (DH, 1998b, p 64)

In pursuit of these aims, the government has introduced a range of measures to ensure that care staff are appropriately regulated, inspected and checked for previous criminal activity. While commentators such as NCIL have welcomed many of these policies, they have emphasised that disabled people should be allowed to take risks on a par with non-disabled people and that greater regulation should not restrict the rights of disabled people to employ PAs of their choice, regardless of training or registration (NCIL, 1999). Thus, direct payments seem to raise something of a dilemma in which safeguarding disabled people against abuse has to be balanced against the right of individuals to exercise choice and control over their own lives (see DH, 2008i for a recent consultation). Although this may prove a difficult balance to achieve, there are three key issues to highlight:

- One possible solution may be for local authorities and central government to ensure that there is adequate funding available for support mechanisms so that PA users can consider issues of risk in advance and develop preventative strategies. With the correct support, disabled people beginning to receive direct payments can adopt employment practices that minimise risk (such as not giving out personal contact details in advertisements, asking appropriate questions at interviews, following up references and so on). When problems arise, direct payment recipients could share their experiences and develop their own solutions through peer support.
- Local authorities should make sure that the necessary mechanisms are in place for direct payment recipients to design support that is safe (for example, by ensuring that people can make Criminal Record Bureau (CRB) checks if they wish). However, this is different from insisting that all PAs *must* be CRB-checked (or that people cannot employ people of their choosing), which arguably runs counter to the spirit of the choice and control at the heart of direct payments.
- Provided that sensible precautions are taken, it is difficult to see how receiving direct payments could be any more risky than receiving direct services. In Box 7.13 the disabled person would have been just as vulnerable to physical assault had a local authority employee arrived drunk as she was with a PA that she employed herself. In this particular case, the PA had worked for the woman for 11 months, had shown herself to be reliable and was presumably a trusted worker. As a result, the fact that the PA was employed through a direct payment

rather than by the local authority or a private agency seems to be irrelevant, and this incident could presumably have occurred just as easily if the woman was receiving directly provided services.

Despite this, concerns about risk have continued to be expressed as direct payments have spread and as personal budgets have been developed. Essentially, a range of different commentators remain concerned that this way of working could expose individual service users, often deemed to be 'vulnerable', to risk of financial exploitation or of designing support that leaves their needs unmet (see, for example, Henwood and Hudson, 2007b, pp 48-52; Ahmed, 2008; Samuel, 2008). Certainly, evidence to date suggests that much more needs to be done in order for current adult protection processes to engage fully with the personalisation agenda (see, for example, Glendinning et al, 2008; Manthorpe et al, 2008b). This is a complex issue – but we remain convinced that it is possible to design systems of self-directed support in which issues of risk can be appropriately managed and reduced as much as is possible. As the director-general for Social Care has commented: "I believe we have conflated safety and quality in our thinking over the past few years and the debate about quality [of service] has played second fiddle to the debate about safety. I think we need to square that off in some way" (quoted in Brindle, 2008b).

For us, one of the limitations of the current system is that it assumes that most people are either untrustworthy or incapable, and thus is overly bureaucratic and cumbersome. By shifting to a system where we assume that most people are capable and can be trusted, we are then able to focus scarce resources on the small number of cases where this may not be true (for example, where there are concerns about adult protection). By supporting people to exercise greater choice and control, we arguably put them at less risk of abuse – because they are more confident, have more community links and are better able to recognise and respond to potential abuse when it occurs. Finally, we also believe that new ways of working are often subject to greater scrutiny than current approaches, with the result that we criticise the 'new' without ever really subjecting the 'old' to the same standards. Thus, as one person remarked in Henwood and Hudson's (2007b, p 51) study: "we don't worry about all the money we waste on crap institutional provision, but yet we will worry about giving someone £20!"

'Offloading troublemakers'

Although there is little direct evidence, there is a danger that 'difficult' service users may be encouraged to receive direct payments so that local authority services do not have to have ongoing contact with them. In this scenario, 'difficult' is often a shorthand term to refer to potentially violent or verbally/sexually abusive users, and the suggestion is that some authorities may be tempted to 'offload' such 'troublemakers'. Of course, it was precisely for this reason that disabled people welcomed the emphasis of the 1996 Community Care (Direct Payments) Act and subsequent guidance on disabled people being 'willing' to receive payments – a requirement that should stop local authorities from making payments to alleged 'troublemakers' without their consent. However, the example cited in Box 7.14 does suggest that at least one local authority may have been relatively proactive in recommending direct payments for service users it feels are a threat to its own staff. Although this must remain conjecture without further research, it does raise questions about the possible use and abuse of direct payments. With the development of personal budgets, this probably becomes less of an issue, since self-directed support transforms the system as a whole and may therefore be perceived as less of a 'bolt-on' than was the case with direct payments in some areas of the country.

Box 7.14: 'Offloading troublemakers'

In one local authority, the social services department found it difficult to reconcile the rights of service users with the health and safety of its staff. Where users are deemed to be violent and aggressive, the department is very aware that it has a duty to meet the needs of users while at the same time protecting its employees. In such a situation, legal advice suggested that the department could try to discharge its responsibilities by purchasing care from a private agency. If private care was not available for any particular reason, legal advisors recommended that the social services department considered direct payments as a means of ensuring that an appropriate service is provided to the individual service user without jeopardising the safety of workers or exposing them to unacceptable verbal abuse. This seems to be an abuse of the concept of direct payments, which should be based on the empowerment of disabled people and the enhancement of user choice and control, not on attempts by social services departments to 'offload troublemakers'.

Practical challenges and support mechanisms

Managing direct payments is not easy and recipients face a number of practical challenges to overcome, including:

- employment legislation
- tax and National Insurance
- accounting
- recruitment
- miscellaneous issues such as arranging cover and the training/support needs of PAs.

Although many of these issues are dealt with in much greater detail in the practical resources listed at the end of this chapter, it is important that service users and their social workers are aware of the practical challenges that direct payments can raise and are clear about the way in which these challenges are to be overcome. Unless these issues are carefully considered, the result can be a situation in which service users unused to managing their own payments may be left to struggle on alone without adequate support. At best, this will be stressful for the individuals concerned and may prejudice them against direct payments in the future. At worst, it could lead to a breakdown in care arrangements, with potential financial and legal implications for the service user and/or their social services department. Certainly the alleged complexity of direct payments is something that some people (particularly, the evidence suggests, older people and people with mental health problems) may find daunting – at least at first. Managing a payment and (possibly) employing staff are new skills for many people, and most of us would need significant information, training and support to take on these roles. While some studies suggest that such complexity can be perceived as a barrier (see, for example, Help the Aged, 2002; Ridley and Jones, 2003; CSCI, 2004), others argue that people are put off by difficulties in accessing direct payments – not a lack of desire to try this way of working (see, for example, Stainton and Boyce, 2004). Moreover, there is also evidence to suggest that many people do not perceive direct payments to be overly daunting, particularly when they have had a chance to build their confidence over time (see, for example, IFF Research, 2008). Overall, there are two key ways in which the perceived complexity of direct payments can be reduced:

- Local authorities should ensure that the procedures they put in place are no more onerous than is absolutely essential. In some areas, direct payments seem so difficult and bureaucratic to access that numbers remain low. While this may be to do with the culture of individual local authorities, it can sometimes be the result of a deliberate attempt to pay lip-service to the concept of direct payments whilst also restricting access.
- The success of direct payments depends significantly on access to support – particularly peer support (see below for further discussion).

Throughout the literature, the need for adequate support structures is an almost constant theme (see, for example, Simpson with Campbell, 1996; Dunnicliff, 1999; Hasler et al, 1999; Dawson, 2000; Glendinning et al, 2000c; Leece, 2000), and the absence of such support can be a major barrier that is difficult to overcome (Witcher et al, 2000). This was recognised by the Department of Health (1997, 2000a) from the very beginning, and has also been highlighted through evaluations undertaken by the Social Services Inspectorate (Fruin, 2000, p 16). In six authorities where direct payments were in place, users were found to need assistance in starting to receive payments and managing them on an ongoing basis, both in terms of administrative issues and psychological support. This was sometimes provided by a local disability organisation, by other voluntary agencies or by specialist social services staff, although there was no evidence of peer support or self-help groups in any of the authorities concerned. However, nowhere is the importance of adequate support more apparent than in PSI/NCIL guidance for local authorities seeking to implement and manage direct payment schemes (Hasler et al, 1999). To emphasise the centrality of effective support mechanisms, the guidance notes that in areas where disabled people are successfully managing direct payments, there is nearly always an established support service to assist them:

> Support services are perhaps the most fundamental part of a successful direct payments scheme. The purpose of direct payments support services is to ensure that adequate advice, information and support are available to disabled people so that they may feel confident to undertake the complexities of using direct payments to employ and manage their own staff. Such support also ensures that individuals using a direct payment are operating legally and efficiently. The support service has to be properly funded and responsive. (Hasler et al, 1999, p 11)

After the Community Care (Direct Payments) Act came into force in 1997, more and more schemes have developed, often provided by Centres for Independent Living, and disabled people have proved extremely capable of rising to the practical issues that direct payments raise. Although managing direct payments may be difficult at times, this should not stop disabled people from attempting to do so. Above all, this is the resounding message that emerges from NCIL's *Rough guide to managing personal assistants*:

> Direct Payments really represent a golden opportunity for disabled people. They are the means by which we close the chapter of disability history called 'Institutions' and move on to the part of the story where we get a crack at living just like everybody else. With the right facilitation any disabled person, whatever their impairment, can take control and be free to get on with life. It all seems so simple, but of course like so many things it is just a bit more complicated than it first appears … We are all wrestling with the same issues. Everybody finds it an effort, at least some of the time, because it is basically management work that we are involved in here and management is rarely easy. In business, managers are paid large sums and then often do it badly. We get paid nothing and cannot afford to fail, not only because our living arrangements will instantly be in tatters, but because there is a view widely held by the powers that be that we are not up to the job. This book [The rough guide] is a celebration of disabled people's undoubted ability to get on with a difficult job in order to get a life. (Vasey, 2000, pp 7-8)

Although they may have different names, all support services should include four core features:

- peer support (so that disabled people can share information and experiences, develop practical solutions to problems and support each other);
- information (covering all aspects of independent living and direct payments, available in a range of formats and languages);
- advice and/or advocacy (to assist disabled people to manage their payments and find solutions to any problems);
- training (about independent living, recruiting staff, time management, building relationships with staff, legal responsibilities and administrative duties) (Hasler et al, 1999, pp 12-15).

In addition to this, some support schemes may offer a payroll service, employ staff on behalf of the service user and hold registers of PAs. More recent guidance from CIPFA (2007) also offers a helpful summary (see Box 7.15).

Box 7.15: CIPFA guidance regarding support services

Whatever approach local authorities decide to adopt locally, support should be available to cover the following areas as a minimum:

- support to help people think and plan creatively to make the best use of resources they have available;
- support to navigate the market place and choose goods and services to achieve outcomes;
- support to help people set up and maintain their support and manage their finances;
- support to help people troubleshoot problems and resolve difficulties with managing their support;
- help for people to participate fully in reviewing and refining their support plans to achieve outcomes;
- training for people to learn skills to plan and take control of meeting their support needs.

(CIPFA, 2007, pp 9-10)

Despite the undoubted need for adequate support, there is evidence to suggest that some direct payment recipients may not always receive the assistance they require to make their care packages work successfully. In two audits by the former Social Services Inspectorate, the local authorities concerned had attempted to identify disability organisations to take on a support role, but were unable to find any agencies available/willing to do so (Fruin, 2000, pp 16-17). Elsewhere, some support schemes have found it difficult to survive as a result of funding difficulties (Hasler et al, 1999, p 23), and some direct payments schemes are felt to be floundering because the local authority is using social workers to advise service users, rather than organisations of disabled people (McCurry, 1999).While some support is presumably better than none at all, there are concerns that many social workers are not trained in issues such as employment legislation or financial management and feel stressed about having to offer this support in addition to their normal case loads. Certainly, this is an issue that has been highlighted time and time again by organisations of disabled people, and one which has been re-emphasised following the various extensions of direct payments to new user groups:

> NCIL welcomes the extension of Direct Payments … but are very concerned that a budget has not been forthcoming to develop an infrastructure of support to new payment users. Currently, such support schemes are funded from existing Social Services budgets, which we are told are insufficient to meet the need of essential services, let alone new development. (NCIL, 1999, p 4)

More recently, a number of national surveys have continued to illustrate the patchy nature of support services. Thus, research by Barnes and Mercer (2006) suggests that many user-led Centres for Independent Living are finding it virtually impossible to provide the full range of support needed to achieve independent living, with some struggling to survive year on year. While there were many causes, the key difficulty was funding that was insufficient and short term. In the same way, a national survey of direct payment support schemes suggests that over 50% of all people receiving a direct payment are not covered by a support scheme (Davey et al, 2007a). While the reasons for this are not fully clear, possible explanations may be to do with the fact that people's need for support can sometimes be temporary, that people may be seeking other sources of assistance, that some people may not be able to access current services and/or that the support available varies so much by user group and by local authority. In addition to this, some authorities have seemingly been reluctant to fund appropriate support, whether due to political differences in the make-up of local councils, a desire to protect in-house services, a perception that there are insufficient local disabled people's organisations or a belief that many people are fully satisfied with existing services (Davey et al, 2007a). Even where authorities do seek to fund appropriate support, there can be additional problems due to unsophisticated commissioning arrangements, with payments to support organisations not always seeming to reflect the volume of people supported, the type of service provided or the levels of support offered to individuals (Davey et al, 2007a). To some extent, the future now looks slightly more positive following the initial example of the Direct Payments Development Fund (see Chapters Three and Four) and a more recent government commitment to create a national network of user-led organisations (Prime Minister's Strategy Unit, 2005). However, delivering this will be difficult and possibly expensive, as all the available evidence suggests that there is not enough support available and that some of the support that does exist is vulnerable.

With the advent of personal budgets, the need for support probably becomes more straightforward and more complex at the same time (if that is possible). With everyone receiving a personal budget able to play a greater role in planning their support, there is now a much broader range of choices with regard to how much control people want over the resources that are available to meet their needs (see Chapter Five for more detailed discussion). For those who want to control how their needs are met, but do not want to manage the practicalities of this themselves, the concept of self-directed support offers a new and exciting way forward. Of course, within this there will still be many people who want to receive at least part of their personal budget in the form of a direct payment – and these people in particular will need access to the same practical support as in the early days of direct payments. However, a system of self-directed support seems to point to a potential future where there is a much broader range of options available locally, and where people can choose which sort of support will be best for them – whether this be from a social worker, a family member, a service provider, a broker, a high street solicitor, a Centre for Independent Living or another source altogether. To us, this is both exciting and potentially liberating (for staff and service users alike), but also daunting – if the history of direct payments tells us just one thing, it is that failure to ensure that adequate support is available can set people up to fail and be a way of undermining the very choice and control that should be at the heart of this way of working.

Recruitment

For some direct payment recipients, recruiting staff can be a major source of difficulty and consternation. This is particularly the case in some rural areas (where population is sparse and the pool of potential workers small) and in areas of the country where wages are relatively high and direct payment recipients are not always able to pay competitive wages. While many disabled people are able to recruit PAs by word of mouth (Morris, 1993a, pp 128-30) and through informal social networks (Dawson, 1995, 2000), this can be an area of potential concern for some disabled people otherwise interested in using direct payments to employ their own care staff.

Prior to the 1996 Community Care (Direct Payments) Act, interviews with ILF recipients found that around one-quarter of participants reported difficulties recruiting carers (Kestenbaum, 1993b). In London, one 66-year-old woman with rheumatoid arthritis spent months trying to recruit someone to help with domestic care, advertising in shops and church magazines: "It was an absolute nightmare. Everybody [was] very understanding but nothing [was] forthcoming. I couldn't understand it. I couldn't believe there wasn't someone within the area that would fit in, whether morning, afternoon or evening" (Kestenbaum, 1993b, p 12).

While trying to recruit workers, some of the disabled people questioned felt that they had been unsupported by their social workers and many were reluctant to advertise too widely for fear of publicising their vulnerability and attracting 'the wrong sort of person' (Kestenbaum, 1993b, p 17). Difficulties recruiting staff were also reported in research conducted by the PSI, with 43% of payment recipients identifying problems in finding suitable workers:

> "I think any employer finds it difficult choosing the right person to come and do the job."

> "I am having difficulty recruiting staff at the moment. But I guess that's something I am always going to have difficulties with – recruiting staff. I wish there was somewhere you could phone up and say, have you got anyone on your books at the moment who is looking for a position? If there is, I don't know of it."

> "The most difficult thing is recruiting staff. I would just love to see a system where you could phone up somewhere and say, have you got something that might be suitable."

(Zarb and Nadash, 1994, pp 45, 108)

After the legalisation of direct payments in 1996/97, recruitment difficulties have often persisted. In Staffordshire, two out of five direct payment recipients who responded to an evaluation of a pilot project wished to employ PAs but were unable to recruit suitable workers (Leece, 2000). In Scotland, nine out of the 12 authorities where direct payment recipients employed their own staff or used agencies reported that service users experienced difficulties identifying an appropriate individual or agency to meet their care needs. Key issues included low levels of pay, recruiting people of a particular age/gender, recruiting people to work a small number of hours or split shifts, and finding PAs with the right characteristics for individual recipients (Witcher et al, 2000, para 2.44). In Norfolk, direct payment recipients sometimes encountered difficulties with people not turning up to interviews and found it hard to attract people who were sufficiently flexible (Dawson, 2000). Some disabled people also found that they had a high turnover of workers (for example, where the worker was a student and left university), having to go through the difficult process of recruiting workers again and again. Elsewhere, disabled employers may find that they have too few care hours to recruit workers on a full-time basis, that there is an insufficient supply of suitably qualified workers and that it is difficult to attract quality applicants because of low pay (Leece, 2000; Valios, 2000). Where responses to advertisements are low, disabled people may feel that it is unrealistic to ask for minimum qualifications or experience and find themselves lowering their initial expectations about the quality of worker they are able to employ (Glendinning et al, 2000a).

Once a group of potential employees have been identified, disabled people need to ensure that they select the most appropriate person for the job. For some disabled people, this can often depend on the personality of the individuals involved rather than on previous skills or experience. Since PAs will be coming into people's homes and may be providing a range of intimate personal care tasks, it is important that the disabled employer chooses staff that they will be able to trust and get on with. Certainly, this was a key finding of an evaluation of the experience of ILF recipients:

"The chemistry has to be right."

"You have to think – are they physically capable of doing the care? Are you going to get on with them? Are they going to fit in with your family? – they'll be in your house seven days a week. You have to have some sort of rapport going. It doesn't work otherwise."

"It comes quite hard to both of us to have someone else intruding in your own very private life and home. That's why it's very important to get the right person."

(Kestenbaum, 1993b, p 12)

Over time, the importance of reliable, trustworthy PAs capable of fitting into the disabled person's lifestyle has been re-emphasised in a number of research studies and first-hand accounts by disabled people (see, for example, Lakey, 1994; Zarb and Nadash, 1994; Glendinning et al, 2000c; Vasey, 2000). Despite the importance of recruiting suitable workers, finding such individuals can be difficult, and disabled employers often find that they do not always make the right choice when interviewing potential staff, or that the 'right' person simply does not come forward. In one study, one disabled person felt that "for 99 frogs there was one prince" (quoted in Glendinning et al, 2000c, p 206). Nowhere is the difficulty of recruiting staff more clearly illustrated than in NCIL's *Rough guide to managing personal assistants* (Vasey, 2000), which provides numerous examples of what can go wrong when recruiting, interviewing and selecting PAs (see Box 7.16).

Although direct payments have now been established for some time, difficulties recruiting PAs nevertheless remain an ongoing issue (see, for example, CSCI, 2004; Davey et al, 2007b), although this can vary – in a 2008 study of direct payment recipients in 16 local authorities, 66% of people were able to find an appropriate PA quickly (IFF Research, 2008, p 56). In light of this, some disabled people have expressed a desire to employ household members and relatives as PAs (see, for example, Elkington, 1996; Age Concern, 1998; Leece, 2000) – something that was prohibited by initial direct payments guidance (see Chapters Three and Four). Whether or not direct payments should be used to employ family members is a complex issue. On the one hand, there may be a risk of family members exploiting their disabled relatives or of informal carers being pressured to give up work (DH/Scottish Office/Welsh Office/Northern Ireland Office, 1996). At the same time, many European payment schemes permit the employment of close relatives (Halloran, 1998; Schunk, 1998; Pijl, 2000), as does the ILF (as long as the relative does not live in the same household) (ILF, 2000). Preventing the employment of family members also limits the choice that direct payments are supposed to promote (Age Concern, 1998), and the evidence to date suggests that direct payments may make some disabled people more comfortable about asking their families for things to be done, giving them an opportunity to give something back to people who have previously provided unpaid care (Stainton and Boyce, 2004). This is particularly problematic for people with progressive or fluctuating conditions, who can experience a sudden deterioration and may want their family to care for them during one-off crisis periods or at short notice (NCIL, ndc).

Box 7.16: Recruiting PAs

"I will never forget my feeling of total amazement when an applicant turned up on my doorstep with her Italian husband and her mother. The reason given for this was that they wanted to check me out to make sure I was genuine ... Needless to say, she did not get the job."

"Peter arrived one Saturday afternoon for an interview. A pleasant young man, immaculately dressed. ... After two hours and cups of tea we were still talking. ... He was asked to start the following Saturday and has never been seen from that day to this."

"I used to employ PAs directly myself, but ... the standard of applicants was poor. Most who applied were women who could not get shop or factory work – generally because of unreliability."

"Being a PA user is not something I'm comfortable with or very good at. I struggle with the business of recruiting ... I am getting better as I have learnt from some bad experiences."

One PA user recalls some of the responses given to him in interviews:

"I've healed all my clients, usually in the first week."

"So I don't have to nag you then about taking your tablets and eating your food?"

(Vasey, 2000, pp 19-21, 26-7)

While there are no easy answers to this dilemma, more recent guidance and the advent of self-directed support seem to have simplified (if not entirely resolved) many of these tensions. Under current approaches, there is scope for close relatives living in the same household to be employed using direct payments under *exceptional circumstances*, and this may well prove to be a helpful compromise (although the exact meaning of the guidance may benefit from being clarified).

Certainly the emerging evidence suggests that this change has been helpful (particularly for older people and people from minority ethnic communities), in spite of some concerns persisting about the extent to which employing relatives might put pressure on people to accept family members as employees or 'open the floodgates' in terms of payment to informal carers (see, for example, Vick et al, 2006, pp 36-7). With personal budgets, moreover, there is now much greater flexibility as to how people make use of the money available to meet their needs – with the emphasis shifting away from the detail of how people use these resources to whether or not needs are met and the outcomes that are achieved. In this way, self-directed support offers a helpful overarching framework that seems better able to respond to the individual needs and circumstances of people with different types of family, social and community life.

SUMMARY

Despite the positives emphasised in Chapter Six, direct payments and personal budgets (as currently conceived) may also bring a number of disadvantages that need to be acknowledged and overcome. Introduced by a Conservative government committed to rolling back the frontiers of the welfare state, there is a potential contradiction between the emphasis of the Independent Living Movement on choice and control, and an initial (and perhaps ongoing?) government agenda influenced by flawed notions of consumerism. Implemented against the backdrop of attempts to curtail public expenditure, direct payment schemes may not have received sufficient funding, resulting in financial difficulties for some local authorities, inadequate payments and support arrangements, low wages for PAs and the potential exploitation of women. Following the advent of personal budgets, moreover, other difficulties have included the need to balance empowerment against risk, the danger of local authorities viewing direct payments in particular as a means of 'offloading troublemakers' and the perceived danger that these ways of working may exacerbate existing inequalities.

Throughout, a key barrier has been the attitude and practices of frontline social workers, who occupy an important gatekeeping role and can sometimes hinder rather than facilitate the dissemination of information about direct payments and personal budgets. All this is not to suggest that direct payments or personal budgets are a 'bad thing' – on the contrary, the authors are firm supporters and believe that the advantages of direct payments and personal budgets far outweigh the potential disadvantages. However, it is important that some of the negative features of the way in which direct payments and personal budgets are currently operationalised are identified and challenged so that disabled people are adequately informed about the options open to them before they make decisions about their care arrangements and so that the system can be improved. As a result, Box 7.17 sets out some common concerns about both direct payments and personal budgets, providing a short summary of potential answers to these issues from research, policy and practice to date.

Box 7.17: Common concerns

- *Some user groups don't want choice and control – they just want a good service*: while this might be true of some people, there are five key responses.
    - Choice and control are not just ends in themselves, but can sometimes be powerful mechanisms with which to get a 'good service'.
    - As this chapter has demonstrated, local authorities have a key role to play in making their systems as simple as possible and proportionate to risk.
    - Many people do actually want choice and control – but can be put off by how the concepts of direct payments/personal budgets are introduced.
    - The availability of independent support (especially peer support) is an important way of reducing any potential 'hassle'.
    - The advent of self-directed support means that people can still enjoy choice and control without having to manage money/staff themselves (if they don't want to).
- *Direct payments and personal budgets threaten the professional expertise of social workers*: while this is in some ways an understandable reaction, direct payments and personal budgets have the potential to free social workers up to focus on people who most need their support and to reconnect with the value base and core principles of the profession.
- *Direct payments and personal budgets exploit families by expecting them to do the state's job for it*: families already coordinate a large amount of care and are arguably already 'exploited' by some services. Direct payments/personal budgets give the person and their family much more choice and control, allowing them to make decisions about the types of relationship they want with each other. Thus, if people want to keep family as family or only to be supported by close family members, then direct payments/personal budgets can make either possible.
- *Direct payments and personal budgets place too much risk on the individual*: there is a real issue here about what is an appropriate level of risk, about who decides and about whose risk it is anyway. In practice, many service users experience current approaches to risk as profoundly disempowering. With direct payments/personal budgets, risk does not go away, but there is scope to share risk between the person and the system, and to plan more effectively to reduce risk.
- *This is just about privatisation by the back door*: this is about citizenship not about debates about public vs private. People with access to their own resources can already choose (at least in principle) from a range of services – in one way, direct payments/personal budgets 'nationalise' such choices for everyone. With the development of personal budgets, there is nothing to stop a person from receiving all their support from directly provided public services. The key question for providers to ask is: if people could genuinely choose (and had access to funding to make this choice real), why would they choose my service? Service providers that can answer this question easily are likely to prosper in a system of self-directed support; those that can't will struggle.
- *If you give people the money they might misspend it*: all the evidence to date suggests that this is not the case. Often, it is the person with the need for support who has

the biggest vested interest in using available resources as effectively and innovatively as possible. Where someone is not spending money in a way that meets their needs, there is scope to work in a different way (for example, making a personal budget available but managing it via a professional worker rather than a direct payment).

- *This won't work for people whose needs might change suddenly*: on the contrary, directly provided services tend not to work well for people with fluctuating conditions as they are too inflexible to respond quickly. In contrast, direct payments/personal budgets allow people to build up resources when they need less support in order to use when they become particularly unwell. The emphasis also shifts from assessment to support planning/review, thereby allowing people to plan ahead better/learn from periods of intensive needs.

IMPLICATIONS FOR POLICY AND PRACTICE

- Direct payments and personal budgets can appeal across the political spectrum, and there is some evidence to suggest that different groups may promote these ways of working for different reasons. In the short term, this has built momentum for change; in the longer term it could lead to tensions if the interests of the different groups diverge.
- Frontline workers have a key role to play in the development of direct payments/ personal budgets – either in promoting these ways of working or in restricting access.
- Calculating the appropriate level of direct payments is crucial if people are to be able to meet their needs and to be good employers. Making inadequate payments sets people up to fail.
- Direct payments and personal budgets change the nature of the relationship between the disabled person and the workers who may meet their needs (in a way that can be liberating but which is also contentious).
- Critics of direct payments/personal budgets often say that they are concerned about risk. While risk does not go away, direct payments/personal budgets enable better support/contingency planning. Ultimately, people may be less at risk if they have greater choice and control over their lives.
- Although direct payments and personal budgets are potentially very empowering, there is scope for some local authorities to promote them for their own local reasons – including for reasons that are not within the spirit of this way of working.
- Direct payments in particular have a series of practical implications in terms of managing and administering resources. This can become a barrier to access if systems are unnecessarily restrictive/onerous or if appropriate support is not available.
- Linked to this, access to practical support (especially peer support) is a crucial component of the success of many direct payment schemes. This is also true of personal budgets, although self-directed support arguably allows the individual to choose from a broader range of support mechanisms.

Recommended reading and useful websites

Of all the critiques of direct payments and the discussions of differences between civil rights and consumerist approaches, Spandler's (2004) review provides one of the most helpful summaries. For more general discussion of issues to do with rights, empowerment and consumerism, a range of different views and contributions are provided by Ellis (2005), Ferguson (2007), Rummery (2006), Sapey and Pearson (2004), Stainton (2002, 2005), Riddell et al (2005) and Scourfield (2007).

Ellis's (2007) study of frontline assessment and care management practice provides a fascinating insight into the pressures practitioners face, the way they ration access to direct payments and the justifications they put forward to legitimise this practice.

Simon Duffy's (2007) paper on 'Care management and self-directed support' is a concise and helpful summary of the implications of personal budgets for care management and professional social work.

For a discussion of the financial implications of direct payments/personal budgets, see the Audit Commission (2006) and Duffy and Waters' (2008) 'The economics of self-directed support'. Practical guidance is also available from CIPFA (2007).

Julian Le Grand (2007) reviews different strategies for public sector reform, including discussion of issues of equity.

For discussions on the workforce, see the debate between Jenny Morris (1997) and Clare Ungerson (1997). More recent sources include:

- ongoing research into this topic by Ungerson (1999, 2003, 2004, 2006; Ungerson and Yeandle, 2007);
- a study on the workforce implications of direct payments commissioned by Skills for Care (IFF Research, 2008). Skills for Care have also produced a training code for individuals buying training for their own staff (Skills for Care, nd).

Sources of practical support include the National Centre for Independent Living (www.ncil.org.uk), who also provide an online directory of local support services.

For a national overview of the state of play with regard to the provision of support services, see:

- Barnes and Mercer's (2006) *Independent futures*;
- Davey et al's (2007a) survey of direct payment support schemes.

For policy commitments on the funding of the user-led organisations, see the Prime Minister's Strategy Unit (2005) report on *Improving the Life Chances of Disabled People*. Further information is also available via the Office for Disability Issues (www.officefordisability.gov.uk).

Reflective exercises

1. Re-read the key social care policy documents that commit to a policy of direct payments and personal budgets (see Chapters Three and Five) – to what extent do these reflect a consumer model and to what extent do they reflect a commitment to citizenship? Do they sometimes do both at the same time? What words are used to justify these policies, and does the reality of the policy commitment match the rhetoric of the policy document?

   If possible, talk to your team manager and other senior people within the social care directorate – what are their motivations for promoting direct payments and personal budgets? Are all these motives fully compatible and consistent?

2. At a team meeting, raise the issue of the role of frontline staff in rationing access to direct payments and personal budgets. What information do you give out? How enthusiastic are colleagues about these ways of working? Where there seems to be resistance, how is this rationalised and expressed? What can you do personally to promote direct payments and personal budgets with the people you meet?

3. On a blank piece of paper, list the reasons why you decided to work in social care (or, if you don't work in social care, why someone might make this choice). Compare this list to the potential advantages of direct payments and personal budgets set out in this book. For many people, the lists are often almost identical. Was this the case for you and, if so, what can you do to help colleagues to explore these issues for themselves?

4. How does your department calculate its direct payment rates, and when were they last reviewed and changed? What is this rate meant to include? How does this compare to private sector agencies and to in-house unit costs?

5. Reflect on the people who receive direct payments or have a personal budget within your team. Do they reflect fears that these ways of working will appeal only to articulate and well-educated service users? What can your team do to promote these options to everyone and to focus support on those who need it most?

6. Does your team, support service or local authority have any information about the people who work as personal assistants in your area? Do you know anything about who these people are or why they choose to do these jobs? If you work with a disabled person who employs their own staff, ask them about who they employ, how they recruited them, and what they think the person gets out of the role. Ask similar questions of colleagues from the in-house home care service – to what extent do the answers differ?

7. Reflecting on individuals with whom you work or have read about, write a list of the potential risks that direct payments and personal budgets might entail. Compare this with the risks that receiving direct services might entail. To what extent do the risks differ, and are they worth it (given the potential

outcomes of direct payments/personal budgets discussed in this book)? What would your colleagues say if you asked them? What would disabled people say?

8. Reflect on the section above about 'offloading troublemakers'. Are you aware of any situations from your practice or from the literature where a local authority has promoted direct payments as a means not of promoting choice and control, but to solve a problem on behalf of the authority? If this is an example from direct experience, what did you do/could you have done to challenge this?

9. What support services are available in your local area and how familiar are you with what they offer? Where you work in frontline practice, what information does your team have available to update itself on the support available and to communicate this to potential service users? If possible, visit your local support service to discuss the issues raised in this chapter.

10. Talk to your local support service and to direct payment recipients about their experiences of recruiting staff. What worked well/did not work so well, and what sources of support were available? What role could the local authority play in making this easier?

EIGHT

Conclusion – implications for community care

At their best, direct payments and personal budgets have the capacity to transform the lives of disabled people and to enrich the jobs of social care staff. Implemented after a sustained campaign by disabled people's organisations, direct payments are potentially revolutionary in terms of the opportunities they offer to enhance the choice, control, health and well-being of previously marginalised groups of disabled people. In some local authorities, direct payments have been implemented with enthusiasm, benefiting service users, improving satisfaction with care arrangements and leading to greater cost-efficiency. However, this has not always been the case, and some local authorities have been slow to recognise and capitalise on the advantages that direct payments offer. Often, patterns of implementation have been strongly affected by regional variations, with particular areas of the country dragging their heels and hindering progress. Early on in particular, little consideration seemed to have been given to the needs of user groups other than people with physical impairments; access to payments has often been denied to certain categories of people altogether (despite government guidance). While this is partly due to the initial wording and focus of legislation and official documentation, it is also the result of discriminatory attitudes and a failure to provide appropriate and accessible information to a range of user groups. Although their contribution was and continues to be significant, the fact remains that direct payments often felt like something bolted on to the current system and their capacity to transform the system as a whole was too often constrained.

More recently, the development of personal budgets has built on what was good about direct payments in order to create a new system of social care. Although it is still very early days, the emerging evidence is so positive that this way of working has now become a key part of the government's personalisation agenda and may even spread to other areas of the welfare state. Behind all the complexities debated in this book remain a small number of very simple but profound concepts and principles – staying true to these is likely to be the biggest challenge of all as we move forward (see below for further discussion).

Throughout this book, we have attempted to highlight the strengths and the limitations of direct payments and personal budgets, arguing that any potential shortcomings often tend to be the result of the way in which these concepts have been implemented, not necessarily of the concepts themselves. However, if we are to maximise the positive aspects of direct payments and personal budgets (and minimise any potential negatives), a number of changes will be required, both in policy and practice.

Practice

The attitude of frontline workers is crucial to the success or failure of direct payments and personal budgets. Disabled people currently rely on social workers and care staff for a great deal of information and cannot be expected to make informed choices without accurate and accessible advice about the options available to them. Evidence to date suggests that social workers play an important gatekeeping role, and that those people who receive direct payments/personal budgets often do so at least in part because of information and support provided by a social worker. At the same time, research also suggests that many practitioners may be either relatively uninformed about direct payments and personal budgets and/or suspicious about the implications for their work. In many cases, fears about an erosion of public services, about losing power and status, about workload implications and about the dangers of creating demands that cannot be met may be hindering the progress of direct payments and personal budgets. In this scenario, it is not disabled people making informed decisions to reject new ways of working, but their social workers effectively depriving them of access to direct payments and personal budgets by failing to provide support and information. If direct payments and personal budgets really are to become a central feature of mainstream social care, there needs to be much greater emphasis on training for frontline workers and on the provision of accessible information. Although we hope that this book goes some way towards promoting the concepts of direct payments and personal budgets, much more work will be required by social work trainers and educators to ensure that staff are appropriately trained, informed and have the right value base for the job they occupy. It will then be down to individual workers to ensure that the people with whom they work:

- are fully informed about the options available to them;
- have the opportunity to think and talk through the advantages and disadvantages of direct payments and personal budgets;
- have sufficient time to make a decision about the type of support they would like to receive;
- have access to peer support so that they can benefit from the experiences of other disabled people.

Overall, despite all the complexities, it is our firm belief that direct payments/personal budgets offer practitioners a new and extremely exciting way of working, empowering service users to be more in control of their own lives. If we get this right, this could be a way of helping workers to reconnect to the value base of the profession, and could free up scarce resources to focus on those most in need of support. Whether or not individual social workers are prepared to accept these challenges and changes is ultimately down to them.

Policy

In addition to changes in the training and attitudes of frontline workers, a number of policy measures will be required to promote direct payments and personal budgets, removing existing limitations while at the same time retaining the many advantages that these ways of working have to offer. Throughout, the key test will be the extent to which the system as a whole can hold on to the underlying value bases of direct payments and personal budgets, allowing them to remain sufficiently flexible to be effective and preventing the old system from reinventing itself. Ironically, neither direct payments nor personal budgets were at their most vulnerable when they began in humble circumstances as good ideas for future policy and practice, and started to spread from the bottom up. Instead, the biggest risk comes now that both are central features of national policy, and there seems a real danger that either/both could become incorporated into mainstream practice, but get watered down to such an extent that they lose most of their power and potential impact. As Dowson (2002, p 57, quoted in Spandler and Vick, 2006, p 113) has previously warned: 'Little by little, the necessary ingredients of IF [independent funding] will be omitted, weakened, re-defined, downgraded; until IF has become something that no longer poses a threat to the system.'

The history of community care is full of new developments that promised much during pilots, but failed to deliver because of the way in which they were implemented. The challenge for policy makers, managers, practitioners, service users and students alike is now to make sure that this does not happen again.

Joint NCIL/in Control statement

Our goal is Independent Living

Working in Partnership

Statement of Agreed Position and Actions

The National Centre for Independent Living (NCIL) and in Control have come together to share good practice and to state their jointly held view that:

- the goal for disabled people, whatever their age or impairment, is **Independent Living** – to have choice and control in how support needs are met;
- **Self-Directed Support** is the route to achieving Independent Living.

In this context the term 'disabled people' refers to all people with an impairment, whatever their age, and their families.

The principles of Independent Living

The phrase **Independent Living** first entered the English language during the 1970s following its adoption by disabled activists in the United States. Since then it has become an established term in the United Kingdom, across Europe, and in many other parts of the world. There is general agreement that the philosophy of Independent Living is founded on four principles:

- That all human life, regardless of the nature, complexity and/or severity of impairment is of equal worth.
- That anyone, whatever the nature, complexity and/or severity of their impairment, has the capacity to make choices and should be enabled to make those choices.
- That people who are disabled by societal responses to any form of accredited impairment – physical, sensory or cognitive – have the right to exercise control over their lives.
- That people with perceived impairments and labelled 'disabled' have the right to participate fully in all areas – economic, political and cultural – of mainstream community, living on a par with non-disabled peers.

From these principles it follows that, in promoting Independent Living, we are promoting the right of all disabled people to exercise choice and control over how their support and assistance needs are met – not only in health and social care but in all aspects of life.

Self-Directed Support

The route to achieving Independent Living is through Self-Directed Support.

In a rapidly changing social policy field it is inevitable that particular terms will be used in different ways. This inconsistency in use can lead to confusion and misunderstanding. Language is constantly evolving and to some extent reflects the motives of those using the term. For example, disabled people are more likely to use the term 'personal assistant' to refer to someone giving support because they reject the concept of care, which to them suggests a passive relationship of disabled people to their support. On the other hand, a family member may prefer the term 'carer' because they believe caring is the natural function of family members. Because of the potential for confusion, it is essential to clarify use of the term 'Self-Directed Support'.

'Self-Directed Support' is used here to denote any situation where support needs are being met through a system that allows the individual to have choice and control over how that support is met. The term 'personalisation' is also sometimes used to describe such situations – particularly by Government. However, the term 'personalisation' is not used here because of its common use in the so-called consumerist agenda, in which the standards of public service are increased through consumer choice. Self-Directed Support is about disabled people exercising their rights to determine their own lives with the clear goal of achieving Independent Living.

Self-Directed Support began, after a sustained campaign by disabled people, with the passing of the Community Care (Direct Payments) Act 1996. For the first time local authorities were granted the legal power to give a cash payment to disabled people with a physical or sensory impairment under the age of 65 in lieu of commissioned services. Since that time direct payments have been rolled out to all groups. They have made possible an improved quality of life because people are able to choose their support. Direct payments have also (arguably) much improved efficiency in the provision of social care, and have ensured that disabled people have a relationship with personal assistants that is rooted in dignity and respect.

Direct payments have created some problems; not because there is anything fundamentally wrong with the concept, but because of the way they have been implemented. Commissioning has continued to operate relatively unchanged with the result that local authorities still rely to a large extent on block contracts for service provision. Also, those people considered by the authority to be incapable of managing a direct payment have not been offered an alternative that would bring similar benefits. Finally, monitoring processes developed by local authorities have been onerous. All these factors have created barriers to the beneficial implementation of direct payments.

Partly to overcome these barriers in Control has developed a system of Self-Directed Support. This system involves setting personal budgets so that people know up front what funding they are entitled to for support. It also reduces restrictions on what the money can be spent on so that people can plan the creative use of their budget, meet their support needs in a way that makes sense to them and exercise their rights as citizens.

In 2006 the Department of Health (DH) began a project to pilot individual budgets in 13 local authority areas. In these pilots there are many similarities with in Control's system but also one significant difference – individual budgets in the DH pilot areas are attempting to integrate a number of funding streams alongside social care.

These systems of support – direct payments, in Control's system of Self-Directed Support and the DH's individual budgets pilot programme – stem from the same philosophical base. People should be able to enjoy Independent Living and this can only be achieved by having choice and control over how support needs are met.

Integration

If the systems of Self-Directed Support outlined above all have the same intended outcomes, it follows that these systems are not opposed to one another.

In fact, it is possible to have a 'mix and match' situation where, for example, part of a personal budget can be received as a direct payment. It therefore makes sense for local authorities to be integrating direct payments with personal budgets.

Support

To get the most benefit from Self-Directed Support, disabled people and families need support in exploring ideas of how support needs can be met, how to put together a support plan, and how to manage support (including support with employing personal assistance if that is the chosen route).

Experience of direct payments indicates that such support is more likely to be successful if it is provided by organisations controlled by disabled people or people who use social care services. This is because these organisations are able to offer peer support – support provided by people who may have had similar experiences and have practical ideas about what does and does not work.

People who receive direct payments and personal budgets should have a portion of their payment that can be used to buy help with planning and managing support. They should be freed to choose where they get this help. This arrangement will have implications for providers of direct payment support services working under contract to local authorities – not least that these providers will need to move to marketing their services to individuals who can shop around for support.

Some interim arrangements may be needed in order to help these organisations make the transition. In particular, work needs to be done with user-led organisations to ensure they are able to get their message across about the support they offer. Despite the difficulties of change, the logic of Self-Directed Support determines that people should be able to choose who provides their support.

Agreed Actions

- NCIL will promote more widely the value of in Control and personal budgets as a means to achieving Independent Living
- NCIL will work with its member organisations to ensure they are informed about personal budgets and can offer support and advice
- in Control will promote more widely the goal of Independent Living through Self-Directed Support
- in Control will promote the value of user-led organisations in providing support for Self-Directed Support
- NCIL/in Control will work with the Association of Directors of [Adult] Social Services (ADASS) to revise NCIL's existing protocol with ADASS to cover all areas of Self-Directed Support
- NCIL/in Control will meet regularly to share ideas, good practice, and to plan joint approaches to public bodies and Government.

November 2007 – reproduced with permission from Hatton et al, 2008, pp 141-4.

References

Abbott, D. (2003) *Direct payments for young disabled people*, York: Joseph Rowntree Foundation.

Abbott, P. (2000) 'Gender', in G. Payne (ed) *Social divisions*, Basingstoke: Macmillan.

Adams, I. (1998) *Ideology and politics in Britain today*, Manchester: Manchester University Press.

Age Concern (1998) 'Extend direct payments to over 65s', *Care Plan*, vol 5, no 2, pp 14-16.

Age Concern (2000) *Direct payments from social services*, Factsheet 24, London: Age Concern England.

Ahmed, M. (2008) 'Nearly all adult social workers want personal assistants to be regulated', *Community Care*, 23 October, p 5.

Alakeson, V. (2007) *The case for extending self-direction in the NHS*, London: Social Market Foundation.

Alcock, P. (1996) *Social policy in Britain: Themes and issues*, Basingstoke: Macmillan.

Andrisani, P. and Nestel, G. (1976) 'Internal–external control as contributor to and outcome of work experience', *Journal of Applied Psychology*, vol 61, no 2, pp 156–65.

Arber, S. and Ginn, J. (1995a) 'Gender differences in informal caring', *Health and Social Care in the Community*, vol 3, no 1, pp 19–31.

Arber, S. and Ginn, J. (1995b) 'Gender differences in the relationship between paid employment and informal care', *Work, Employment & Society*, vol 9, no 3, pp 445–71.

Askheim, O.P. (2003) 'Empowerment as guidance for professional social work: an act of balancing on a slack rope', *European Journal of Social Work*, vol 6, no 3, pp 229-40.

Audit Commission (1986) *Making a reality of community care*, London: HMSO.

Audit Commission (1992) *Community care: Managing the cascade of change*, London: HMSO.

Audit Commission (2006) *Choosing well: Analysing the costs and benefits of choice in local public services*, London: Audit Commission.

Auld, F. (1999) *Community Care (Direct Payments) Act 1996: Analysis of responses to local authority questionnaire on implementation – England*, London: Department of Health.

Bailey, R. (2000) 'Don't forget the police', *Personal Assistants Users' Newsletter*, October, pp 9–10.

Balloch, S., McLean, J. and Fisher, M. (eds) (1999) *Social services: Working under pressure*, Bristol: The Policy Press.

Barnes, C. (1995) *From national to local: An evaluation of the effectiveness of national disablement information providers' information services to local disablement information providers*, London: British Council of Disabled People.

Barnes, C. (1997) *Older people's perceptions of direct payments and self-operated support schemes*, Leeds: British Council of Disabled People Research Unit.

Barnes, C. and Mercer, G. (2006) *Independent futures: Creating user-led disability services in a disabling society*, Bristol: The Policy Press.

Barnes, M. (1997) *Care, communities and citizens*, London: Longman.

Barnes, M. (2006) *Caring and social justice*, Basingstoke: Palgrave.

Barnes, M. and Walker, A. (1996) 'Consumerism versus empowerment: a principled approach to the involvement of older service users', *Policy & Politics*, vol 24, no 4, pp 375–94.

Barnett, H. (1918) *Canon Barnett: His life, work and friends – volume one*, London: John Murray.

Barret, G. and Hudson, M. (1997) 'Changes in district nursing workload', *Journal of Community Nursing*, vol 11, no 3, pp 4–8.

Baxter, K., Glendinning, C., Clarke, S. et al (2008) *Domiciliary care agency responses to increased user choice*, York: Social Policy Research Unit.

Beardshaw, V. (1988) *Last on the list: Community services for people with physical disabilities*, London: King's Fund.

Becker, S. (1997) *Responding to poverty: The politics of cash and care*, Basingstoke: Macmillan.

Becker, S. and MacPherson, S. (eds) (1988) *Public issues, private pain: Poverty, social work and social policy*, London: Insight/Carematters Books.

Bennett, S. (2008) *Commissioning for personalisation: A framework for local authority commissioners*, London: DH.

Beresford, P. (1996) 'Meet the diversity of need', *Care Plan*, vol 2, no 4, p 14.

Beresford, P., Shamash, M., Forrest, V. et al (2005) *Developing social care: Service users' vision for adult support*, London: Social Care Institute for Excellence.

Bewley, C. (1998) *Choice and control: Decision-making and people with learning difficulties*, London: Values Into Action.

Bewley, C. (2000) 'Care managers can be champions for direct payments', *Care Plan*, vol 6, no 4, pp 13–16.

Bewley, C. and McCulloch, L. (2004) *Helping ourselves: Direct payments and the development of peer support*, York: Joseph Rowntree Foundation.

Bignall, T. and Butt, J. (2000) *Between ambition and achievement: Young black disabled people's views and experiences of independence and independent living*, Bristol/York: The Policy Press/JRF.

Blyth, C. and Gardner, A. (2007) '"We're not asking for anything special": direct payments and the carers of disabled children', *Disability and Society*, vol 22, no 3, pp 235–49.

Bond, H. (1996) 'State of independence', *Community Care*, 4–10 April, pp 20–1.

Bosanquet, H. (1914) *Social work in London 1869–1912: A history of the Charity Organisation Society*, London: John Murray.

Brandon, D. (1998) 'What is direct payment?', *Breakthrough*, vol 2, no 3, pp 25–6.

Brandon, D., Maglajlic, R. and Given, D. (2000) 'The information deficit hinders progress', *Care Plan*, vol 6, no 4, pp 17–20.

Brindle, D. (2008a) 'Tireless champion of autonomy', *Guardian Society*, 22 October, available online via www.guardiansociety.co.uk (accessed 24 October 2008).

Brindle, D. (2008b) 'Registering disapproval', *Guardian Society*, 2 July, available online via www.guardian.co.uk (accessed 4 July 2008).

Brown, G. (2008) 'Speech on the National Health Service', 7 January, London, King's College London/Florence Nightingale School of Nursing, available online via www.number10.gov.uk.

Browne, L. (1990) *Survey of local authorities direct payments*, London: RADAR.

Browning, D. (2007) *Evaluation of the self-directed support network: A review of progress up to 31st March 2007*, London: Care Services Improvement Partnership.

Burgess, P. (1994) 'Welfare rights', in C. Hanvey and T. Philpot (eds) *Practising social work*, London: Routledge.

Burrows, G. (2001) 'Charities criticise draft home care standards', *Community Care*, 21–27 June, p 3.

Butcher, T. (2002) *Delivering welfare* (2nd edn), Buckingham: Open University Press.

Butt, J. and Box, L. (1997) *Supportive services, effective strategies: The views of black-led organisations and social care agencies on the future of social care for black communities*, London: Race Equalities Unit.

Butt, J., Bignall, T. and Stone, E. (eds) (2000) *Directing support: Report from a workshop on direct payments and black and minority ethnic disabled people*, York: Joseph Rowntree Foundation.

Campbell, J. (nd) 'Promoting personal assistance to enable independent living', Social Services Conference, 29 October, London: National Centre for Independent Living.

Campbell, J. (1996) 'Implementing direct payments: towards the next millennium', National Institute of Social Work Conference, 12 November.

Carlin, J. and Lenehan, C. (2004) *Direct experience: A guide for councils on the implementation of direct payments in children's services*, London: Council for Disabled Children.

Carlin, J. and Lenehan, C. (2006) 'Overcoming barriers to the take-up of direct payments by parents of disabled children', in J. Leece and J. Bornat (eds) *Developments in direct payments*, Bristol: The Policy Press.

Carlin, J., Winters, L., Lenehan, C. et al (2006) *Individual budgets and children's services – a pre pilot scoping report*, London: Council for Disabled Children in partnership with Contact a Family and the Children's Society.

Carmichael, A. and Brown, L. (2002) 'The future challenge for direct payments', *Disability and Society*, vol 17, no 7, pp 797–808.

Carmichael, F. and Charles, S. (1998) 'The labour market costs of community care', *Journal of Health Economics*, vol 17, no 6, pp 747–65.

Chinn, C. (1995) *Poverty amidst prosperity: The urban poor in England, 1834–1914*, Manchester: Manchester University Press.

CIPFA (Chartered Institute of Public Finance and Accountancy) (1998) *Community care direct payments: Accounting and financial management guidelines*, London: CIPFA.

CIPFA (2007) *Direct payments and individual budgets: Managing the finances*, London: CIPFA (supported by in Control and the Department of Health).

Clark, H. and Spafford, H. (2002) 'Adapting to the culture of user control?', *Social Work Education*, vol 21, no 2, pp 247–57.

Clark, H., Dyer, S. and Horwood, J. (1998) *That bit of help: The high value of low level preventative services for older people*, Bristol/York: The Policy Press/Joseph Rowntree Foundation.

Clark, H., Gough, H. and Macfarlane, A. (2004) *'It pays dividends': Direct payments and older people*, Bristol: The Policy Press.

Cochrane, S. (2008) 'Use of direct payments by local authorities and health organisations (Letter)', Cardiff: Welsh Assembly Government, available online via www.wales.gov.uk/docrepos/40371/403823111/Direct_Payments_and_Health_1.doc?lang=en (accessed 29 September 2008).

Commission for Rural Communities (2008) *Tailor made? The implications of the personalisation of social care for older people living in rural communities*, London: Commission for Rural Communities.

Conservative Party (2007) *NHS autonomy and accountability: Proposals for legislation*, London: Conservative Party.

Coolen, J. and Weekers, S. (1998) 'Long-term care in the Netherlands: public funding and private provision within a universalistic welfare state', in C. Glendinning (ed) *Rights and realities: Comparing new developments in long-term care for older people*, Bristol: The Policy Press.

Cozens, A. (2002) *Findings of ADSS Survey on the implementation of the Carers and Disabled Children Act (2000)*, Leicester: ADSS.

Craig, G. (1992) *Cash or care: A question of choice? Cash, community care and user participation*, York: Social Policy Research Unit, University of York.

Crosby, N. (2008) 'Children and families in control', in C. Hatton, J. Waters, S. Duffy et al *A report on in Control's second phase: Evaluation and learning 2005–2007*, London: in Control Publications.

CSCI (Commission for Social Care Inspection) (2004) *Direct payments: What are the barriers?*, London: CSCI.

CSCI (2006a) *Time to care? An overview of home care services for older people in England, 2006*, London: CSCI.

CSCI (2006b) *Performance assessment handbook 2006 – adult services*, London: CSCI.

CSCI (2006c) *State of social care in England 2005–06*, London: CSCI.

CSCI (2008) *State of social care in England 2006–07*, London: CSCI.

CSIP (Care Services Improvement Partnership) (2008) 'Micro markets project: Report on progress after one year', available online via http://individualbudgets. csip.org.uk (accessed 29 August 2008).

Daly, G. and Roebuck, A. (2008) 'Gaining independence: an evaluation of service users' accounts of the individual budgets pilots', *Journal of Integrated Care*, vol 16, no 3, pp 17–25.

Darzi, A. (2008) *High quality care for all: NHS next stage review final report* (Darzi Report), London: The Stationery Office.

Davey, V., Snell, T., Fernandez, J. et al (2007a) *Schemes providing support to people using direct payments: A UK survey*, London: Personal Social Services Research Unit, London School of Economics and Political Science.

Davey, V., Fernandez, J., Knapp, M. et al (2007b) *Direct payments: A national survey of direct payments policy and practice*, London: Personal Social Services Research Unit, London School of Economics and Political Science.

Davidson, D. and Luckhurst, L. (2002) *Making choices taking control: Direct payments and mental health service users/survivors*, London: National Centre for Independent Living/Joseph Rowntree Foundation.

Davis, A. (1996) 'Women and the personal social services', in C. Hallett (ed) *Women and social policy*, London: Harvester Wheatsheaf.

Davis, A. and Wainwright, S. (1996) 'Poverty work and the mental health services', *Breakthrough*, vol 1, no 1, pp 47–55.

Davis, A., Ellis, K. and Rummery, K. (1997) *Access to assessment: Perspectives of practitioners, disabled people and carers*, Bristol: The Policy Press.

Dawson, C. (1995) *Report of the Independent Living Project (Norfolk)*, Cambridge: Daniels Publications/Joseph Rowntree Foundation.

Dawson, C. (2000) *Independent successes: Implementing direct payments*, York: Jospeh Rowntree Foundation.

DfES (Department for Education and Skills) (2006) *A parent's guide to direct payments*, London: DfES.

DH (Department of Health) (1989) *Caring for people: Community care in the next decade and beyond*, London: HMSO.

DH (1990) *Community care in the next decade and beyond: Policy guidance*, London: DH.

DH (1994) 'Virginia Bottomley gives direct payments to disabled people the go ahead', 24 November, press release 94/537, London: DH.

DH (1997) *Community Care (Direct Payments) Act 1996: Policy and practice guidance*, London: DH.

DH (1998a) *Independence pays: Community Care (Direct Payments) Act 1996*, DH information video, London: DH.

DH (1998b) *Modernising Social Services: Promoting independence, improving protection, raising standards*, London: The Stationery Office.

DH (2000a) *Community Care (Direct Payments) Act 1996: Policy and practice guidance* (2nd edn), London: DH.

DH (2000b) *Caring about carers: A national strategy for carers* (2nd edn), London: DH.

DH (2001a) *Carers and Disabled Children Act 2000: Carers and people with parental responsibility for disabled children – practice guidance*, London: DH.

DH (2001b) *Carers and Disabled Children Act 2000: Carers and people with parental responsibility for disabled children – policy guidance*, London: DH.

DH (2001c) *Carers and Disabled Children Act 2000: Direct payments for young disabled people – policy guidance and practice guidance*, London: DH.

DH (2001d) *A practitioner's guide to carers' assessments under the Carers and Disabled Children Act 2000*, London: DH.

DH (2001e) *Explanatory notes to Health and Social Care Act 2001*, available online via http://www.opsi.gov.uk/Acts/acts2001/en/ukpgaen_20010015_en_1 (accessed 19 June 2001).

DH (2001f) *Valuing People: A new strategy for learning disability for the 21st century*, London: DH.

DH (2003a) *Direct payments guidance: community care, services for carers and children's services (direct payments) guidance England*, London: DH.

DH (2003b) *Social services performance assessment framework indicators 2002–2003*, London: DH.

DH (2004a) *Direct choices – what councils need to make direct payments happen for people with learning disabilities*, London: DH.

DH (2004b) *An easy guide to direct payments*, London: DH.

DH (2005a) *Independence, Well-being and Choice*, London: The Stationery Office.

DH (2005b) *Community care statistics 2003–2004: Referrals, assessments and packages of care, for adults: Report of findings from the 2003–04 RAP collection – information for England for the period 1 April 2003 to 31 March 2004*, London: National Statistics.

DH (2006) *Our Health, Our Care, Our Say*, London: The Stationery Office.

DH (2007) *Direct payments uptake project: An easy words leaflet*, London: DH.

DH (2008a) *Transforming social care*, local authority circular LAC(DH)(2008)1.

DH (2008b) *Consultation on direct payments regulations*, London: DH.

DH (2008c) *Impact assessment of extending direct payments*, available online via www.dh.gov.uk/en/Consultations/liveconsultations/DH_087108 (accessed 6 September 2008).

DH (2008d) *The case for change – why England needs a new care and support system*, London: HM Government.

DH (2008e) *A guide to receiving direct payments from your local council – a route to independent living*, London: DH.

DH (2008f) *Moving Forward: Using the learning from the individual budget pilots*, London: DH.

DH (2008g) *Making Personal Budgets Work for Older People: Developing experience*, London: DH.

DH (2008h) *Putting People First – working to make it happen: Adult social care workforce strategy – interim statement*, London: DH.

DH (2008i) *Safeguarding Adults: A consultation on the review of the 'No Secrets' guidance*, London: DH.

DH/Care Services Improvement Partnership/in Control (2008) *Individual budgets: Living your life, your way*, DH DVD.

DH/Scottish Office/Welsh Office/Northern Ireland Office (1996) *Community Care (Direct Payments) Bill: Consultation paper*, London: DH.

DH/SSI (Social Services Inspectorate) (1996) *Progressing services with physically disabled people: Report on inspections of community services for physically disabled people*, London: DH.

DH/SSI (1997) *Inspection of community care services for black and minority ethnic older people: Birmingham*, Nottingham: Central Inspection Group, SSI.

DH/SSI (1999a) *Inspection of independent living arrangements for younger disabled people: Poole Borough Council*, Bristol: South and West Inspection Group, SSI.

DH/SSI (1999b) *Inspection of independent living arrangements for younger disabled people: Middlesbrough Borough Council*, Gateshead: North East Inspection Group, SSI.

DH/SSI (1999c) *Inspection of independent living arrangements for younger disabled people: County of Herefordshire District Council*, Bristol: South and West Inspection Group, SSI.

DH/SSI (1999d) *Inspection of independent living arrangements for younger disabled people: Oxfordshire County Council*, Bristol: South and West Inspection Group, SSI.

DHSS (Department of Health and Social Security) (1981) *Growing Older*, London: HMSO.

DHSSPS (Department of Health, Social Services and Public Safety) (1997) *Personal Social Services (Direct Payments) (Northern Ireland) Order 1996: Guidance for boards and trusts*, Belfast: DHSSPS.

DHSSPS (2000a) *A guide to receiving direct payments*, Belfast: The Stationery Office.

DHSSPS (2000b) *Personal Social Services (Direct Payments) (Northern Ireland) Order 1996: Guidance for boards and trusts*, Belfast: DHSSPS.

DHSSPS (2004) *Direct payments legislation and guidance for Boards and Trusts*, Belfast: DHSSPS.

DHSSPS (2007) *Direct payments statistics, 31 December 2007*, available online via www.dhsspsni.gov.uk/direct_payments_dec_07.xls (accessed 29.9.2008).

DHSSPS (2008) *Direct payments statistics, 31 March 2008*, available online via www.dhsspsni.gov.uk/direct_payments_report__mar_08__read_only.xls (accessed 29 September 2008).

Dickens, C. (1867) *Oliver Twist*, London: Chapman and Hall.

Dowson, S. (2002) *Not just about the money: Reshaping social care for social determination*, Stockport: Community Living and Emprise International Training and Consultancy.

Drew, E. (1995) 'Employment prospects of carers of dependent adults', *Health and Social Care in the Community*, vol 3, no 5, pp 325–31.

Duffy, S. (1996) *Unlocking the imagination, purchasing services for people with learning difficulties*, London: Choice Press.

Duffy, S. (2004) 'in Control', *Journal of Integrated Care*, vol 12, no 6, pp 7–13.

Duffy, S. (2005a) *Keys to citizenship: A guide to getting good support for people with learning disabilities* (reprinted from 2003 edition, with additional new chapter), Birkenhead: Paradigm.

Duffy, S. (2005b) 'Will "in Control" at last put people in charge of their lives?', *Community Living*, vol 18, no 4, pp 10–13.

Duffy, S. (2005c) 'Individual budgets: transforming the allocation of resources for care', *Journal of Integrated Care*, vol 13, no 1, pp 8–16.

Duffy, S. (2006) 'The implications of individual budgets', *Journal of Integrated Care*, vol 14, no 2, pp 3–10.

Duffy, S. (2007) 'Care management and self-directed support', *Journal of Integrated Care*, vol 15, no 5, pp 3–14.

Duffy, S. (2008) 'Self-directed support is for everyone', in C. Hatton, J. Waters, S. Duffy et al *A report on in Control's second phase: Evaluation and learning 2005–2007*, London: in Control Publications.

Duffy, S. and Waters, J. (2008) 'The economics of self-directed support', in C. Hatton, J. Waters, S. Duffy et al *A report on in Control's second phase: Evaluation and learning 2005–2007*, London: in Control Publications.

Dunnicliff, J. (1999) *Funding for personal assistance support services: The key to making personal assistance schemes work*, London: NCIL.

DWP (Department for Work and Pensions) (2005) *Opportunity Age: Meeting the challenges of ageing in the 21st century*, London: DWP.

Edsall, N.C. (1971) *The anti-Poor Law movement, 1834–1844*, Manchester: Manchester University Press.

Elkington, G. (1996) 'Exceptions to the rule', *Care Plan*, vol 2, no 4, p 12.

Ellis, K. (2005) 'Disability rights in practice: The relationship between human rights and social rights in contemporary social care', *Disability and Society*, vol 20, no 7, pp 691–704.

Ellis, K. (2007) 'Direct payments and social work practice: the significance of "street-level bureaucracy" in determining eligibility', *British Journal of Social Work*, vol 37, pp 405–22.

Ellis, K., Davis, A. and Rummery, K. (1999) 'Needs assessment, street-level bureaucracy and the new community care', *Social Policy and Administration*, vol 33, no 3, pp 262–80.

Englander, D. (1998) *Poverty and Poor Law reform in 19th century Britain, 1834–1914: From Chadwick to Booth*, London: Longman.

ENIL (European Network on Independent Living) (1997) *Training on direct payments for personal assistance*, Report from the ENIL Seminar, Berlin, 1–4 May, available online via www.independentliving.org/docs2/enilreport9705.html (accessed 1 March 2001).

Evans, J. (1993) 'The role of centres of independent/integrated living and networks of disabled people', in C. Barnes (ed) *Making our own choices: Independent living, personal assistance and disabled people*, Belper: British Council of Disabled People.

Evans, J. (2000) 'Direct payments in the United Kingdom', presentation at the International Conference on Self-Determination and Individualised Funding, Seattle, 29–31 July.

Evans, J. and Hasler, F. (1996) 'Direct Payments Campaign in the UK', presentation for the European Network on Independent Living Seminar, Stockholm, 9–11 June.

Ferguson, I. (2007) 'Increasing user choice or privatizing risk? The antimonies of personalization', *British Journal of Social Work*, vol 37, pp 387-403.

Fernandez, J.L., Kendall, J., Davey, V. et al (2007) 'Direct payments in England: factors linked to variations in local provision', *Journal of Social Policy*, vol 36, no 1, pp 97–121.

Fletcher, M. (2006) 'Carers and direct payments', in J. Leece and J. Bornat (eds) *Developments in direct payments*, Bristol: The Policy Press.

Fraser, D. (1984) *The evolution of the British welfare state* (2nd edn), Basingstoke: Macmillan.

Friedman, M. (1962) *Capitalism and freedom*, Chicago: University of Chicago Press.

Fruin, D. (1998) *Moving into the mainstream: The report of a national inspection of services for adults with learning disabilities*, London: DH.

Fruin, D. (2000) *New directions for independent living*, London: DH.

Fryer, R. (1998) *Signposts to services: Inspection of social services information to the public*, London: DH.

Gainsbury, S. (2008) 'Councils could lose £7bn social care funds to DWP', *Health Service Journal*, 29 May, available online via www.hsj.co.uk (accessed 7 July 2008).

Gardner, A. (1999) *Making direct payments a reality for people with learning difficulties*, Whalley: North West Training and Development Team.

George, M. (1994) 'Flexible choices', *Community Care*, 24–30 November, pp 14-15.

George, M. (1996) 'Cash on the nail', *Community Care*, 17–23 October, pp 24-5.

George, M. (2001) 'Our way or no way', *Community Care*, 12–18 July, pp 32–3.

Ginn, J. and Sandell, J. (1997) 'Balancing home and employment: stress reported by social services staff', *Work, Employment & Society*, vol 11, no 3, pp 413–34.

Glasby, J. (2007) *Understanding health and social care*, Bristol: The Policy Press.

Glasby, J. (2008a) *'Who cares?' Policy options for the reform of long-term care*, Birmingham: Health Services Management Centre.

Glasby, J. (2008b) *Individual budgets and the interface with health: A discussion paper for the Care Services Improvement Partnership*, Birmingham: Health Services Management Centre.

Glasby, J. and Beresford, P. (2006) 'Who knows best? Evidence-based practice and the service user contribution', *Critical Social Policy*, vol 26, no 1, pp 268–84.

Glasby, J. and Duffy, S. (2007) *'Our Health, Our Care, Our Say' – what could the NHS learn from individual budgets and direct payments?*, Birmingham: Health Services Management Centre/in Control.

Glasby, J. and Hasler, F. (2004) *A healthy option? Direct payments and the implications for health care*, Birmingham: Health Services Management Centre/National Centre for Independent Living.

Glasby, J. and Littlechild, R. (2004) *The health and social care divide: The experiences of older people* (2nd edn), Bristol: The Policy Press.

Glasby, J., Walshe, K. and Harvey, G. (eds) (2007) 'Evidence-based practice', special edition of *Evidence and Policy*, vol 3, no 3, pp 323–457.

Glendinning, C. and Kemp, P. (eds) (2006) *Cash and care: Policy challenges in the welfare state*, Bristol: The Policy Press.

Glendinning, C., Halliwell, S., Jacobs, S. et al (2000a) *Buying independence: Using direct payments to integrate health and social services*, Bristol: The Policy Press.

Glendinning, C., Halliwell, S., Jacobs, S. et al (2000b) 'Bridging the gap: using direct payments to purchase integrated care', *Health and Social Care in the Community*, vol 8, no 3, pp 192–200.

Glendinning, C., Halliwell, S., Jacobs, S. et al (2000c) 'New kinds of care, new kinds of relationships: how purchasing services affects relationships in giving and receiving personal assistance', *Health and Social Care in the Community*, vol 8, no 3, pp 201–11.

Glendinning, C., Challis, D., Fernandez, J. et al (2008) *Evaluation of the individual budgets pilot programme*, York: Social Policy Research Unit.

Glynn, M. and Beresford, P, with Bewley, C. et al (2008) *Person-centred support: What service users and practitioners say*, York: Joseph Rowntree Foundation.

Goodinge, S. (2000) *A jigsaw of services: Inspection of services to support disabled adults in their parenting role*, London: DH.

Goodman, C. (1986) 'Research on the informal carer: a selected literature review', *Journal of Advanced Nursing*, vol 11, pp 705–12.

Greenwood, W. (1969) *Love on the dole*, Harmondsworth: Penguin.

Grimshaw, J. and Fletcher, S. (nd) *Direct payments: People with HIV – the way forward*, London: National AIDS Trust/National Centre for Independent Living.

Hallett, C. (ed) (1989) *Women and social services departments*, London: Harvester Wheatsheaf.

Halloran, J. (ed) (1998) *Towards a people's Europe: A report on the development of direct payments in 10 member states of the European Union*, Vienna: European Social Network.

Hancock, R. and Jarvis, C. (1995) 'Care free? The after effects of being a carer', *Reviews in Clinical Gerontology*, vol 5, no 3, pp 245–6.

Harding, M.L. (2005) 'Patients could get their own budgets, Number 10 says', *Health Service Journal*, 18 May, available online via www.hsj.co.uk. (accessed 02 December 2008).

Hasler, F. (1997) 'Living is about more than bed and breakfast', *Health Matters*, vol 32, pp 12-13.

Hasler, F. (1999) 'Exercising the right to freedom of choice', *Professional Social Work*, June, pp 6-7.

Hasler, F. (2000) 'What is direct payments', in J. Butt, T. Bignall and E. Stone (eds) *Directing support: Report from a workshop on direct payments and black and minority ethnic disabled people*, York: Joseph Rowntree Foundation.

Hasler, F. (2006) 'The Direct Payments Development Fund', in J. Leece and J. Bornat (eds) *Developments in direct payments*, Bristol: The Policy Press.

Hasler, F., Campbell, J. and Zarb, G. (1999) *Direct routes to independence: A guide to local authority implementation and management of direct payments*, London: Policy Studies Institute.

Hasler, F., Zarb, G. and Campbell, J. (1998) *Key issues for local authority implementation of direct payments* (first published 1998, revised 1999), available online via www.psi. org.uk/publications/DISAB/key%20issues.htm (accessed 18 January 2001).

Hatchett, W. (1991) 'Cash on delivery?', *Community Care*, 30 May, pp 14-15.

Hatton, C., Waters, J., Duffy, S. et al (2008) *A report on in Control's second phase: Evaluation and learning 2005–2007*, London: in Control Publications.

Hayek, F. (1944) *The road to serfdom*, London: Routledge and Kegan Paul.

Health and Social Care Information Centre (2008) *Community care statistics 2006–07: Referrals, assessments and packages of care for adults, England*, London: The Health and Social Care Information Centre.

Help the Aged (2002) *Direct payments, direct control: Enabling older people to manage their own care*, London: Help the Aged.

Henwood, M. (1998) *Ignored and invisible? Carers' experience of the NHS*, London: Carers National Association.

Henwood, M. and Hudson, B. (2007a) *Review of the Independent Living Funds*, London: Department for Work and Pensions.

Henwood, M. and Hudson, B. (2007b) *Here to stay? Self-directed support: Aspiration and implementation (a review for the Department of Health)*, Heathencote: Melanie Henwood Associates.

Heslop, P. (2001) 'Direct payments for people with mental health support needs', *The Advocate*, May, pp 8-9.

Hirst, J. (1997) 'Direct benefit?', *Community Care*, 1 May, pp 10-11.

HM Government (2007) *Putting People First: A shared vision and commitment to the transformation of adult social care*, London: HM Government.

HM Treasury and the Department for Education and Skills (DfES) (2007) *Aiming High for Disabled Children: Better support for families*, London: HM Treasury.

Hoffmann, R. and Mitchell, A. (1998) 'Caregiver burden: historical development', *Nursing Forum*, vol 33, no 4, pp 5–11.

Holman, A. and Bewley, C. (1999) *Funding freedom 2000: People with learning difficulties using direct payments*, London: Values into Action.

Holman, A. and Bewley, C. (2001) *Trusting independence: A practical guide to independent living trusts*, London: Values into Action.

House of Commons Health Committee (1993) *Community Care: The Way Forward – volume I* (Sixth Report), London: HMSO.

Howe, D. (1986) 'The segregation of women and their work in the personal social services', *Critical Social Policy*, vol 5, no 3, pp 21-35.

Hudson, B. (1988) 'Doomed from the start?', *Health Service Journal*, 23 June, pp 708-9.

Hudson, B. (1993) 'The Icarus effect', *Health Service Journal*, 18 November, pp 27-9.

Hudson, B. (1994) 'Independent living for people in Britain: too successful by half? The case of the Independent Living Fund', *Critical Social Policy*, vol 40, pp 88-96.

Hunter, M. (1999) 'Case threatens direct payments', *Community Care*, 12–18 August, pp 10-11.

Hutchinson, P., Lord, J. and Salisbury, B. (2006) 'North American approaches to individualised planning and direct funding', in J. Leece and J. Bornat (eds) *Developments in direct payments*, Bristol: The Policy Press.

IBSEN (2008) *The national evaluation of the individual budgets pilot programme* (research findings series), York: Social Policy Research Unit.

IFF Research (2008) *Employment aspects and workforce implications of direct payments*, London: IFF Research.

ILF (Independent Living Fund) (2000) *Guidance notes for the 93 Fund and Extension Fund*, Nottingham: ILF.

Irish, H. (1998) 'Direct payments', *Breakthrough*, vol 2, no 3, pp 27-32.

Jones, G. (1989) Women in social care: the invisible army', in C. Hallett (ed) *Women and social services departments*, London: Harvester Wheatsheaf.

Jones, R. (2000) *Getting going on direct payments*, Trowbridge: Wiltshire Social Services, on behalf of the Association of Directors of Social Services.

Jordan, B. (1974) *Poor parents: Social policy and the 'cycle of deprivation'*, London: Routledge and Kegan Paul.

Kestenbaum, A. (1993a) *Making community care a reality: The Independent Living Fund, 1988–1993*, London: RADAR.

Kestenbaum, A. (1993b) *Cash for care: A report on the experience of Independent Living Fund clients* (2nd edn), London: RADAR/Disablement Income Group.

Kestenbaum, A. (1999) *What price independence? Independent living and people with high support needs*, Bristol/York: The Policy Press/Joseph Rowntree Foundation.

Killin, D. (1993) 'Independent living, personal assistance, disabled lesbians and gay men', in C. Barnes (ed) *Making our own choices: Independent living, personal assistance and disabled people*, Belper: British Council of Disabled People.

Kobasa, S. (1979) 'Stressful life events, personality and health: an inquiry into hardiness', *Journal of Personality and Social Psychology*, vol 37, no 1, pp 1–11.

Labour Party (2005) *The Labour Party 2005 manifesto: Britain forwards, not back*, London: Labour Party.

Lakey, J. (1994) *Caring about independence: Disabled people and the Independent Living Fund*, London: Policy Studies Institute.

Leadbeater, C., Bartlett, J. and Gallagher, N. (2008) *Making it personal*, London: Demos.

Leece, D. and Leece, J. (2006) 'Direct payments: creating a two-tiered system in social care?', *British Journal of Social Work*, vol 36, pp 1379-93.

Leece, J. (2000) 'It's a matter of choice: making direct payments work in Staffordshire', *Practice*, vol 12, no 4, pp 37-48.

Leece, J. (2002) 'Extending direct payments to informal carers: Some issues for local authorities', *Practice*, vol 14, no 2, pp 31-44.

Leece, J. (2003) *Direct payments*, Birmingham: Venture Press.

Leece, J. (2004) 'Money talks but what does it say? Direct payments and the commodification of care', *Practice*, vol 16, no 3, pp 211-21.

Leece, J. (2006a) 'Direct payments and user-controlled support: the challenges for social care commissioning', *Practice*, vol 19, no 3, pp 185-98.

Leece, J. (2006b) '"It's not like being at work": a study to investigate stress and job satisfaction in employees of direct payment users', in J. Leece and J. Bornat (eds) *Developments in direct payments*, Bristol: The Policy Press.

Leece, J. and Bornat, J. (eds) (2006) *Developments in direct payments*, Bristol: The Policy Press.

Leece, J., Babb, C. and Leece, D. (2003) 'Money matters: An evaluation of the direct payment pilot project for parents of disabled children in Staffordshire', *Journal of Integrated Care*, vol 11, no 1, pp 33-8.

Le Grand, J. (2007) *The other invisible hand: Delivering public services through choice and competition*, Princeton: Princeton University Press.

Lewis, J. (1995) *The voluntary sector, the state and social work in Britain*, Aldershot: Edward Elgar.

Lewis, J. (1996) 'What does contracting do to voluntary agencies?', in D. Billis and M. Harris (eds) *Voluntary agencies: Challenges of organisations and management*, Basingstoke: Macmillan.

Lindblom, C. (1959) 'The science of muddling through', *Public Administration Review*, vol 19, no 2, pp 78-88.

Lipsky, M. (1980) *Street-level bureaucracy: Dilemmas of the individual in public services*, New York: Russell Sage Foundation.

Lister, R. (2008) 'Citizenship and access to welfare', in P. Alcock, M. May and K. Rowlingson (eds) *The student's companion to social policy* (2nd edn), Oxford: Blackwell Publishing.

Local Government Association (2008) *Our Lives, Our Choices: Fit for the future – a new vision for adult social care and support*, London: Local Government Association.

Lombard, D. (2008) 'Self-directed care schemes in Scotland break employment law', *Community Care*, 17 June.

Lord, P. and Hutchinson, P. (2003) 'Individualised support and funding: building blocks for capacity building and inclusion', *Disability and Society*, vol 18, no 1, pp 71-86.

Luckhurst, L. (2000) 'Survivors explore direct payments', *Personal Assistants Users' Newsletter*, August, pp 11-12.

Lundsgaard, J. (2005) *Consumer direction and choice in long-term care for older persons, including payments for informal care: How can it help improve care outcomes, employment and fiscal sustainability?* OECD Health Working Paper no 20, Paris: OECD.

Macfarlane, A. (1990) 'The right to make choices', *Community Care*, 1 November, pp 14-15.

Maglajlic, R. (1999) 'The silent treatment', *Openmind*, September/October, pp 12-13.

Maglajlic, R., Brandon, D. and Given, D. (2000) 'Making direct payments a choice: a report on the research findings', *Disability & Society*, vol 15, no 1, pp 99-113.

Maglajlic, R., Bryant, M., Brandon, D. et al (1998) 'Direct payments in mental health – a research report', *Breakthrough*, vol 2, no 3, pp 33-43.

Mandelstam, M. (1999) *Community care practice and the law* (2nd edn), London: Jessica Kingsley.

Manthorpe, J., Jacobs, S., Rapaport, J. et al (2008a) 'Training for change: early days of individual budgets and the implications for social work and care management practice', *British Journal of Social Work* (advance access, published 7 March 2008).

Manthorpe, J., Stevens, M., Rapaport, J. et al (2008b) 'Safeguarding and system change: early perceptions of the implications for adult protection services of the English individual budgets pilots – a qualitative study', *British Journal of Social Work* (advance access, published 26 March 2008).

Marchant, R., Lefevre, M., Jones, M. et al (2007) *'Necessary stuff'* – the social care needs of children with complex health care needs and their families, London: SCIE.

McCurry, P. (1999) 'The direct route', *Community Care*, 9–15 September, pp 20-1.

McKay, S. and Rowlingson, K. (1999) *Social security in Britain*, Basingstoke: Macmillan.

McLaughlin, E. and Ritchie, J. (1994) 'Legacies of caring: the experiences and circumstances of ex-carers', *Health and Social Care in the Community*, vol 2, no 4, pp 241-53.

McMullen, M. (2003) *The direct approach*, London: SCOPE.

Means, R. and Smith, R. (1998a) *Community care: Policy and practice* (2nd edn), Basingstoke: Macmillan.

Means, R. and Smith, R. (1998b) *From Poor Law to community care: The development of welfare services for elderly people, 1939–1971* (2nd edn), Bristol: The Policy Press.

Means, R., Richards, S. and Smith, R. (2008) *Community care: Policy and practice* (4th edn), Bristol: The Policy Press.

Mickel, A. (2008) 'What's the outlook for adult care?', *Community Care*, 23 October, pp 28-30.

Milburn, A. (2007) 'A 2020 vision for public services', speech at the London School of Economics, 16 May.

Morris, J. (1993a) *Independent lives: Community care and disabled people*, Basingstoke: Macmillan.

Morris, J. (1993b) 'Advocating true reform', *Community Care*, 4 February, pp 16-17.

Morris, J. (1995) 'How to get money to pay for personal assistance and have control over how its spent', in British Council of Disabled People (ed) *Controlling your own personal assistance services*, available online via wwwindependentliving. org/docs/enilbcodppayschemes2.html (accessed 30 January 2001).

Morris, J. (1997) 'Care or empowerment? A disability rights perspective', *Social Policy and Administration*, vol 31, no 1, pp 54-60.

Morris, J. and Wates, M. (2006) *Supporting disabled parents and parents with additional support needs*, London: SCIE.

Morris, J. and Wates, M. (2007) *Working together to support disabled parents,* London: SCIE.

Murray, C. (1984) *Losing ground: American social policy 1950–1980*, New York: Basic Books.

Murray, K., Tyson, A. and Murray-Neill, R. (2006) *Increasing the uptake of direct payments: A self-assessment and action planning guide for local councils with social services responsibilities and their partners*, London: DH.

National Assembly for Wales (1997) *Community Care (Direct Payments) Act 1996: Policy and practice guidance*, Cardiff: National Assembly for Wales.

National Assembly for Wales (2000) *Community Care (Direct Payments) Act 1996: Policy and practice guidance*, Cardiff: National Assembly for Wales.

National Statistics/Information Centre (2007) *Personal social services staff of social services departments at 30 September 2007, England*, Leeds: Information Centre.

NCIL (National Centre for Independent Living) (nda) *Promoting personal assistance to enable independent living*, unpublished information sheet, London: NCIL.

NCIL (ndb) *Direct payments for mental health users/survivors*, London: NCIL.

NCIL (ndc) *Community Care (Direct Payments) Act 1996 government review: Response by the British Council of Disabled People's National Centre for Independent Living*, London, NCIL.

NCIL (ndd) *Response to consultation on CIPFA draft guidance on direct payments*, London: NCIL.

NCIL (1999) *Government White Paper: Modernising social services – response by the British Council of Disabled People's National Centre for Independent Living*, London: NCIL.

NCIL (2000) *NCIL Briefing on the Carers and Disabled Children Bill*, London: NCIL.

NCIL (2003) Transcript of speech by Stephen Ladyman, Parliamentary Under Secretary of State, Department of Health, at NCIL launch event, 30 October, London.

NCIL (2006) *The Direct Payments Development Fund*, London: NCIL/DH.

Newbigging, K. with Lowe, J. (2005) *Direct payments and mental health: New directions*, Brighton: Pavilion Publishing.

NIMHE (National Institute for Mental Health in England) (2006) *Direct payments for people with mental health problems: A guide to action*, London: DH.

Novak, T. (1988) *Poverty and the state: An historical sociology*, Buckingham: Open University Press.

OPM (Office for Public Management) (2006) *Budget-holding lead professionals: Literature review – report for the Department for Education and Skills*, London: OPM.

OPM (2007) *The implications of individual budgets for service providers*, London: OPM.

Oliver, M. (1990) *The politics of disablement*, Basingstoke: Macmillan.

Oliver, M. (1996) *Understanding disability: From theory to practice*, Basingstoke: Macmillan.

Oliver, M. and Sapey, B. (1999) *Social work with disabled people* (2nd edn), Basingstoke: Macmillan.

Oliver, M. and Zarb, G. (1992) *Greenwich personal assistance schemes: Second year evaluation*, London: Greenwich Association of Disabled People.

Patmore, C. and McNulty, A. (2005) *Making home care for older people more flexible and person-centred*, York: University of York.

Payne, M. (2005) *The origins of social work: Continuity and change*, Basingstoke: Palgrave.

Pearson, C. (2000) 'Money talks? Competing discourses in the role of direct payments', *Critical Social Policy*, vol 20, no 4, pp 459-77.

Pearson, C. (2004) 'Keeping the cash under control: What's the problem with direct payments in Scotland?', *Disability and Society*, vol 19, no 1, pp 3-14.

Pearson, C. (2006) 'Direct payments in Scotland', in J. Leece and J. Bornat (eds) *Developments in direct payments*, Bristol: The Policy Press.

Pijl, M. (1997) 'Quality of care: on whose terms?', in A. Evers, R. Haverinen, K. Leichsenring et al (eds) *Developing quality in personal social services: Concepts, cases and comments*, Aldershot: Ashgate.

Pijl, M. (2000) 'Home care allowances: good for many but not for all', *Practice*, vol 12, no 2, pp 55-65.

Poll, C., Duffy, S., Hatton, C. et al (2006) *A report on in Control's first phase, 2003–2005*, London: in Control Publications.

Poole, T. (2006) *Direct payments and older people* (background paper commissioned by the Wanless Review), London: King's Fund.

Priestley, M., Jolly, D., Pearson, C. et al (2007) 'Direct payments and disabled people in the UK: supply, demand and devolution', *British Journal of Social Work*, vol 37, pp 1189-204.

Prime Minister's Strategy Unit (2005) *Improving the Life Chances of Disabled People*, London: Prime Minister's Strategy Unit.

Project 81 (nd) *Project 81 – one step up*, Petersfield: HCIL Papers.

Rabiee, P., Moran, N. and Glendinning, C. (2008) 'Individual budgets: lessons from early users' experience', *British Journal of Social Work*, advance online access.

Ratzka, A. (nd) *What is independent living?*, unpublished information sheet, London: NCIL.

Raynes, N., Temple, B., Glenister, C. et al (2001) *Quality at home for older people: Involving service users in defining home care specifications*, Bristol: The Policy Press/ Joseph Rowntree Foundation.

Rees, S. (1978) *Social work face to face*, London: Edward Arnold.

Revans, L. (2000) 'Payments reform stalls', *Community Care*, 28 September– 4 October, p 12.

Riddell, S., Pearson, C., Jolly, D. et al (2005) 'The development of direct payments in the UK: implications for social justice', *Social Policy and Society*, vol 4, no 1, pp 75-85.

Riddell, S., Priestley, M., Pearson, C. et al (2006) *Disabled people and direct payments: A UK comparative study*, Economics and Social Research Council award RES-000-23-0263.

Ridley, J. (2006) '"Direct what?" Exploring the suitability of direct payments for people with mental health problems', in J. Leece and J. Bornat (eds) *Developments in direct payments*, Bristol: The Policy Press.

Ridley, J. and Jones, L. (2003) 'Direct what? The untapped potential of direct payments to mental health service users', *Disability and Society*, vol 18, no 5, pp 643-58.

Riley, C. (1999) *Directly involved? A study of direct payments*, unpublished Masters dissertation, Department of Social Policy and Social Work, University of Birmingham.

Rooff, M. (1972) *One hundred years of family social work: A study of the family welfare society 1869–1969*, London: Michael Joseph.

Rose, M.E. (1988) *The relief of poverty, 1834–1914* (2nd edn), Basingstoke: Macmillan.

Royal Commission on Long Term Care (1999) *With respect to old age: Long term care – rights and responsibilities*, London: The Stationery Office.

Rummery, K. (2006) 'Disabled citizens and social exclusion: the role of direct payments', *Policy & Politics*, vol 34, no 4, pp 633–50.

Ryan, T. and Holman, A. (1998a) *Able and willing? Supporting people with learning difficulties to use direct payments*, London: Values Into Action.

Ryan, T. and Holman, A. (1998b) 'Questions of control and consent', *Care Plan*, vol 5, no 2, pp 10–14.

Ryan, T. and Holman, A. (1998c) *Pointers to control: People with learning difficulties using direct payments*, London: Values Into Action.

Samuel, M. (2008) 'Alarm over plans to expand direct payments', *Community Care*, 28 August, p 5.

Sapey, B. and Pearson, J. (2004) 'Do disabled people need social workers?', *Social Work and Social Sciences Review*, vol 11, no 3, pp 52–70.

Satyamurti, C. (1981) *Occupational survival*, Oxford: Blackwell.

Schunk, M. (1998) 'The social insurance model of care for older people in Germany', in C. Glendinning (ed) *Rights and realities: Comparing new developments in long-term care for older people*, Bristol: The Policy Press.

SCIE (Social Care Institute for Excellence) (2005) *Direct payments: Answering frequently asked questions*, London: SCIE.

SCIE (2007) *Choice, control and individual budgets: Emerging themes*, London: SCIE.

SCIE (2008) *Personalisation: A rough guide*, London: SCIE.

Scottish Executive (2000) *Community Care (Direct Payments) Act 1996 – Community Care (Direct Payments) (Scotland) Amendment Regulations 2000, circular no. CCD4/2000*, Edinburgh: Scottish Executive.

Scottish Executive (2001) 'Chisholm announces £530,000 to promote direct payments', Scottish Executive press release SE0940/2001, 06/04/2001, Edinburgh: Scottish Executive.

Scottish Executive (2003) *Direct Payments and Social Work (Scotland) Act 1968: Sections 12B and C: Policy and practice guidance*, Edinburgh: Scottish Executive Health Department, Community Care Division.

Scottish Executive (2006) 'Statistics release: Direct payments Scotland 2006', available online via www.scotland.gov.uk/Resource/Doc/149651/0039854.pdf (accessed 29 September 2008).

Scottish Executive (2007) *National guidance on self-directed support*, Edinburgh: Primary and Community Care Directorate Adult Care and Support Change Team, available online via www.scotland.gov.uk/Publications/2007/07/04093127/10 (accessed 11 September 2008).

Scottish Office (1997) *Community Care (Direct Payments) Act 1996: Policy and practice guidance*, Edinburgh: Scottish Office Social Work Services Group.

Scourfield, P. (2005a) 'Implementing the Community Care (Direct Payments) Act: will the supply of personal assistants meet the demand and at what price?', *Journal of Social Policy*, vol 34, no 3, pp 1-20.

Scourfield, P. (2005b) 'Direct payments', *Working with Older People*, vol 9, issue 4, pp 20-3.

Scourfield, P. (2007) 'Social care and the modern citizen: client, consumer, service user, manager and entrepreneur', *British Journal of Social Work*, vol 37, pp 107-22.

Seddon, D., Robinson, C., Tommis, Y. et al (nd) *The modernisation of social care services: A study of the effectiveness of the national strategy for carers in meeting carer needs*, Bangor: University of Wales.

Seligman, M.E.P. (1975) *Helplessness: On depression, development and death*, San Francisco, CA: W.H. Freeman.

Senker, J. (2008) 'Enabling people to plan and arrange support', in C. Hatton, J. Waters, S. Duffy et al *A report on in Control's second phase: Evaluation and learning 2005–2007*, London: in Control Publications.

Shearer, A. (1984) 'Independence is the name of the game', *Voluntary Action*, vol 2, no 3, pp 10-11.

Simpson, F. with Campbell, J. (1996) *Facilitating and supporting independent living: A guide to setting up a personal assistance support scheme*, London: Disablement Income Group.

Skills for Care (nd) *Care training code: A guide for individuals buying in training for their own staff*, Leeds: Skills for Care.

Social Exclusion Unit (2004) *Mental health and social exclusion*, London: Office of the Deputy Prime Minister.

Social Interface (2007) *A survey on the implementation of the current direct payments scheme in Wales*, Bangor: Social Interface.

Social Services Improvement Agency (nd) *Number of direct payments service users in Wales*, available online via www.ssiacymru.org.uk/media/excel/7/r/Authority_Annual_Comparison.xls (accessed 29 September 2008).

Spandler, H. (2004) 'Friend or foe? Towards a critical assessment of direct payments', *Critical Social Policy*, vol 24, no 2, pp 187-209.

Spandler, H. and Vick, N. (2006) 'Opportunities for independent living using direct payments in mental health', *Health and Social Care in the Community*, vol 14, no 2, pp 107–15.

Stainton, T. (2002) 'Taking rights structurally: rights, disability and social worker responses to direct payments', *British Journal of Social Work*, vol 32, pp 751-63.

Stainton, T. (2005) 'Empowerment and the architecture of rights based social policy', *Journal of Intellectual Disabilities*, vol 9, no 4, pp 289-98.

Stainton, T. and Boyce, S. (2004) '"I have got my life back": users' experience of direct payments', *Disability and Society*, vol 19, no 5, pp 443-54.

Stevens, S. (2008) 'My problem with trade unions', *Community Care*, 2 June.

Stuart, O. (2006) *Will community-based support services make direct payments a viable option for black and minority ethnic service users and carers?*, London: SCIE.

Taylor, N. (2008) 'Obstacles and dilemmas in the delivery of direct payments to service users with poor mental health', *Practice*, vol 20, no 1, pp 43-55.

Taylor, R. (1994) 'Putting the cash upfront', *ADSS News*, November, pp 16-17.

Taylor, R. (1995) *Community Care (Direct Payments) Bill: Briefing paper*, Kingston-upon-Thames: ADSS Disabilities Committee.

Taylor, R. (1996a) 'Independent living and direct payments', speech delivered to the ADSS Spring Conference, Cambridge, April.

Taylor, R. (1996b) 'A coherent policy for direct payments', *ADSS News*, vol 5, no 4, p 20.

Taylor, R. (1996c) 'To the beat of a different drum', *Care Plan*, vol 2, no 4, pp 9-10.

Taylor, R. (1997) 'Funding freedom', presentation to the Values Into Action Funding Freedom Conference, 19 March.

Thane, P. (1996) *Foundations of the welfare state* (2nd edn), London: Longman.

Thompson, N., Murphy, M. and Stradling, S. (1994) *Dealing with stress*, Basingstoke: Macmillan.

Tomlinson, C. (2006) 'An individual budget in practice', *Journal of Integrated Care*, vol 14, no 1, pp 35-7.

Twigg, J. (1998) 'Informal care of older people', in M. Bernard and J. Phillips (eds) *The social policy of old age: Moving into the 21st century*, London: Centre for Policy on Ageing.

Tyson, A. (nd) *Strategic commissioning and self-directed support*, London: CSIP.

UK Home Care Association (2008) *An overview of the UK domiciliary care sector*, Sutton: UK Home Care Association.

Ungerson, C. (1997) 'Give them the money: is cash a route to empowerment?', *Social Policy and Administration*, vol 31, no 1, pp 45–53.

Ungerson, C. (1999) 'Personal assistants and disabled people: an examination of a hybrid form of work and care', *Work, Employment and Society*, vol 13, no 4, pp 583–600.

Ungerson, C. (2003) 'Commodified care work in European labour markets', *European Societies*, vol 5, no 4, pp 377–96.

Ungerson, C. (2004) 'Whose empowerment and independence? A cross-national perspective on "cash for care" schemes', *Ageing and Society*, vol 24, pp 189–212.

Ungerson, C. (2006) 'Direct payments and the employment relationship: some insight from cross-national research', in J. Leece and J. Bornat (eds) *Developments in direct payments*, Bristol: The Policy Press.

Ungerson, C. and Yeandle, S. (eds) (2007) *Cash for care systems in developed welfare states*, Basingstoke: Palgrave Macmillan.

Unison (2001) *Home care: The forgotten service*, London: Unison.

Valios, N. (1997) 'Direct payments delayed in Ulster', *Community Care*, 24–30 April, p 3.

Valios, N. (2000) 'Wanted: caring employees', *Community Care*, 1–7 June, pp 20-1.

Vasey, S. (2000) *The rough guide to managing personal assistants*, London: NCIL.

Vevers, S. (2007) 'Carers of disabled children and direct payments', *Community Care*, 6 December.

Vick, N., Tobin, R., Swift, P. et al (2006) *An evaluation of the impact of the social care modernisation programme on the implementation of direct payments*, London: Health and Social Care Advisory Service (with University of Central Lancashire and the Foundation for People with Learning Disabilities).

Wanless, D. (2006) *Securing good care for older people: Taking a long-term view*, London: King's Fund.

Waters, J. and Duffy, S. (2007) *Individual budgets: Report on individual budget integration*, London, in Control Publications.

Weekers, S. and Pijl, M. (1998) *Home care and care allowances in the European Union*, Utrecht: Netherlands Institute of Care and Welfare.

Wellard, S. (1999) 'The costs of control', *Community Care*, 21–27 January, p 23.

Welsh Assembly Government (2004) *Community Care, Services for Carers and Children's Services (Direct Payments) Guidance, Wales*, Cardiff: Welsh Assembly Government.

Williams, V. and Holman, A. (2006) 'Direct payments and autonomy: issues for people with learning difficulties', in J. Leece and J. Bornat (eds) *Developments in direct payments*, Bristol: The Policy Press.

Winter, J. (2008) 'The personalisation revolution', plenary presentation, Community Care Live, 14 May 2008, Business Design Centre, Islington, London.

Witcher, S., Stalker, K., Roadburg, M. et al (2000) *Direct payments: The impact on choice and control for disabled people*, Edinburgh: Scottish Executive Central Research Unit.

Zarb, G. (1998) 'What price independence?', paper presented to the 'Shaping our Futures' Conference, London, 5 June.

Zarb, G. and Nadash, P. (1994) *Cashing in on independence: Comparing the costs and benefits of cash and services*, London: BCODP.

Zarb, G. and Oliver, M. (1993) *Ageing with a disability: What do you expect after all these years?*, London: University of Greenwich.

Zarb, G., Hasler, F., Campbell, J. et al (1997) *Implementation and management of direct payment schemes: First findings – Summary*, London: PSI.

6, P. (2003) 'Giving consumers of British public services more choice: what can be learned from recent history?', *Journal of Social Policy*, vol 32, no 2, pp 239–70.

Statutory instruments/rules

Statutory Instrument 2000/11 *The Community Care (Direct Payments) Amendment Regulations 2000*

Statutory Instrument 2000/1868 (W127) *The Community Care (Direct Payments) Amendment (Wales) Regulations 2000*

Scottish Statutory Instrument 2000/183 *The Community Care (Direct Payments) (Scotland) Amendment Regulations 2000*

Statutory Rule 2000/114 *The Personal Social Services (Direct Payments) (Amendment) Regulations (Northern Ireland) 2000*

Scottish Statutory Instrument 2003/243 *The Community Care (Direct Payments) (Scotland) Amendment Regulations 2003*

Scottish Statutory Instrument 2005/114 *The Community Care (Direct Payments) (Scotland) Amendment Regulations 2005*

Scottish Statutory Instrument 2007/458 *The Community Care (Direct Payments) (Scotland) Amendment Regulations 2007*

Index

Witcher, S. 114, 124
Wonter, Julia 107
workhouse 6

Y

young carers 55, 64
young people
  direct payments 66
  self-directed support 102, 103

Z

Zarb, G. 9, 10, 27, 28-9, 47, 48, 113, 118,
    122-3, 124, 141, 157, 159, 171